Dear Jason and Jodi

A MEMOIR

William H. Gilmore

ISBN-13: 9780692857014 (POWERUP)
ISBN-10: 069285701X
Library of Congress Control Number: 2017945391
POWERUP, Morgan Hill, CA
Printed in the United States of America

Dedication

Lee VanNamen was my friend and fellow crewmember on the RF-4 Phantom aircraft during the Vietnam War. We were stationed in Thailand from April 1972 to April 1973, and he was the best RF-4 reconnaissance system operator any pilot could ever hope for or imagine. Rest in peace, my friend, and thanks for saving my life on at least three occasions. You were the best.

I also want to dedicate this memoir to Patricia, Jo, Jack, Judy, and my mother, Alice Marie Gilmore.

And to the members of the Fourteenth Tactical Reconnaissance Squadron who served in Southeast Asia.

Contents

Preface

WHY THIS MEMOIR? I GUESS there are many reasons. Several people have suggested to me that I write about my life, and I have always said that many people I know should write about their own. At this stage of my life, I wish I had known more about our family members and wish *they* had written about *their* lives. And so, for these reasons and more, I am writing this memoir.

Somewhere along the line, I have learned that writing is often cathartic for the writer. This writing likely will be just that for me, especially on the topic of Vietnam. Jason and Jodi, dear nephew and niece, I hope you don't find this an egotistical endeavor. All I want is to let you know more about who I was and what I did when I was around. With no kids or grandkids, I want you, at least, to know what I did with my life. If you choose to share it with anybody, so be it.

Rather than think of chapter names, I have decided to lay the book out mostly according to my age. Chapter 9 takes on a character of its own and has no age moniker associated with it. I know some literary types think naming chapters according to the author's age is very boring, but on the other hand, you should understand, quite easily, what I was doing during each decade of my life.

About twenty years ago, I wrote a considerable amount about my life in the air force. Despite some very serious times, I came at it from a humorous perspective, of all things. At the time, I thought readers would get all the military humor, be it light or dark. I read some of it years later, however, and it was not very funny. I will refrain from trying to be funny here, but those who know me know I enjoy the lighter side of life, even if it comes in the middle of some very serious times. This may show up here.

Conversely, you may find limited or no discussion of certain other subjects in this writing. Love stories in movies, novels, biographies, or memoirs really are interesting, and I believe love is the central theme around which all life revolves. If love is not a part of the story, then something is missing. Be that as it may, I will avoid the details of that part of my life—at least the intimacies. The two main women in my life were Jo, my first wife, and Pat, my second wife. I hope to preserve the integrity of those relationships without delving into the personal parts. My mother and grandmother were the other two women in my life, of course, and I don't know what I would have done without all four of these women. Any firm ground I stand on is because of them, my grandfather, my father, and my brother.

For each decade of my life and therefore each chapter (except chapter 9), I have noted the beginning and ending prices of the Dow Jones Industrial Average. "Strange," you might say, but I'm doing this for a couple of reasons. One is that, regardless of what I was doing, from the time I was about ten years old, I have always wondered what was happening with the stock market from day to day. This was because of a single visit my grandfather and I made to a stockbrokerage office when I was still a kid. I have chosen to annotate each chapter with the Dow readings as a reminder to readers that I have spent an enormous amount of my life watching, reading about, discussing, cheering on, and—yes—agonizing over the financial markets. Another reason I have posted these numbers is for readers to see what would happen over a lifetime—or, more specifically, over *my* lifetime—to an invested dollar, though I do not include dividends in these numbers. The source material for most of the Dow numbers came from Jeffrey and Yale Hirsch's *Stock Trader's Almanac.*

As I wrote, the subject of the Vietnam War loomed large, just as it has in my life. Likewise, I found myself extensively referencing a few books about Vietnam, and my biggest challenge in writing this memoir was to boil the Vietnam material down to something acceptable. Perhaps I failed in this effort, because after hours of compressing this material, I finally brought the Vietnam writing to a close by remembering that I was writing a memoir, not a study of the Vietnam War. Thus, I have placed the heart of what I thought about Vietnam in chapter 9 and the rest of my Vietnam reference material in five appendixes toward the very end of the book.

In writing about the airplanes I flew, I have tried to give you an idea of a number of things, including airspeed capabilities. Throughout this memoir, I occasionally write about certain airspeeds, but I have not gone to any great lengths to convert these speeds for you (e.g., true airspeed, indicated airspeed, ground speed, or Mach). They are readily available on the Internet. The speeds I cite in these pages usually come from my memory or from aircrew conversations back in the day. Other than in a few places, I am not dedicating myself to exact speeds.

Also, I want readers to be aware that about five of seventy-one endnote references are from *Wikipedia*: a couple regarding aircraft information, two regarding refugee material, and one regarding the aftermath of the Paris Peace Accords. I mention this in keeping with *Wikipedia*'s own caution that "*Wikipedia*'s articles should be used for background information, as a reference for correct terminology and search terms, and as a starting point for further research. There is a possibility for error in content." I also used *Wikipedia* for some terms in my glossary.

I want to say something to my audience. Obviously this memoir has been written for my niece and nephew, but it is also for anybody else who chooses to read it. Sometimes I address myself to my niece and nephew, and sometimes I address myself to the "reader." I hope this doesn't confuse my niece or nephew—or my other readers. My overall message is for Jason and Jodi but also for *anyone* willing to read the memoir.

Also, I'd like to say a few things about the image on the cover of this memoir. It is more meaningful to me than it will be to most readers. The location of the image is in (South) Vietnam at a place called Linh Quy Phap An, in Lam Dong Province. Google maps say it is about 133 miles northeast of Saigon (Ho Chi Minh City). To me it represents how tranquil things often appear while flying near sunset or sunrise, even in Vietnam during the war. I like the fact that it is a landscape of Vietnam since I spent so much time there. Also the cover designers inserted those high jet contrails into the image for me. The contrails are very meaningful to me, as they represent the contrails I saw in a book while sitting in a freshman Air Force ROTC class. I paused that day to wonder whether I would ever be able to fly for a living, especially as a pilot in the US Air Force. Of course the contrails are also reminiscent of all the contrails that I saw as an aviator during my life. An eagle was also inserted into the image both because of my fascination with the bird itself and because of the metaphor that it represents and which I talk about herein—the beauty of flight.

On the back cover I asked to have an image of a US flag positioned with a South Vietnamese flag. The reasons for the US flag are obvious. To have a South Vietnamese flag presented, I thought would be a tribute to all who fought in the conflict to make South Vietnam free. I also think it a tribute to those South Vietnamese, and others, who fled their country after the communists took over in 1975, especially those living and working in America now and who still have memories of the flag that waved before they lost their country.

Writing a memoir requires, of course, that you write about yourself. I did not enjoy that aspect of this journey. It reminds me of narcissism and arrogance—to write about oneself. Those are two characteristics that offend me more than anything. I hope you will go easy on judging me and the memoir when it comes to those two characteristics. Because I feel so strongly about this, you will likely see another paragraph along these lines in the epilogue at the end of the book.

Acknowledgments

AT THE END OF THIS memoir, I have presented five appendixes. In three of the five, I have included summaries or quotes on an abundance of other people's work. Here I would like to acknowledge those people for granting me permission to reprint their material.

Appendix A includes the transcript of a speech by Bruce Herschensohn, "The Truth about the Vietnam War." I thank Prager University for allowing me to print the transcript in this memoir, and I'd like to mention the university's website, www.prageru.com, where readers can find the speech in both transcript and video form.

In appendix B, I present a significant amount of material from *Intellectuals and Society* by Thomas Sowell, an economist, political philosopher, and author, among other things. The book's publisher, Basic Books, has granted me permission to use this material, and I would like to credit the book as follows: *Intellectuals and Society* by Thomas Sowell, copyright 2010. Reprinted by permission of Basic Books, an imprint of Perseus Books, LLC, a subsidiary of Hachette Book Group, Inc.

Appendix C includes a significant amount of material from two other books. The first, *Thoughts of a Philosophical Fighter Pilot*, is a compendium of speeches, writings, and thoughts by Jim Stockdale, a naval aviator, Vietnam veteran, prisoner of war, scholar, retired vice admiral, and vice presidential contender. I received permission to use this material from a representative of the publication's copyright holder, the Board of Trustees of the Leland Stanford Junior University.

The second book also cited extensively in appendix C is *Stolen Valor* by B. G. Burkett and Glenna Whitley. Burkett, the former cochairman of the Texas Vietnam Memorial, has been the subject of an award-winning segment on ABC's *20/20* and of much-acclaimed articles in *Texas Monthly* and *Reader's Digest*. Burkett is a combat veteran of the Vietnam War. He served with the 199th Light Infantry Brigade and was awarded the Bronze Star Medal, Vietnamese Honor Medal, and Vietnamese Cross of Gallantry with Palm. I received his direct permission to reprint material from his book in this memoir. Glenna Whitley, Burkett's coauthor, used to be an investigative reporter and was a senior editor at *D Magazine* in Dallas, Texas, when she and Burkett wrote *Stolen Valor*. As she said to me on the phone one day, "The story in *Stolen Valor* is Burkett's." I thank Glenna for putting me in touch with B. G. Burkett.

These three books and the Herschensohn transcript helped me frame my thoughts about my own experiences in Vietnam, even though I waited more than forty years to write them down. My respect and admiration for Thomas Sowell, Jim Stockdale, B. G. Burkett, Glenna Whitley, and Bruce

Herschensohn are unconditional. In their own way, they told much of my story.

I must acknowledge two others, Mike McGill and Max Peacock, as well. These young men approached me separately and unknown to each other to ask, in essence, what I thought about the Vietnam War. Both were involved in senior class projects on Vietnam at the time. Mike and Max were the catalysts for me writing chapter 9 of this memoir as well as the supporting material/appendixes near the end.

CHAPTER 1

Ages Zero to Ten: 1942–1952

Dow Jones Industrial Average
119.71–291.90
143.8% Gain

THE FAMILY

DEAR JASON, AND JODI,

Before I was born in March of 1942, my grandfather Bill and grandmother Ma were busy working at the Gilmore & Manning Grocery Store in Sharon, Pennsylvania. Bill's sister Hazel and her husband, Joe Manning, were their joint business partners—hence their store's name. They were all hard workers.

As I understand it, Bill had been a welder before this, and I remember both he and Hazel were very down-to-earth, savvy, and wise—they always seemed to know what was going on. Ma and Bill had a fairly large house for a middle-class family, and it sat back-to-back with Hazel's house, separated by only a picket fence with a gate and lock. Bill could not have been very old when he went into the grocery business, so I often wondered where he'd found the capital for such a venture. Bill had gone as far as sixth grade in school, though I don't know what level of education Ma, Hazel, and Joe attained. Bill was about forty-three years old when I was born, and my parents were barely twenty years old. In 1942, I lived in Ma and Bill's house with my mom, Alice, and a man named Howard Abersold.* Dad was off with the navy, and I was a newborn at the time.

Dad was serving on a Patrol Torpedo (PT) boat in the navy. He had quit school in the ninth grade and was deaf in one ear from some childhood infection or disease, but he faked his hearing test to get into the navy. That's what men did then; it was hard to keep them out of the war. Mom had graduated from high school, making her the only one in the house with a high school education. Later I would ask the family about Howard Abersold, and I learned only that Bill had decided to raise him. Where Howard came from, I still don't know, even though my parents chose my middle name in his honor.

My mother, the most disciplined member of our family, cared for me in fine fashion while my dad was involved in World War II. My grandfather Bill was also disciplined, but this was more in terms of his business. As I've mentioned already, Bill was also the wise one: methodical, well-read, and very capable. Aside from my grandmother, he was also the most content one. My grandmother Ma, or Margaret, was the loving one. She always had a friendly smile—much like yours, Jodi— and no one dared to say anything bad about the family when Ma was around. When I grew older, I became aware that the whole town felt the same as I did about my grandmother. And as I did, the townsfolk also greatly respected my grandfather

---

* I'm not sure of the spelling of Howard's last name.

as a wise and capable businessman. My father was also a loving man but probably the least disciplined of the family. He would spend a while finding himself.

It was easy to remember names in the house. There was my grandfather, Big Bill; his son and my dad, Little Bill; and me, Billy. Jack, my brother, was not born yet. Ironically, Little Bill was now more than six feet tall, while Big Bill was only five foot nine. Later, when Dad came home from the war, he started calling me Butch, and I stopped going by Billy. I renamed my grandmother Ma, because I couldn't pronounce Margaret. And Alice remained Alice or Mom to me.

Because both Mom and Dad were only children, all my aunts and uncles were grandaunts and granduncles; that is, they were Ma's and Bill's brothers and sisters. I guess Mom's father, Mac, had no brothers or sisters, and Mom's mother died while Mom was a very young teenager. I don't know if my maternal grandmother had any siblings, but I guess not.

Can you think of what your first memory is? Mine is looking at the lock on the gate that separated Bill's backyard from Aunt Hazel's. I think I had finally figured out how to open that lock, though I doubt I was more than three years old at the time. The mechanics of the lock fascinated me for some reason, and I can still see it in my mind's eye.

Grandfather Bill and his sister Hazel circa 1904

Grandfather Bill and Grandmother Ma

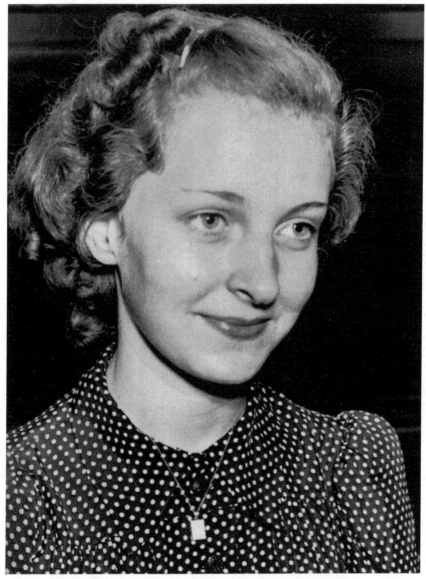

Mom, Alice Marie Gilmore—the picture doesn't do her justice.

Dad's navy class. Dad (W. J. Gilmore III) is second from the left in the top row. He always enjoyed saying he had been in PT boats, and he revered his chief petty officer. All notes on the picture are his.

The next memory I have is from about 1945, when I was three years old. I recall standing in the back seat of my grandfather's car as we drove to our new living quarters and store in Hubbard, Ohio. (At least, it was a new store to us.) The car had a big hump on the floor, and I held on to a fabric-like rope that attached to the back of the front seat. I would compare it to the velvet ropes common in movie theaters, but Jason and Jodi, I'm not sure you remember those either.

Anyway, we were going to the general store my grandfather had just purchased after selling the one in Sharon, Pennsylvania. Years later, when I asked Aunt Hazel why they'd sold the Pennsylvania store, she paused and said some individual had *really* wanted the store. That meant they could get a good price, so they sold it. We would live in two apartments above the new store at 431 East Liberty Street. My grandparents took the apartment to the left at the top of the stairs, and Mom and I lived in the one to the right.

Next I remember playing out in front of the store—in uniform. Yes, I would wear a navy outfit in those days. I was still only three to four years old.

The young sailor

As you can see in the picture, the stairs to the apartments were fairly steep and included quite a few steps. At the bottom of the stairs, a water pipe came out of the floor and went about twenty feet up into the high ceiling. I later would ride that water pipe down the stairs, after leaping through the air, grabbing it, and then sliding down to the floor like a fireman. I always thought that someday that water pipe was going to break; after all, I jumped on it from increasingly higher heights to get to the bottom of the apartment stairs. Amazingly, it never did break.

Mom and I seemed to be doing fine in the apartment. I had a bedroom way in the back, and she slept in a bed just beyond the living room. Her bedroom had no door—only a curtain that kept it a little bit private when she wanted—but it did have two windows, which overlooked East Liberty Street. This was the early 1940s; we had no TV. Neither did anybody else. I don't remember a washing machine, and nobody had a clothes dryer in those days either. In fact, I don't remember even a radio there, though I do remember a music box of my mom's that I would play with—or, to be more accurate, that I would take apart. The kitchen had a linoleum floor and was pretty sparse, and our small table sat next to a window overlooking the flat roof of the garage, where my grandfather stored oil for his business. In the winter, we would watch the snow collect on the top of that flat roof, and in the summer, we would watch the rain or sun beat against the garage's tar roof. A small fridge and a very small stove served our basic needs, and our home was quiet and peaceful. And Mom and I would talk; she was pretty young, maybe twenty-four or twenty-five.

I was probably five years old when I experienced what I would call a defining moment. World War II had just ended, although I don't remember Dad being around at all during these years. One day, there at the kitchen table, my mother talked to me about national defense and men's duty to serve the country. And then she said it: "Sometimes men have to give their lives for their country, and you might have to do that someday." As a little kid, I thought and thought and thought about what that meant. It stayed with me forever. Today, I am sure many would feel she had no right to say something like that to a little kid. Perhaps it was a little early, but it served me well in the future and was the basis for my value structure for the rest of my life. *Sometimes men* [do] *have to give their lives for their country.*

I remember that Mom had a birthday party for me when I was six years old. We still lived in the apartment, and she had the neighborhood kids over. I specifically remember she gave out some horns and other noisemakers, and I fondly recall a cowboy shirt she had made for me. She sewed most of her life and had sewn that shirt specifically for me on my birthday. Sewing seemed to be an escape for her.

I don't remember Dad's being around during this period. Bill and Ma continued working in Gilmore's General Store downstairs, and Mom would help out too. I played everywhere, as any kid would—in the store, in front of the store, behind the store, back where all the potatoes and lettuce came into the store, and back where Bill had his desk and each day methodically took out his penknife to open his mail. I still have that penknife of Bill's here on my desk as I write, as well as the leather zip-up case in which Bill carried cash for the store. He had a professional-looking florescent light over his desk too. Past Bill's desk and up some stairs were some old store materials that no one seemed to care about anymore, mostly cardboard boxes of all sizes. A few steps beyond that, I found a place I could go for hours without anybody finding or intruding upon me, mostly because it was too hot and dusty.

Other important memories of these early years for me included bike parts, nails, hammers, bolts, and washers; paint cans and brushes; candy, ice cream, and five-cent pies; bread and butter, potatoes, eggs, and other assorted groceries; the produce deliveryman; Fred, the butcher; Jimmy, the bread man; Mrs. Finney, the store clerk; and Bob McKim, a salesman and my grandfather's friend.

My biggest problem as a youngster was getting around Mrs. Finney to the candy in the cabinets behind her as she checked out customers. Jimmy, the bread man, would load six to ten neighborhood kids in his bread truck and take us on the journey to our elementary school—what a kick. Oh, and Bill called potatoes, lettuce, cabbage, bananas, and the like "produce," so I did too. I bagged potatoes a few times and marked the prices on the tops of cans of vegetables with a grease pencil. I didn't get the feeling that Bill thought much of my grease-pencil efforts and he didn't say anything after looking at some of my work. Nor did he offer me any more grease-pencil jobs. So my work devolved back to eating candy and ice cream.

Back then, I also had a fear of falling into the ice-cream freezer. To get to the ice cream, as little as I was, I had to jump up onto the freezer, balance myself on my stomach, and open the freezer with one hand. Then I would stick my whole upper body into the freezer and grab the ice-cream bars with my other hand. I always expected Bill to say something about this activity, but he never did. Years later, my brother would tell me *his* fortune in this area was not as good.

Gradually, for one reason or another, Mom and I moved across the hallway, joining Ma and Bill in their larger apartment. I remember a man and woman, the Bolands, moved into the apartment Mom and I had just vacated. Thinking back on the Bolands now, I realize they kind of reminded me of

Fred and Ethel Mertz of *I Love Lucy*. They looked like Fred and Ethel, they were about the same age, and they even dressed like them. I remember Bill saying they likely would be good tenants, because the man, Jess, was retired from the railroad and had a pension. And they *were* good tenants.

In the meantime, Mom and I settled into living with Ma and Bill. The apartment had three bedrooms and a miniature bowling-alley-like hallway that went from the first bedroom, past the other two bedrooms, and to the kitchen in the rear. By today's standards the hallway was very narrow yet was wide enough for us to travel throughout the apartment. After the kitchen came a little storage area, and after that came a fairly big porch, complete with a set of stairs down to the back of the store. Below the porch was a garage, and behind that were maybe two or three acres of open land Bill had bought as part of the store deal. Beside the store and the land was a dirt road, Fox Street. It was a dead-end street with maybe seven or eight families on it, and I came to love that street and the families living there.

I don't exactly remember when I first saw Dad again. Maybe it was when he appeared at the bottom of the stairs in his navy uniform. He was on crutches, and I think he had been in a car accident. Mom seemed to keep him at the foot of the stairs and then ushered me off. I guess they talked.

After that, I remember Dad in the apartment with us all. He was in civilian clothes and had two tattoos. One, on his forearm, was a large anchor with some dates on it. *US Navy* was inscribed below the anchor. On the inside of his other arm, he had a smaller tattoo, which was my mother's name, Alice, inscribed in the middle of an anchor. Many military guys had tattoos back in the day, and it seemed like a rite of passage for all the young men who had served in the military. This was around the time he started calling me Butch; I didn't know why. I didn't call him anything. If I wanted to ask him a question, I would just ask the question looking at him. I'd never called him "Dad."

Years later I would find out that, in this relative time frame, Dad took Mom and me to Michigan to try to start a new life after the war. Mom later told me she had become so close to Ma and Bill that—particularly with her mother dead—she felt really homesick for them. Over the years, she felt guilty for not having tried harder to adapt to the new life in Michigan. I do not remember ever being there. That is a total blank for me. We returned to the apartment above the store in Hubbard with Ma and Bill in a very short time, probably within a few months.

As a little kid, I stayed busy in the apartment. I remember taking the kitchen chairs apart with a screwdriver and putting them back together again. Mom, who provided the screwdriver and the advice on how to do it, was cool. I would also busy myself with turning orange crates from the store into "chairs" with a storage area on the bottom of the crate used for comic books. Bill, Ma, and Mom remained busy in the store, and sometimes Dad was there too.

I remember Bill putting a sign in front of the store that said Gilmore and Son Groceries, and I remember thinking that maybe someday I'd get *my* name on the store too. Dad worked as a radio repairman of sorts for the store and tried to become a part of Gilmore and Son Groceries. But later he tried to sell insurance, and after that, he tried to sell ice cream out of a freezer attached to the front of a bicycle? He had bought a couple freezers that could be strapped to your body or hooked on to a bicycle. I think he tried to hire a couple people to sell frozen ice cream out of these but that did not last long at all. These money making efforts all seemed separate from the Gilmore and Son store. And then he wasn't around for a while. For the most part, I didn't remember when he was gone or when he was home. Bill was my role model, and he was always there and always working, and I always knew where he was. Little did I know how I would be influenced by these four people in the apartment above the store.

I also remember Mom and Ma doing the ironing back in Ma and Bill's bedroom. They both would be back there, one with an iron and the other working on the "mangle." The mangle was a pretty fancy machine for those days, and Mom or Ma would operate it by using their hands and knees to press pants or other large items. The machine was at least a yard wide, and by raising the hot rolling device up and down, they could insert the pants or whatever they were pressing. The item they were working on would roll through the mangle and come out the top with a finished dry-cleaner look, including knife-edge creases on pants and shirtsleeves. I remember them pressing underwear, shirts, and handkerchiefs along with everything else. Of course I went to school with a pressed handkerchief in my back pocket as a youngster! And I know none of the neighbors had a mangle.

Ma and Mom seemed to get along really well. They were always laughing and having a good time. Ma was spending time with a daughter she'd never had, and Mom was having time with a mother she hadn't had since she was a young teenager. There was a radio there in the bedroom too, and it was always on and usually tuned to some type of newscast, such as Edward R. Murrow or Art Linkletter. Sometimes the radio was inaudible because of all the chatter and laughter going on during these ironing days.

The back porch above the store became a sanctuary of sorts. It was very high off the ground and gave me my first taste of being above sea level, so to speak. It was on this porch that my grandfather taught me to tell time, and it was also where I would learn to launch "rockets." I found somehow that if I wrapped a match tip with tin foil, opened a tiny airway in the tin foil with a needle, and heated the tip of the match, eventually it would fly off the porch, trailing smoke. I would guess that I launched about five thousand of these off the porch or its steps. Ma and Mom tended to their geraniums on the porch in the summer and hung all our clothes out to dry up there. It seemed they were always talking and laughing. Just standing up there on the porch, looking down on things on Fox Street, and feeling the breeze—be it summer or winter— was mesmerizing for a little guy.

In about 1948, our family was the first of all the Fox Street people to get a TV. This was back in the day when there was a "test pattern" on early in the day and late at night. It was of course, black and white. No color back then. It also had an antenna that you turned by hand near the TV, known as "rabbit ears" because it consisted of two metal projections split apart much like...rabbit ears. We had a good time sitting around and watching TV together, but the TV picture and the programming, by today's standards, were abysmal. We watched wrestling a lot and even went to see some matches when famous wrestlers were in town—in Youngstown, that is.

In fact, I still have Don Eagle's autograph. He wore an Indian headdress into the ring. Farmer Don Marlin and Argentina Rocca were other interesting wrestling characters. We didn't realize that professional wrestling, especially in those early days, was all fake; so color us—and many like us—naïve.

A PIPER CUB

Eventually I went to school and seemed to do pretty well, at least for the first three grades. Mom had spent a fair amount of time reading to me and correcting my small vocabulary and I knew that was making a difference for me in school.

In the summers, she would take me to Yankee Lake, and we'd swim and lie on the "beach." The lake was located out on Route 7, about seven miles out of Hubbard. I loved going to the lake with her and remember her drying my head off with a towel after I came out of the water. It always felt warm and soothing, and I wouldn't move until she was done.

Then she'd take me over to the YMCA, where I'd swim. Eventually the neighborhood boys and I would take the bus to Youngstown and go to the Y without adult supervision. When I was only six or seven years old, I won two swimming ribbons; one for holding my breath longer than anyone else and one for swimming with my head down. I can remember looking up after one of these races, and there Mom was as usual, smiling down at me. I loved her.

Jack Mason, our neighbor, had a cottage up on Lake Erie, near the town of Geneva-on-the-Lake. Occasionally he'd ask if I wanted to go with their family to the cottage for the weekend, and I remember Mom and I spent a day or two there with them. Life was about as good as it could get. We swam in Lake Erie, where the big waves were. With all this swimming, I became very comfortable in the water and grew to love it. And Mom was always nearby, it seemed.

About this time, I found myself looking at scrapbooks my mother was keeping. In one of them, I saw a picture of her and Dad leaning up against a Piper Cub airplane. Mom was holding a baby. I asked, time and time again, who the baby was, and she always smiled and responded, "You." And I would look at it and wonder about my dad, my mom, that airplane, and me. My dad had taken flying lessons on the GI bill, and this was proof that he had flown. This picture would be a catalyst for me, I think, for the rest of my life, though I had no idea of that at the time.

DISCIPLINE

In those days, if I did something outside that I shouldn't, Mom would call for me. With young kids playing outside all the time, mothers were always *calling* their kids for various reasons. If I looked up and saw her with her hand on her hip and a finger pointed high in the air toward the stairs, I knew what was about to happen. I would approach, and she would take me by a hand, stretch it above my head until I was on my tiptoes, and then commence whipping my behind, all the way up the stairs. She would explain why she was doing this as we went up the stairs. She used this method of discipline for a long time until I learned a few years later that if I could get up a head of steam running as I approached her, she would have some difficulty catching up with me. One day I made it all the way to the top without her laying a single hand on me, and we laughed all the way up the stairs because we both knew that she would never catch me again on any race up the stairs. That was the last time she attempted that kind of discipline. To this day, I am glad for the discipline she instilled in me, though the liberals of the world might cringe to hear me say that. I guess the new word for a liberal is *progressive*. As far as I can tell, they mean the same thing.

WHEELS

Somewhere along the line, my next-door neighbor, Dick Mason started pushing a scooter around. It wasn't an ordinary scooter, though; it was quite a bit larger than an ordinary scooter, the tires were a lot bigger than ordinary, and the back end of it contained a rather large empty compartment. In short, it was a motor scooter without a motor in it. Dick and I would push each other around on it, taking turns as rider or pusher, while sweating in the Ohio summer humidity. Eventually we found a large hill on a dusty dirt road. It seemed to take us an hour or so to push the scooter up the hill, but once atop the hill, we would both climb on the scooter and ride it down. The trip down seemed to take only thirty seconds, though perhaps it lasted a minute. And then we'd push the scooter back up the hill. You get the picture. I'm sure Jack Mason, Dick's father, is the one who found that old scooter, but I don't know where he got it.

Jack was a machinist, as I understood it. He seemed to be a kind and methodical guy. When I look back on it, he seemed to know my dad wasn't around much. I remember Jack taking a quick shot of whiskey from time to time but never saw him even approach being under the influence.

He was the first person I ever saw drink alcohol. Jack had a little darkroom in the basement of their house, where he often produced professional-quality pictures. Dick and I developed some pictures down there too, using the required chemicals to produce them. Dick seemed to know what he was doing. Jack seemed to be able to balance his work life and his family life, and he seemed almost as happy as Bill seemed—though to be as happy or content as Bill was impossible.

I can't jump ahead without drawing this scene. At about age six, I was walking up East Hill toward the store, coming home from school. As I crested the hill, I saw Mom holding a twenty-six-inch bike. It was green and white and brand-new. It was a Schwinn with a built-in light, a built-in horn, and New Departure brakes. I ran to her and jumped on the bike; feeling her light hand on my back, I pushed off. And away I went. As I learned later, she had saved some of the money Bill had given her from working in the store to buy it, though at the time, I didn't have a clue about what was going on with my mom and dad. Up until this point, I had talked Dick Mason into letting me ride his twenty-inch bike, which as I remember, had no fenders. It felt like a little hot rod, was very maneuverable, and looked cool.

Soon I was taking longer and longer bike rides. My friend AG—short for Addison Guy—lived out in the country. I remember riding my bike a couple of miles out to his house one day. AG's mother said he was down in the little barn, and I walked the fifty or so yards to get there. I had never been there before and didn't know what to expect inside the barn. What I saw was AG sitting on a stool, milking a cow. Now this was different from anything I had seen on Fox Street. AG wanted me to try milking the cow, but I don't think I did.

Mom used to drive my school friend Paul Leach and me to Sharon to go roller-skating. Hey, roller skates qualified as *wheels*! We got pretty good and eventually entered a lot of races as a two-man (boy) team. The idea was if anybody passed you, you were eliminated. Paul and I became unbeatable. After several months, the roller-rink management decided we would all compete individually. In the end, Paul beat me for the coveted prize: a Coke. I knew he would—I was too fat. But I could beat everyone else there, except Paul. Like bikes and scooters, even roller skates seemed to be all about speed.

Paul offered me lunch one day. We ran down to his house from school. I noticed nobody was there, but that was normal for him, as both his parents worked, and his sisters were in school. He got out a ladder, climbed up, and began pulling cans of soup out of the cabinet, asking what kind I wanted. I didn't care, and eventually Paul turned on the stove. We ate together in the quiet house on a spring day in Ohio. It was very peaceful.

Many of us youngsters used to go to the movies at the theater in downtown Hubbard. They always had a drawing on Saturdays: if you bought popcorn, you could tear off part of the cardboard box, put your name on it, and then drop that into a large container full of other entries for the big prize, a free ticket to the movies. The motives for the theater, of course, were to see that you bought a lot of popcorn in order to enter the drawing. Well, I found out that Paul's mother often worked at the theater. In that job, she found a lot of empty popcorn boxes on the floor.

Paul told me he could get as many as I wanted. I took a lot of them when Paul's mother provided them, and I stuffed the large container with all my entries for the weekly contest. My name was called for the first five prizes. It took that many wins for me to realize that what I was doing was just not right, and I shut down the popcorn operation. And I would feel guilty about it for the rest of my life. Although we didn't keep in touch through the years, later I became reacquainted with Paul. And I will always remember those roller skating days.

THE NEIGHBORHOOD

At six years old or so, I became aware of the rest of the neighborhood. I was fascinated by the kids on the street and their families and was obsessed with knowing them—I mean, *really* knowing them. They, too, would influence me greatly. Our neighbor Jack Mason and his son, Dick, were part of this influence, but others on Fox Street would affect me too.

Farther up Fox Street lived the McBrides. Bill and Gladys McBride had at least four kids: Huey, Kathleen, Billy (I think), and Bobby. Bill worked in the steel mills of Youngstown, like most people in the area. Each day I would see him walk down the street with his black lunch bucket in hand. Bill was very interested in sports and became the coach of my Little League team, the Tigers. One day he suggested I throw some balls to him in their front yard—little did I know that he was going to let me come off my first-base position and pitch a few games for the Tigers. I never learned how to get any heat on the ball, though, and I never learned to hit a fast pitch, even though I had been an outstanding hitter in softball. The McBrides seemed to struggle financially, and I always figured it was because of having all those kids. Huey, two years my senior, would become known as "Golden Arm," because of his quarterbacking prowess on the local high school football team. He played the trumpet too, and the McBrides had a piano in their house, though nobody I knew of played it. Huey and I later tried to jam, with me on the piano and him on the trumpet. That didn't work out.

Farther up the street were the Collers. Robert Coller was my buddy, even though he was four years older. His dad was never around, and his mother was as cool as could be. Tall and very lean, she would fix us tea and crackers. Or we would just eat crackers and mayonnaise. Robert and I would lie on the living-room floor and listen to the *Green Hornet*, a radio program about the adventures of a supposed newspaper reporter who would don a mask and fight crime at night. A few years later, Robert's dad showed up and stayed awhile, later becoming a sheriff. I often took my record player up to Robert's house, where we hooked up an extension cord and placed the device on a banister overlooking the yard and Fox Street. Then we would play the record *Rock around the Clock* by Bill Haley and the Comets until we couldn't stand it anymore.

A few years later, when my family talked of moving from Hubbard, I announced that I would not leave the town. Mom asked where I would live, and I quickly said, "I'll live at the Collers'." Mom asked what I would eat, and I answered, "Mayonnaise and crackers and tea." The Collers had little money, but their house sure was quiet and peaceful, and Mrs. Coller did a lot of smiling and giggling. In the years since, I've realized why it was so quiet there: there were only two people in the house—Robert and his mom—versus the five or six of us in the Gilmore house.

The Harley boys: Robert Coller, Butch Gilmore, Dick Mason (about 1948)

Across the street from the Collers lived the Corals, who had two daughters, Bev and Midge. Mrs. Coral worked in Bill's store once in a while, but I don't know what Mr. Coral did for a living, though I noticed he tended to beehives out back in the summer. I watched him closely one day as he walked toward the bees. He'd obviously had some kind of problem, likely a birth defect or maybe an accident, and it affected the way he walked. He had a limp with a pause in the middle, and it seemed to take twice as long for him to get one leg forward as it took his other leg. Up close, he seemed a handsome man to me, his sun-browned face and athletic look making up for his labored gait. He also would repair things around Bill's store from time to time. I never got inside their house, but from the outside, it looked like the Corals had a good thing going on. Bev, who played tag football with the rest of the neighborhood kids in the Corals' front yard when we were under ten, would become a physical-education teacher. I don't know what Midge ended up doing.

Not far from the Corals' house was an open field that was everything to the kids of Fox Street—"my kids," as I called them. It was our baseball field, complete with a dugout, and our football field. It was the place where we held a "carnival," during which I remember lying on the ground and rolling over completely while Dick Mason balanced on my back. What an act. We had a pole-vault operation going on in that field as well, and I think eventually we all could jump more than four feet in this effort.

In the early, early years, we all decided we were going to dig our way from our field down to China. Somehow all of us found shovels, and we dug and dug and dug. We didn't get to China—the hole seemed to get wider than it did deep—but we talked a lot about it and a lot of other things too. Maybe we learned to philosophize right there. Kids will do some amazing things. We had no adult supervisors, and there was no worry that something would happen to us there on Fox Street in Hubbard, Ohio, as we tried to dig to China.

Walt and Katherine Johnson lived across the street from what would later be our house at 33 Fox Street. The Johnsons had four kids: Janice, Marilyn, Kathy, and Jimmy. Walt was seldom there, but when he was, I noticed he wore a starched white shirt. He was a handsome man. Mrs. Johnson was pretty heavyset, and despite caring for four kids with no visible support, she had a great sense of humor. Janice was two years older than I was and eventually gave me my first kiss. I had no idea what that was all about and curtailed the relationship. Marilyn was my age and eventually had at least four kids herself. Kathy was a pretty little girl, but I never really knew her. Jim, I heard, ran a bar in Hubbard years later. Early on, I'd wondered who had served as his model while growing up.

The Johnsons' front porch was a good place to spend summer evenings, and we would all sit, talk, and laugh—just the Johnsons and me. Mrs. Johnson would sweat because of the humidity and because she laughed so hard. Of course, we all sweated during those hot and very humid nights in northeast Ohio. Again, I thought, here was a family who seemed to have it pretty good despite their economic situation. They enjoyed one another and were kind enough to let me have a brief view into their life. The three girls jumped rope a lot and played hopscotch on the sidewalk in front of their house. Although it was not the manly thing to do, I often joined in. The "two rope" jump rope was cool, and it all had a rhythm to it.

Around the corner on Liberty Street were the Featsants. They had two kids, Paul and Kathleen. When Paul and Kathleen finished growing, the whole family was very tall, at least six feet each, and I thought they were all good-looking. They were Catholics, and I used to listen to Paul talk about learning about Catholicism while at school. It seemed odd to me to be learning religion at school, and I didn't quite get why he and his sister weren't in public school. Later that all became clear, but I will hand it to Paul for making me stop and think a little bit about religion.

At the same time, I was being exposed to religion through Mom, who took me to the Methodist church sometimes and to Bible school quite a bit. I didn't understand how I was a sinner, like the preacher said, and I still have a bit of a problem with a preacher including kids in the sinner thing. I know: some Bible study would clear this issue up for me. In first grade and in Bible school, I'd meet up with the Fluent brothers, AG and Fran, and they became my friends. We would remain good friends throughout my life, and eventually, my brother would be a friend to them as well.

On the next street up from Fox lived the Tobeys, who had three boys: Emmerson, Gerome, and Art. Art was the youngest, and he was two years older than I was. His mom would be our Cub Scout den mother. The Tobeys seemed very industrious. Emmerson or Gerome, I forget which, played the piano, and I wanted to play the piano too. They had a horse or two, and Gerome would later get an Austin Healy and allow Art to drive me around in it. Now *that* was a car. That engine sounded different from US-produced cars, and there was a gearshift on the floor. The new leather smelled good, and the engine had a smell I liked as well. I noticed things like that. Their garage was full of tools, bolts and nuts, and many other things. I liked the tools.

I guess I'm getting ridiculous in describing all the neighbors, but I've always felt that, in one way or another, I was shaped by them all. For my last portrait of these folks, I will describe what I call the Three Grocers of Hubbard. Bill was one grocer. Mr. Patton was another, and Mr. Thiel was a third. Dick Patton and Jack Thiel were my age, and consequently, we all went to school together and were in the same class. The Pattons had six kids and seemed to be doing fine economically. The Thiels had two kids and were doing well economically too. I developed a crush on Jane Patton, like most other boys in the school, but nothing happened from that. Dick, Jack, and I became friends in grade school but drifted apart later. It seemed that we were aware of the grocery business as an underlying commonality among us, even though we never talked about it.

I later learned to jitterbug in Jack Thiel's basement out on West Liberty in Hubbard. We played a lot of Ping-Pong down there as well. I would sit and watch TV with Dick Patton and his dad in their family room in the basement of their house, but we never talked to his dad, who seemed like he was busy thinking all the time. I think I was in love with Mrs. Patton too. She and her daughter Jane had eyes so blue they seemed to flash. I knew she had a big job taking care of all those kids, but she would smile and listen to anything you wanted to say. I tried to wash dishes there a few times, but they soon knew I didn't know what I was doing...yet they pretended not to know I had never washed a dish in my life.

THE STORE, BILL, AND CLODHOPPERS

Another important part of my life from ages six to ten was my interaction with Bill's store. Bill ran a true general store, because he had generally anything you wanted: groceries, meats, milk, canned goods, produce, ice cream, candy, paint, beer, wine, nuts, bolts, nails, hammers, baseballs, ball gloves, catcher's mitts, catcher's masks, chest protectors, and probably many other things I don't remember. I partook of most everything in the store, and Bill never slowed me down. I regularly ate ice cream, drank soft drinks, and chewed bubble gum to my heart's content. As I've mentioned, my biggest problem in life here was scooting around Mrs. Finney's behind to get to the candy counter. Mrs. Finney was a clerk at the store for many years. I never knew if there was a Mr. Finney.

When I was six, I walked or rode my bike to school all the time, a trip of about a mile each way. On my way to school, I would go by some of the small shops in town before turning up the street to get to Roosevelt Grade School. At the time, some kids wore "clodhoppers," shoes that came up over the ankles and were made of thick leather. They also had cleats on the heels to keep the heels from wearing down, but more importantly, they gave off an audible click-click-click as wearers walked down the concrete sidewalk.

Well, every day I would walk past this clothing store and see a pair of clodhoppers displayed in the window. Eventually I took action. I walked into the store, and the owner greeted me. He was tall, slender; and, of course, well dressed. I smiled at him and said, "Hello," as my mother had taught me to do with people. He responded in kind and, with a smile, asked if he could help. I asked, "Yes, may I borrow your phone?" He smiled and showed me where the phone was, way in the back of the store. I dialed the number for Bill's store. The phone rang, and then Mrs. Finney answered.

"Hi, Mrs. Finney. Is Bill there?" I asked.

She gave the phone to Bill.

"Hi, Bill," I said. "This is Butch."

"Hi," he said. "How are you?"

"I'm good…I'm down here at so-and-so's store, and I was just wondering if you could come buy me these shoes I have been looking at."

"Well, I'll be right down there. I want to see these shoes," he said.

Of course he bought them for me. Maybe he knew what an impact that had on me, but I seriously doubt it. I knew I might be going over the line in asking him to buy me something like that, but for the rest of my life, I appreciated what he did. He was probably up to his eyeballs in work at the store, but he showed up in about ten minutes. And after the purchase, he smiled. And I had my new clodhoppers and made a lot of noise everywhere I walked. I thought I was cool. I wasn't. It was my grandfather who was cool.

Somewhere along the line, Bill and Ma started hanging around the Baums. Mr. Baum's name was Harry, but I forget hers. Harry was the first man I had seen who was bigger around the waist than Bill. (When Bill was in his fifties, he weighed around 255 pounds.) When Harry talked, he sounded something like the godfather—that is, he seemed to need a lot of air to talk. Bill and Harry were always talking about business. Eventually Harry would own a pawnshop, and Bill said Harry reached under his counter one day and pulled out a shoe box. It was full of diamonds.

Then there was the story about Bill and Harry going on some trip. They stopped for lunch. After they finished eating, the waitress brought over the tab, but Harry told her they were not done and wanted an ice-cream sundae for dessert.

Then the waitress brought over the tab again, and Harry told her they were still not done. He said they wanted another sundae. This continued until they had each eaten four sundaes. As the waitress walked away to get the fifth, Harry leaned over and said to Bill, "We'll show these bastards how to eat sundaes."

Later the Baums and Ma and Bill would make a trip out west. They came back with a sombrero for me and a leather holster for two toy guns, one on the right and one on the left. The white holsters had my name inscribed on them: Billy Gilmore. No, I never realized how spoiled I was. I didn't ask for the sombrero or the guns, mind you.

One day, after some bicycles with hand brakes started to appear in America, a new bike appeared in the back of the store near where the produce came in. It was another Schwinn. Bill had bought it for me—probably after I made it known that I wanted it, though I don't remember doing that. The bike was reddish. Bill didn't make any fanfare out of things like this. By the time I was finished admiring it, he was back at work in the store. I tried helping with stocking shelves, bagging potatoes, labeling prices on canned goods, and other tasks, but I never seemed to solidify a job at the store. Bill did everything. He would become the butcher if he had to, and at one time, I think we even had live chickens in the basement of the store. He waited on customers, stocked shelves, cleaned and put up produce, talked to salesmen, hired and fired people, and always knew what was going on with the family. He liked to play cards, especially poker, canasta, or bridge. And he would go on a fishing trip to Canada every year for a week with his guy friends.

There was a small bathroom in the basement of the store. I noticed after Dad came home that a "Kilroy Was Here" caricature was penciled in on the bathroom wall; this phrase became associated with GIs in the 1940s and was usually written below a cartoonlike man with a bald head and large nose peeking over a wall and clutching the wall with the fingers of each hand.

At night, I noticed Ma would look at each and every bill that showed what the customers had purchased that day and what price they had been charged. As each bill was made out during the day, the cashiers would place it on a device that looked like an upside-down nail. At the end of the day, the stack of bills could easily be carried home via this device. Ma would add up each number on every bill every night to see if any errors had been made. She did it quietly on her own. I never heard Bill tell her to do this; she just always did it.

RECIPROCATING ENGINES

Something happened with that scooter of Dick Mason's. All of a sudden, it had a motor in the back where the open compartment had been, and a twist grip on the right side that regulated the carburetor and allowed the rider to go faster if he or she wanted. We probably got up to fifteen miles an hour, and this was a life changer for me. I found the smell of gas and oil intoxicating, both literally and figuratively. I began imagining the places I could go on that scooter if Dick allowed me to ride it. We didn't have to push it anymore, which I found totally amazing. In the beginning, I rode on the back with

Dick driving. One day, we had too much fuel in the tank, and because I was sitting on that tank, the fuel leaked onto my butt. I learned the hard way about the effects of gasoline on human skin. My butt burned for days, it seemed.

Eventually, Dick would let me take the scooter out by myself—OMG, as kids say nowadays. When I would get to take the scooter by myself, I always traveled the same route: down Fox Street, over to a path behind Bill's store, up the path to where it intersected with Creed Avenue, and up to the cemetery. Yes, the cemetery. And then around and around and around the cemetery I would go. The biggest reason for this was that there were no cops at the cemetery, and Dick and I weren't more than seven or eight years old at the time—not old enough to be driving a motorized vehicle on the road. It was quiet at the cemetery with only the sound of the *putt...putt...putt...*coming from the little scooter engine. The hot summer days and rain had ensured that the cemetery grounds were brilliantly green, and the robins were always busy pulling worms out of the ground.

Even at that age, with the little engine putting along, I often thought about how alive I felt on the scooter. That feeling contrasted sharply with my thoughts about all the people under the tombstones. But it was my time to live, and life on the scooter was good. The gravel around the cemetery was not very stable, but it was good to learn how to handle the scooter on this type of road. (Generally speaking, it was a good thing for my future in motorized vehicles.) It was always painful—*really* painful—to turn the scooter back over to Dick, but to this day, I am thankful to him for letting me experience that scooter with the real live engine in it.

Although the scooter dominated our lives, there were still things going on at school.

When I was about eight, I got into a discussion with Huey McBride and Robert Coller, who told me I ought to join the "early class" and get out of the "late class." This was a scheme for me to get home from school at the same time they did. This would allow us to commence playing together on Fox Street an hour earlier. I told Mom what I wanted to do, and she made it happen, but I'd forgotten I would be leaving my friends in the late class to do this. The first thing I remember was how dark it was when I started going to school in the early class. The second thing I remember was that the kids were a little different—not much, but a little. I got to know them and enjoyed them all, as I had the kids in the late class. I note this early class/late class thing only to say that because of it, I probably ended up knowing the entire class on a more personal basis than most. As always, I enjoyed studying personalities.

Around fourth grade, my teacher said I was not reading as I should be. This was the first time I had felt pressure to perform in school, but no matter what I did, I still didn't seem to satisfy the teacher. My focus reverted back to enjoying the Fox Street life. I started getting a few Cs from time to time, and I wondered how that was happening but didn't do much to correct it. Mom would review the report cards with me and talk to me about them, but she knew everything was OK with me and Roosevelt Grade School.

JOHN T. GILMORE ARRIVES

When I was eight years old, I heard talk of another child in the family. Mom was pregnant, and I was going to have a sibling. I remember overhearing some talk about the likelihood that I would become jealous, but I honestly don't think that ever happened. It wasn't that I didn't have it in me, but too many years separated us. I was nine years old when Mom went to the hospital to have my brother, Jack. I woke up the next morning and saw the biggest snowfall I'd ever seen. I asked when my mom and new brother would be home, and Ma told me they were stranded in the hospital because of the snowstorm.

Because the schools were closed, I went sledding down East Hill, as we called it. Midway through the afternoon, a hearse or hospital-type ambulance made its way up East Hill. It had chains on it to get through the snow. When I got home, I found that my mom and new brother had been delivered to the apartment. Dad was home too. I don't know when he became a regular in the house, but now he seemed to be around every day.

Jack and I shared a room in the apartment, midway between Mom and Dad's bedroom and Ma and Bill's bedroom. I remember the crib in the room with me, with Liberty Street's yellow caution light blinking and reflecting on a wall in our bedroom. It would illuminate a mirror in my bedroom that had a decal of Jim Hegan, a catcher for the Cleveland Indians, on it. I always wanted to be a catcher but found that left-handers are not catchers. It was something about their throw and the distance between some bases—I forget the details, but you get my drift. Anyway, funny how that little baby in the crib

we immediately headed to some double doors. Bill opened one of the doors and motioned for me to enter. And now came an exposure that would influence me for the rest of my life.

Before me was the following scene: a room one-fourth the size of a basketball court with one wall of blackboards from the floor to the ceiling, divided top and bottom into columns and labeled at the top of each column with the symbols of all the large companies in America. There were ladders pulled up to these blackboards. They looked like those ladders you see in movies that depict libraries of the thirties or forties. The ladders were attached to a rail or something at the top and could be pushed back and forth to where you wanted them to be.

Women were constantly dashing between the blackboards and a ticker-tape machine, which marked current prices of Wall Street stocks onto a tape. The women would pull a yard or so of the ticker tape from the ticker machine and then go and post several of the prices that had just come through. Sometimes they would go directly to a company symbol down low on the blackboard; sometimes they would run up the ladder to get to a company that was up high. Once they found the company they were looking for, they would copy the current price of the company's stock on to the blackboard. You could tell how much the stock price had changed by looking at the previous prices written in chalk. Meanwhile, the men in the room, dressed mostly like my grandfather, were engaged in a ritual of sorts. Many were smoking cigars, and most were conversing with one another about one thing or another, but business was at the heart of their discussions, and their opinions on public companies seemed to receive most of their attention. I also noted that, as the men talked to one another, they often watched the women posting prices. But the focus remained business and the stock market. Bill didn't say much to me about what was going on that day, and it probably took me a few years to realize what I had seen, but that experience changed my life in a profound way.

A Summary and a Defining Moment

In that first decade, I guess I was just busy having fun. I was getting to know people. I had ridden and appreciated a motor scooter, and I seemed to be getting through school OK. My dad was home more often, and I had a new baby brother. I had learned to swim with Mom usually close by, and thanks to her, I was very comfortable in the water. I had seen a stock-brokerage office operating up close and would later note that I had never learned anything about the stock market while in grade school, high school, or college, and I wondered why. Mom remained my disciplinarian, and she continued to watch over me. She and Ma cooked, did the wash, did the ironing, washed the windows, washed the floors, cleaned the house, and generally spoiled the hell out of the men and two boys in the house. The two women worked in the store too. Bill continued to build his business at Gilmore's General Store. And toward the end of this first decade of my life, Dad was spending most, if not all, of his time at home.

In this same time frame, my mother gave me another "defining moment" talk. She said, more than once, that when I grew up, I would go to college, get married, and move away from Hubbard. And I thought about that moment for the rest of my life. It meant above all else that I would eventually move out of the little town that I loved and that I would move away from all my friends that I loved. As for going to college and getting married, I presumed that would be just be a natural process of growing up.

I really didn't like the idea of moving away, ever. But like most things my mother said, I knew it was her notion of what would be best for me. And so I adjusted to that thought.

CHAPTER 2

Ages Ten to Twenty: 1952–1962

Dow Jones Industrial Average
291.9–652.1
123.4% Gain

THE FOX STREET HOUSE

SHORTLY AFTER MY BROTHER WAS born, my grandfather had a house built behind the store—the 33 Fox Street house. He paid about $15,000 for this structure, and it would give the family a little more room; however, we were moving six people into this three-bedroom abode. We eventually would have a yard and a basement. This was a little different from living above the store.

I noticed that Dad was employed as a carpenter on the house, and I think Bill had made that a part of the deal with the builder. He would pay to have the house built, but it would also serve as a training camp for my father to become a carpenter. This seemed to be a good idea.

We eventually moved in.

My brother and I slept in bunk beds, and I got the bottom. Jack was about two or three years old, I guess. It was fun, but nine years is a big age difference between young brothers.

Each night we took our places around the kitchen table with Bill at the head. Ma sat to his right, and Mom sat to *her* right. I sat to her right at the foot of the table. Jack sat to my right, and on his right was usually an empty chair. Sometimes Dad was there.

My brother, Jack, and the fire truck

This is probably my favorite picture of my brother. He used to fly around on this kid-propelled fire engine. That bell on the front was always dinging as he went along, and his favorite thing to do was go as fast as he could and then lock up the pedals so he would skid sideways to a stop. If he is three here, I am twelve years old.

The Gilmore brothers

I would wrestle with Dad now, and eventually, I even began calling him Dad. The first time occurred while we were washing our '53 Chevy out on the driveway of the new Fox Street house. It would take me until I was about eighteen to beat him in arm wrestling, and I remember feeling almost sorry for beating him when I finally did. I noticed he had picked up odd jobs around the house, such as mowing the grass, painting the house's exterior, and the like.

Usually I helped a little. Dad had a lot of tools in the garage, and I found them interesting. The bolts, nuts, screws, and washers all tucked into little drawers were also a part of the garage. Acetylene torches for welding and an electric arc welder were in place to do some work as well. Dad wasn't a very good welder, but he did weld a lot of things. I wasn't good at welding either, but I wanted to be. A fairly large drill press sat on the large workbench too. Gradually, wood-working tools began to appear, and eventually chisels, table saws, handsaws, and other saws were around the garage. I never got into the woodworking deal, though my brother did later.

Dad always talked very respectfully about two subjects: Bill and the US Navy. This would end up in my subconscious, and eventually I had a similar respect for Bill (which I already had) and the navy, or the military in general. Dad would talk of a certain chief petty officer as if he were God. Dad would sing, "Bless 'em all, bless 'em all, the long and the short and the tall." It took me a long time before I realized he was singing about women, though I don't know what *long* meant. It sounded like a navy drinking song to me. He would talk of Shanghai, and he sang something about "the ships in Bombay." I knew only that Bombay and Shanghai were a long way from Hubbard, and that the kids on Fox Street and I had once tried to dig our way there.

Why all the respect for the navy? I would think about that for a long time. Once in a while, I would open his dresser drawer and look in to see his ribbons from the navy. He obviously was proud of them, but we never talked about them or the navy—other than about his chief petty officer. He did tell a story about going absent without leave (AWOL) once, but I don't know how much trouble he got into for that. Although I'm told he did it to come home and see Mom, I still thought for a long, long time about his breaking the rules.

The Masons next door had a new boat: a Yellow Jacket with a forty-horse Mercury engine on it and a "Tee Nee" trailer. Dad was interested, and the two of us gradually started going to Lake Milton and Mosquito Lake just to watch people launching and recovering their boats. I remember it was the first time I'd been in the same car with him. Eventually we would get a boat much like the Masons'. This was all quite a surprise for me, as I was still getting used to having Dad around. I didn't realize he would get involved with boats. He bought the boat in March, I think— and I went water-skiing in March. Yes, March is very cold in Ohio, but it was an adventure, and there was speed associated with taking the skis across the wake when the boat was in a full-throttle turn. And we were around water. Now it was Dad and me and water, instead of Mom and me and water.

Dad did some truck driving once the house was built, and at one point, Bill bought him a diesel truck with two trailers—a set of doubles, as they called it. This was really a big rig. I watched Dad as he taught himself to drive it and, more importantly, to back it up with two trailers attached. That wasn't a small thing. Around and around the store he would go, stopping and backing, stopping and backing; then round and round he'd go again. Eventually he was on the road with it. I heard about tickets from the cops for being overloaded and for speeding. Eventually the truck was gone, and Dad began driving for some different companies. Eventually he got a job with Loblaw's, a grocery chain, which he had for quite some time. He made decent money and seemed to settle down a little. I knew, against this backdrop, that sometime I must decide what I would do with *my* life. I hoped I would like whatever it was.

Dad was not supposed to take riders in the truck, but he picked me up in it anyway, and we went out on one of his runs, delivering grocery products to Loblaw stores. He had picked me up from my hiding place a few miles from where he had signed in for his workday. He knew he shouldn't do this, but when we returned, he pulled into the main office with me in the truck and took me into the office with him. Although it showed no respect for authority, in the end, nothing ever happened. I remember all the truck drivers there that day and the manly humor wafting through the air. Dad liked his buddies and loved fooling around. I guess I liked the same thing, in that regard. These were blue-collar workers, whatever that was, and they seemed to have a good time and drank a whole lot of coffee.

It is hard to think about the Fox Street house without thinking about the beautician that resided therein. Mom decided she was going to become a beautician, and she did a lot of studying to take her state board tests. Dad and I worked to install a beauty shop in the basement. Not bad. It was small, but it was air-conditioned and complete with fluorescent lights, a sink and mirror, and two hair dryers. Little did I know that Mom would spend some thirty years down there in the basement with no windows or sunlight. I think most of the money she made went to pay for an education for me and my brother. Dad placed a sign outside of the house that read Alice's Beauty Shop. She continued to smoke in the little beauty shop, as did most of the women who came to get their hair done. She carried her little white scheduling book with her always. She made breakfast for us, and then she'd fly down the stairs for her appointments, dressed in her white beautician's outfit.

During these years, Howard, my namesake (middle name), and Reva, his wife, would show up at the house. Reva could play the piano by ear, and I wished I could play like she did. And she was one of the most beautiful women I had seen to that point in my life. Maybe her playing for us made me finally bite the bullet and quit my piano lessons, if you know what I mean. I had tried for three years; I had *really* tried. I could play a few songs by memory: "Mr. Sandman," "Autumn Leaves," and my favorite, "Chattanooga Shoe Shine Boy." The last song would help me out years later in college. Sitting for hours practicing did make an impression on me regarding work and discipline, even though I never became a real piano player.

IMAGINE YOU COULD FLY

I don't remember the move from the apartments above the store to 33 Fox Street per se; I just remember everything being fresh and new in the new house. I also remember a maple tree out in front of the house. I'd hang around out there in the summertime and one day decided to climb this tree. It was pretty easy to do, and eventually I made it to the top. I experienced something while up there that was reminiscent of what I'd felt on the high porch above the store. It was that feeling of being up above things. And there was a sound—the sound of the wind—and of the wind moving leaves. Eventually, I returned to the top of the tree with a hammer, some nails, some wood from an orange crate, and a stick. Up the tree I went, and I pounded some nails into the wood and attached it to one of the more horizontal branches near the top of the tree. This would be my seat. Then I hammered a nail into the stick and attached it to a branch in front of me. It would be my stick, or airplane-control column. And then I flew this make-believe airplane. I flew all over the world in my head. The breeze made me feel like I was flying. I was flying and smiling. It was kind of like being on Dick's motor scooter, and as with the scooter in the beginning, I had no engine in my make-believe airplane.

One day I heard a noise outside next door. *What could that be?* I wondered. It was Dick and his dad, Jack, in their garage next to our new house. They had something on the workbench. Jack had welded two steel plates together so that one piece stood up vertically and was supported by a flat piece lying horizontally on the workbench. On that vertical plate was a very small engine. And on the front of the little engine was a propeller. They were turning the prop with their fingers, trying to get it started. Every once in a while, it would snap and reverse and trap their fingers, sometimes drawing blood. Eventually the sound was there. Putt...putt...putt...and then *wrrrrr.* A little 0.049-cubic-inch engine was running on its own with a small fuel tank hooked up to the intake. It was loud for its size, and the power seemed to want to drag the heavy steel plate across the workbench. We all smiled.

Let's see: gas, a spark plug, and a propeller. This was a little different, but like the motor scooter, it had that fuel tank, fuel line, and spark plug. The propeller made it different, but I was interested. And the smell of the fuel was intoxicating.

Dick went through the effort of building a few small airplanes but settled on a plane called a Fire Baby, if memory serves. It was to be flown with some strings attached. The operator would control the elevators to get it to go up and down, and the rudder was aluminum bent just right to cause the nose of the airplane to track to the right as it flew in a circle in a counterclockwise direction.

And to the Fire Baby we mounted the little engine. Dick and his dad worked on a little toolbox for Dick, so he had a battery to hook to the spark plug in order to start the engine. Also, there were wires and clips, fuel, Popsicle sticks, and tape. What? Popsicle sticks? We would tape wooden Popsicle sticks to our fingers to protect them from being beaten up by the propeller during engine start. We were committed to getting this thing going. Crank up the engine. One guy manned the controls (control lines), and the other ran and then threw the airplane into the air when the guy with the control gave the signal. After several attempts, the airplane flew—actually flew—round and round in a circle. What a sight. I knew then how the Wright Brothers must have felt. I'm serious.

Well, that day was just the beginning of a lifetime journey. I got my own Fire Baby, and somehow I got my little toolbox organized too. We flew those planes all day every day for a long time. We got so carried away with it that we eventually flew them at night with a spotlight. At least, we tried to fly them at night once, but the neighbors revolted. They said, "It's one thing for you kids to be making all that noise eight hours a day, every day, but we'll be damned if you're going to do it at night too!" Our night operation was shut down, and we couldn't blame the neighbors.

Then, one sunny summer day, I went by the ball field behind Stiver's Chevrolet at the bottom of East Hill and saw a couple of kids flying control-line airplanes. But these airplanes were much bigger than the ones we had been flying, and the engines on them were much bigger. There was a very athletic-looking kid there, very trim, with blue eyes and blond hair, and he seemed to know what he was doing. His name was Fred Werner, and we would become friends for the rest of our lives. But now I had to think of these bigger, faster airplanes. My budget couldn't hack it, and I wasn't going to ask my family for help. My Fire Baby had cost about three dollars—eight dollars with the engine. I never did fly any of the bigger control-line airplanes, let alone the radio-control planes that were showing up here and there.

MORE WHEELS

Dad was around a lot now. One day he said we ought to build a Soap Box Derby–type car. He said eventually we'd put a motor in it. He was good at bringing some of the neighbor kids into it. I forget which ones, but in the end, we had four names stenciled on the back of the finished product. It had a small grill made out of a screen, a steering system on it, and some tires that would later prove not to be up to the task of "high speed." Dad hooked me up behind the '53 Chevy one day and took me out through the countryside. We probably did thirty-five to forty miles an hour most of the way. We made the first half of the trip with tires and the last half on steel rims. That was the last day for our little unpowered car. I never was in it again. No, we never had an engine in it, but I remembered the wind, the speed, and how Dad made me laugh that day. He had laughed too.

This is the little car Dad helped me and some of "my kids" build. Note the wooden exhaust pipe and lack of engine. Dad and I became friends during this project.

Art Tobey showed up one day on an old Cushman motor scooter—we're talking 1940s vintage here. And then Angie

Perline had a Cushman too. And then Dick Mason showed up on a Whizzer motorbike. AG had a homemade scooter, but it had no brakes. After he went through two pairs of shoes, his mom made him park the scooter until he figured out how to put some brakes on it. Fred Werner was making one also, and Paul Leach showed up on a Whizzer. The long and short of it is that *of course* I wanted one of these motor scooters or motorbikes. I don't really remember asking for one; after all, I'd had it pretty good all along. But the smell of gas and oil was all around me again, as were the sounds of reciprocating engines.

One day Bill asked me to join him in the car. I had no idea where we were going. We pulled into a guy's gravel driveway out in the country; I think we were in Coalburg. This man and my grandfather grinned at each other. *What's going on?* I wondered. We were ushered to a small barn that had no organization to it. There was a huge pile of hay in the corner. The farmer, with a big grin on his face, went over to the pile and started pulling hay off it. Gradually there appeared to be something below, and finally there it was: an old 1948 Cushman motor scooter. The two men smiled and watched me. I didn't know what to say. This couldn't possibly be for me. It was. I was so grateful and happy. Soon it was home and in the garage. Bill had paid the guy seventy-five dollars for it, and soon thereafter, I had it all torn apart to paint it. Mom sewed a red cloth topping for the seat.

I painted the scooter robin's-egg blue. I learned about spark plugs, gas, centrifugal clutches, belts, four-cycle engines, intake, compression, combustion, and exhaust strokes, rings, valves, pistons, piston rings, piston rods, camshafts, and crankshafts. Although I enjoyed the mechanics part of it, driving it or operating it was what I really loved. Wind in the face, the sound of an engine, and a twist grip that connected to a carburetor that would dictate speed were what I seemed to enjoy the most. And yes, speed for speed's sake was becoming an ever-more-unexplainable phenomenon and ever-growing interest for me.

I said I'd get back to Fred Werner again. Well, Fred had made his own scooter, and when I say that, I mean he had made it from scratch. It was a fine scooter, but he told the story of forgetting one thing: a cotter pin for the front axle. He said when he was coming down a hill, the front axle rotated out of the front end, and he saw his front tire rolling down the hill in front of him. I never saw any resultant cuts or bruises, but he said he took a pretty good tumble. Call it operational test and evaluation.

The motor-scooter thing eventually took on a life of its own. Six or seven of us rode around on these Cushman motor scooters, Whizzer motorbikes, or homemade versions of them. We all worked on them, fixed them up the best we could, but mostly we raced them to see who could go the fastest. Eventually, for the most part, it became AG and me, riding around on the hot and humid Ohio summer days. Sometimes I would be by myself and found that it was really something of which the Zen aficionados would be proud. I could think and relax to the *putt...putt...putt* sound of the reciprocating motor, the feel of the breeze on my face, and the warm Ohio summertime air.

AG EARL EDWARDS GILMORE LEACH MASON
ABOUT 1956-57

**The boys on the motor scooters. For a little town, Hubbard
had a lot of motorized vehicles, though none of us were
old enough to have licenses. AG is to the left. Three of
the machines are Wizzer motorbikes, but AG and I both
had Cushmans. (Still no kickstand on my Cushman—
see the block of wood in front of me.) Paul Leach, my
roller-skating pal, is second from the right. Dick Mason,
far right, was our neighbor. I never got to know Earl (on
my right). We were all fourteen or fifteen years old.**

There was one bad accident, when somebody turned a
scooter on its side with a girl on the back. The guy driving
escaped with a few scrapes and bruises, but the girl—who
had been a beauty queen—needed numerous stitches in
her face—enough stitches to significantly alter the way she

looked. But they had survived the accident. Things never were the same after that, because for the first time, most of us realized we could die on these things. Better said, we always knew we could die on these machines, but this was the first up-front and personal, irrefutable, and manifest occurrence of our worst fears. I would later put a scooter on its side one day just screwing around, with AG right behind me. I was paying more attention to him behind me than I was to the curve in front of me. I got slowed down a bit but not quite enough to make the curve. Down I went, bending the scooter a little and scraping a knee and an arm. *You really need to be careful around these reciprocating engines,* I thought.

The Cushman project. There was work to be done.

GETTING SPOILED

I got to take two trips to Canada. The first time was with Ma and Bill. We had an outdoor toilet. It seemed to rain incessantly, and we played a lot of darts. I learned to understand what a Canadian accent was. I remember Bill taking me to a Western Auto store in preparation for the first trip. We bought fishing lures, fishing poles, fishing lines, and tackle boxes. I thought he had spent too much money on this stuff. Mom and Dad stayed home.

On the second trip to Canada, the whole family went. We had a little fifteen-foot boat with a forty-horsepower Mercury engine on it. This trip started very early in the morning. We loaded everything into Bill's 1955 Chrysler the night before in preparation for our trip. Before sunrise we all excitedly climbed into the Chrysler with the boat and boat trailer hooked to it, whereupon we discovered we couldn't get out of the driveway. With the trunk full and the six of us in the car, we were bottoming out on the driveway.

Eventually we put everything into Dad's '53 Chevy, and that worked like a champ. We were a little tight inside the Chevy, but that really wasn't a problem. The whole family still smoked, except Jack and me, but it was summertime, and we rode with the windows down most of the time. Jack learned to swim on that trip after much badgering from the rest of us. I remember listening to my grandmother's wheezing in the middle of the night, as we ended up sleeping in the same room. I knew that wheezing was not a good thing, and I probably knew then that was a result of her smoking for all those years. She was probably in her early fifties at the time. I don't have a lot of clear memories of this trip to Canada, but for the most part, I remember how close the family seemed to be. I do remember that the top speed of our little boat was thirty-two miles per hour. Seemed fast at the time.

Eventually I got a piano—imagine that. I will always hate to admit it but I guess I was getting spoiled. I had a real appreciation for the piano, but I never really could play the piano other than by going over and over a song until I memorized it. I actually had a teacher by the name of Dorsey at one time. (No, no relation to *that* Dorsey.) He knew I was not going far in music, but he always asked how Little League was going. Mom took me to piano lessons for about three years, until I finally quit. Jack would later get interested in the guitar and take lessons for a while too.

One winter day, when Mom was bringing me home from my lesson, she lost control of Bill's 1955 Chrysler as we went down this big hill in Youngstown. The Chrysler slid into a 180-degree turn on the snow and ice. Mom and I looked at each other and then resumed driving back up the hill we had just come down. That was the first time I had seen Mom petrified. Then we laughed real hard. I felt I had learned some more about discipline during my years of trying to play the piano, but as with academics, it seemed that no matter how hard I worked or how much I applied myself, the results seemed only mediocre.

Spoiled? Earlier, while we still lived above the store, Bill took Dad and me to a horse and pony auction. I was surprised to hear the auctioneer doing his thing, and the horses and ponies were beautiful. I had never expressed any interest in them, except when I would go up to Art Toby's house. They had at least one pony. Well, all of a sudden, Bill was bidding for a little pinto pony with a silver mane. He bought Silver, and I was in a state of suspended animation. Now Dad had to build a stall for him in the garage behind the store. Silver was pretty frisky, and to make a long story short, I seldom rode him. But I will never forget my grandfather buying the pony or my dad working to build the stall in the garage behind the store. Sitting in the stall with Silver alone was relaxing, and another Zen-like experience. But I also saw the money it took to keep Silver and the effort it took to keep the stall clean. Horses were expensive and time-consuming. I was sorry I never became a hardcore rider while I had Silver. Bill and my dad were probably a little disappointed too. My only excuse is that I was very young and no match for Silver.

As much as I appreciated Bill buying that pony for me, I appreciated another of his surprise purchases even more. One day when I was about thirteen or fourteen Tom Ennis pulled into the driveway on a brand-new powder-blue Lambretta motor scooter, a scooter originally manufactured in Italy. It had a three-speed transmission that was controlled with the handgrip. It had a horn and a light like the Cushman's, but unlike the Cushman, it had a two-cycle engine. I learned that the intake, compression, combustion, and exhaust events of the four-stroke engine could be combined into two events, instead of four. The two-stroke engine sounded different, and you mixed oil with the gasoline. The *sound* of the two stroke was a little off-putting to me, but the scooter really looked beautiful. To make a long story short, Bill bought me one. I was appreciative, and I don't think I had become obnoxious, like the movie version of the kid who gets all these things. I knew it was expensive, and I knew I couldn't buy it on my own, even though I was working. I loved my grandfather and the new scooter. I think it probably cost him a little over $400.

Tommy Ennis was in our grade school but would later go to Catholic school for his high school years. I lost track

The Lambretta and Mom's beauty shop sign, 1957. More important than the Lambretta is the sign: Alice's Beauty Shop. Dad made that sign and finessed the lettering on it. Mom worked in the beauty shop for maybe thirty years. Two or three months after she retired, she died from cancer.

of him for most of my life, but he called me one day when I was well into my sixties. It would turn out that he was the richest person I would ever know personally. Most of his fortune was from hard work, ingenuity, and persistence within the car-wash business. As an older man, he had numerous patents and said that having ideas and turning them into patents was what he most liked to do. He said he expected to continue with the "idea and patent theme" for the rest of his life. Private business jets and Bentleys had become a routine part of his life, and the *New York Times* had even done a column about his house in southern California. Imagine that: a kid from Hubbard driving Bentleys and flying his own business jet. Good for you, Tom.

From about fourth grade on, school got boring for me, but interacting with the kids never seemed boring. Occasionally, I would try to get serious about school, but most of the time, I became disappointed over the neutral results of my increased study, so I'd go back to the motorized vehicles and my personality studies of literally anyone I met. The personalities were all different, and I found that if I could go to my friends' houses and meet their parents, I usually could figure out why "my kids" had the personalities they did. It's just what I liked to do. And Bill always said, "Everyone has their own peculiarities." I really enjoyed knowing these people. It wasn't until I was about forty years old that I realized my own personality was an amalgamation of those four adults in my family, not to mention some undoubted effects from my brother, the kids of Fox Street, and all the other people I met along the way,.

There was a funny thing about my friends. I hung out with a lot of kids, but they didn't necessarily hang out with one another. I noticed that what their fathers did often indicated who they were going to hang out with. I thought that was, as they say in Thailand, "boooshit." I hung out with the neighborhood kids, the grocers' kids, and some steelworkers' kids. They were different from one another, but they were very similar too. As I look at what I have just written, I realize there really was not that much difference between the families, but to hear some people talk, there was. Well, there certainly was no upper class represented in Hubbard, other than maybe a few doctors.

WORK

Mom got me a job mowing our family doctor's yard. I earned seventy-five cents an hour, I think. Dr. Gross had two very young girls and lived not far from us. I could walk to this job if I wanted to. I am not sure, but I think I used a push mower for that job and trimmed the edges around the property by hand—nothing motorized here. I soon became aware of the clock versus money when I was being paid by the hour. And I did what most people do under the circumstances: I ran up the time a little, but eventually I had more important things to do. I did not like spending more time on the job than was necessary. Like most, I knew it had something to do with integrity. I just didn't know the word back then. Whenever I showed up at the Grosses' house, one of the daughters would yell, "Mom, here comes the worker." I was "the worker" now, and I kind of liked that name.

It's funny how these yard jobs go. The fact that I would mow somebody's yard seemed to spread like wildfire, and before I knew it, I had a full schedule mowing a lot of yards. Mr. Amburenson, who had a glass business, hired me to mow his yard, a fairly large one. And then he started having me wash and wax his car, a '52 Ford, I think. A few years before this, one of my buddies and I had thrown some snowballs at cars. One of them was Mr. Amburenson's. He said we'd cracked the windshield, and Mom found out about it. The whole family found out about it. I really felt awful. Breaking a window was really bad, and I knew it. Mom had taught me better. So it was a surprise, a few years later, when I was hired to do Mr. Amburenson's yard and clean his car.

Somehow the word about my yard business got clear out to Coalburg, and I ended up doing a very big yard out there. I don't even remember who owned the property, but I remember that I did the job on a riding lawn mower, my first experience on one. And that was fun, of course: it had an engine, and I could ride it. And I could smell the gas and oil during those hot summer days.

I remember sitting one day and thinking, *Maybe I could do this yard-mowing thing as an adult, since there are so many people who want their yards done. Maybe I could even hire a bunch of guys to do the work, and I would just do the scheduling.* Those thoughts didn't materialize into reality, but I would be reminded of my early career aspirations through the years, especially every time I saw an adult man in a truck with a lawn mower getting ready to mow somebody's yard. It seemed then, as it does now, a very honest way to make some money.

These jobs were bringing in some spending money, usually for gasoline for the scooter. And eventually I had someone riding on the back of my scooter with me: Jo, who eventually became my wife. She was a year behind me in grade school, and I think I first saw her in the cafeteria in sixth grade.

Eventually Fran Fluent became as much of a friend as his brother AG. One day he told me a buddy of his was quitting a job they held together. They were janitors, in essence, at a restaurant and ballroom in Youngstown called the Mural Room. This job entailed the usual janitorial duties like sweeping and cleaning, but 90 percent of the work was conducted on the second floor, where there was a stage, a huge dance floor and surrounding area, and a bar. It had the usual ladies' room and similar men's room accessible out by an elevator, which connected the first and second floors. If you wanted, you could go up to a third floor, but there wasn't much there. The dance floor and surrounding area required extensive cleaning and buffing as a result of the big parties held there every Friday and Saturday night. There were literally a hundred tables or more that needed to be set up, torn down, or moved for every party the restaurant had.

White tablecloths were the order of the day, and the day after these parties was something to behold: cigarette butts, dirty ashtrays, and corsage pins everywhere; floors sticky from spilled booze and beer; and occasional chewing gum stuck to the dance floor. The telltale odor of the booze, beer, and cigarettes all rolled into one always wafted through the air. And the white tablecloths—well, they weren't very white on these mornings. I needed money for gas and for my new girlfriend, so I told Fran I would take the job.

We would hitchhike together to Youngstown, usually starting out around 5:00 a.m., because we liked to get there no later than 6:00 a.m. That way we could punch in on one of those time clocks, ride the elevator up to the second floor, proceed to the ladies' lounge, and sleep for an hour or so. Sometimes Fran liked to curl up next to one of the wall heaters out by the dance floor, and sometimes when he did, I would fiddle with the baby grand piano on the stage. I mention all this as a precursor to another story.

Mr. Perla was our boss, and as far as I could tell, he was the boss of everybody in the restaurant. He always came up the elevator, and we could hear the elevator doors open, announcing his arrival. By the time he came around the corner, we would be busy doing something—except one day, the noise I was making playing the piano drowned out the telltale sound of the elevator doors. As I looked over the top of the piano, I saw Mr. Perla standing there, looking down at Fran sleeping like a baby. What could I do? Of course, I just went into teenage denial and pretended he didn't exist. I continued to play the piano as Mr. Perla came around and looked straight at the stage, the piano, and me. He paused and then left without saying a word.

Mr. Perla had to be a good guy, I decided, although I never had an actual conversation with him. I should say that Fran, being senior to me in longevity at the Mural Room, did converse with "Perla" once in a while regarding what we were to do on a given day. I'll never forget Mr. Perla's shiny bald head or the immaculate suits he always wore. I wondered how he had become the boss.

The Mural Room became an entity unto itself. Working there taught me a lot and made me think a lot. Fran and I had a wonderful time and became great friends as we grew into young teenagers together. The hitchhiking taught me a lot too. Of course, this was back in the day when kidnappings just didn't happen, and people were trying to help one another. Helping two young teens to get somewhere, literally and figuratively, was very normal back then. There were never more than one or two cars that passed us without stopping. I was amazed at how easily we were getting around and at how nice the people giving us rides were. Each of them had a story, and so did we.

Another thing I became more aware of at the Mural Room was hierarchy and chain of command: Perla at the top, Fran in the middle, and me at the bottom, or Perla at the top, the waitresses in the middle, and Fran and me at the bottom, or Perla at the top, the cooks in the middle, and Fran and me at the bottom, or Perla at the top, the other janitors in the middle, and Fran and me at the bottom. That didn't bother me at all. I was already familiar with the hierarchy at Gilmore's General Store.

Fran used to spend a lot of time practicing throwing corsage pins at the wall. The walls were carpeted, so if he threw the pin just right, it would stick in the wall. One day we were out on the dance floor with a buffer, getting ready to buff the floor, when I noticed everything had gone silent. Fran was looking intently at me, and then he did it. He threw one of those corsage pins at me. And it stuck...in my forehead! I think I chased him almost as far as I did the day he kept tapping me on the head with a broom handle.

Of course we practiced over and over the art of pulling a tablecloth out from under a set table (or trashed table) with dishes, glasses, ashtrays, and silverware. We never did perfect that art.

I had never operated or even seen a floor buffer before. For those who have never operated one, it is different from what you would think. My teacher, Fran, taught me well, but then the minds of two teenage boys went to work. We began riding it, to see who could sit on top of it the longest. One would mount it and grab the handle and lever that turned it on. The comparison might be like sitting on a Harley with a set of high ape handlebars. The other would hold the electric cord high, so that when the buffer started going around and around, the cord would not get tangled up in it. The one sitting atop the buffer would squeeze the lever, and away he would go, round and round. This usually ended with buffer, and buffer rider, tipping over with a finale similar to the final seconds of an unsuccessful competitive bull-riding attempt. The howls and laughter of two teens echoed through the large, otherwise quiet ballroom. It seems like ten seconds might have been the record—and no, Perla never caught us.

Now I'll return to a story of revenge for the aforementioned needle in my forehead and the tap, tap, tap of the broomstick on my head. I decided I'd get back at Fran. I didn't know when, but I thought I would. And then I did one of the five dumbest things I've ever done in my life. Often nature would call us, at the same time, to the men's room for our morning constitutionals. Sitting down side by side, although separated by the usual thin metal wall, we proceeded to do our business. I was traditionally a little faster at this than Fran. (How's this for knowing your friends?)

One day when we were in our respective stalls, I saw a newspaper on the floor. I picked it up, held a lit match to it, and threw the flaming paper over the top of the thin metal wall that separated us. I suppose I could have killed him. I immediately felt awful and knew Mom would have whipped my butt for it. And then I heard Fran let out a big expulsion of air and a "whoaaa." There was silence, and then we started laughing. And I was relieved, because by teen logic, I knew if he was laughing, he was still alive. But there were no more needles or broomstick taps at my head. No, I'm not going to tell you what the other four dumbest things are.

Then there were the people who worked at the Mural Room during normal business hours: the cooks, dishwashers, and other janitors—adult janitors, that is. The cooks were all white, except one black man. Race didn't matter to me then and doesn't now. Although I don't remember his name, the black guy is the only one of the cooks whose face I distinctly remember. Thinking back, he looked a lot like Arsenio Hall. He was the first one we would see when we went downstairs to the kitchen for lunch. He was fairly young, maybe twenty-five, and muscular, with a small, well-groomed mustache. And he always wore a sailor hat—not like a sailor would wear it but turned and folded to make it look cool. His reaction at seeing us was always the same; he would turn his head to loudly announce, "Here come the chooches. Here come the chooches." At that, all the cooks would laugh, and so would we. We had no idea what it meant, but we knew it was likely not an endearing term.

It took me until now, in my seventies, to look up a definition of *chooch*. One definition says it can apply to almost anything, but the following one is probably more of what our cook might have been thinking: Italian slang for hardhead, blockhead, any of a number of similar insults pertaining to one's stubbornness or limited use of common sense.

With that seemingly required announcement out of the way, the cook would look at us smiling and say, "What do you boys want today?" Fran quite often asked for chow mein, and I usually asked for a hamburger. The first time I heard Fran ask for chow mein, I knew I was going to learn some things at the Mural Room, as I had no idea what he was requesting. Despite the derogatory sound of *chooches*, I know the cook meant nothing but good fun in levying that term at us. He laughed, the other cooks laughed, and we laughed. It's the way guys relate with one another, and I knew that already. I suppose today some would call it bullying, and that's a shame. This was the stuff guys do. Besides, the food was free and made with attention to detail. Chow mein? Can't say I ever ate much of it.

And then I discovered or realized something. There were two adult janitors too, one black and one white. They seemed to do most of their work downstairs in the restaurant, but from time to time, they would end up hanging out with us on the second floor. I watched them carefully. They were adults, maybe thirty and forty years old, with wives and children at home, and they were doing a job very similar to what Fran and I were doing. I thought, *God, I hope I'm not a janitor when I'm an adult.* Since I would be an adult soon, I wondered if I could figure out this "life" thing. I was fifteen years old then, so I had only a few years to get prepared.

Like yard mowing, the janitorial profession had many available job opportunities. All you had to do was work, and I liked that. Soon I had a job at Guy's Drug Store as a janitor, where I swept and mopped the floors and took out the trash. Then Mom started giving me a few bucks a week to clean the floor, the mirror, and the hair dryers in her beauty shop. Yard jobs and janitor jobs were plentiful, but I didn't want to do these as an adult. The thoughts of that scrapbook picture with Mom, Dad, me, and the Piper Cub would flash through my mind, but at the time, I didn't know why.

At some point, Mom asked me what I was going to do as an adult for a living. One day I blurted out, "I want to be a military pilot!" I'm not sure where that came from, other than those thoughts about the Piper Cub picture and how much Dad seemed to appreciate the navy.

Mom, being Mom, said, "Well, you know, in order to be a pilot in the military, you need to be an officer first."

I said, "Fine, then I'll be an officer."

She then said, "To be an officer, you must have a college degree."

I responded, "OK, then I'll get a college degree." Little did I know how that conversation would set the stage for much of my life. Maybe I now had some goals.

DRAG RACING

Soon I would be sixteen years old, and Dad kept talking to me about getting a driver's license. I started counting the days until my sixteenth birthday. I already knew how to drive, as Dad had taught me well in an old Studebaker.

Within days after turning sixteen, I got spoiled again. Mac, Mom's dad, gave me his old Nash—a 1942 model, I think. I don't remember Mac being there to give it to me, but Mom was there. I don't remember anyone else in the driveway that day on Fox Street. Like most teenage boys at that time, I was familiar with car-cleaning and waxing products. Soon I had the old Nash looking pretty good. For a long time, however, the horn would blow every time we turned right, so I kept mostly to left-hand turns. You could even change radio stations using a button on the floor in that car.

Like most teenage boys at the time, my friends and I all wanted to see whose car would accelerate the fastest. So early on, we were drag racing one another. It soon seemed that drag racing was all we did and all we thought about. None of our cars were particularly quick, and I remember a lot of blue smoke and gear grinding during these early years. I also remember a lot of laughing, but a theme was developing: first we had raced the small scooters, and now we were racing old dilapidated cars at age sixteen.

I attended Hubbard High, the home of the Eagles. Mom had figured out that I would take college-prep classes, even though I was not Mr. Scholastic. Early on I ran into difficulty with algebra, but Mom found a tutor and had me spend at least an hour a week with him. I remember the quiet of the house where I was tutored, and slowly I began to see the patterns of the math within algebra. Sometimes I even enjoyed it, and I got through Algebra I.

But the kids were still the important thing for me. I hardly was aware of student government, but I learned that our freshman class would choose officers—you know, president, vice president, treasurer, and secretary. The funny thing is that nobody ran for office. One day the teachers told us we were going to vote for classmates to occupy these positions, and I became class president without even running. I thought that was strange. I remember arriving on Fox Street that day, opening the back door to the house, and yelling down the stairs to Mom. (That is where she lived most of her life: downstairs in that beauty shop of hers.) I yelled, "Hey, Mom, guess who's the freshman class president—me!" She came around the corner in her white uniform and smiled up at me from the bottom of the stairs.

Interestingly, the same thing happened in my sophomore year: Nobody ran for any office. Nobody talked of running for office. Everybody voted. I was class president again. *Crazy*, I thought.

As I sat in a classroom staring out the window in my sophomore year, I saw a two-tone, blue 1956 Ford come up the hill toward the school. It disappeared behind the school. It was my dad driving this car, and he would give it to me. Of course I was surprised and felt a little awkward, because there weren't many kids driving cars as nice as this. Not in Hubbard, Ohio. I hadn't asked for it, but sure, I appreciated it. I was lucky, and I knew it.

I had been interested in some sports, but I particularly liked football. We played a lot of football on Fox Street, and so I thought I was ready to play high school football. Early on, however, I had some knee problems. Dr. Gross, the man I had earlier worked for as a yardman, said my knee problems were related to just growing too fast or something like that. The ligaments of my knees were torn and needed some downtime to heal. He taped my knees in a way that required me to walk stiff legged for about six weeks. He was the school athletic doctor and declared that my football days were over. This is the short version of what happened, but I was surprised and guessed I'd never be a football star. But I had plenty to do in learning about cars, engines, and later motorcycles.

Algebra I and II came and went. So did geometry. And the C grades continued, with an occasional B or D. I began noticing the disparity between the good students and the poor ones and was starting to feel like I needed to perform better academically. Again, when I put in an effort, I was seldom rewarded by correspondingly higher grades. I guess my interest was not there, but I didn't want my family to be disappointed. I suppose this was when I was becoming aware of the term *IQ*, or *intelligence quotient*. For some reason, it really interested me. I knew that when I studied hard, it didn't seem to matter much. I still could not perform as well as I wanted. Conversely, I knew some kids were not putting in a big effort but were performing very well.

IQ would become kind of an obsession with me for a long time. Maybe it became an excuse too, but I don't think so. Persistence became my replacement for IQ, I came to think.

It seemed I needed to work very hard to perform even at a minimally acceptable standard, and this was bothersome and frustrating for me.

In these early high school days, I was spending more and more time with Fred Werner. Fred did about as well as I did in algebra, but in his dad's garage, he was master of all things. I was astounded at all the things he could do with a wrench, a carburetor, a motor large or small, an acetylene torch, an electric welder, or a cutting torch. I never found the proper word for what I thought about Fred's ability in mechanics until I reached college. The word was *creativity*—Fred could do anything mechanically, and he would do most things creatively. He also was a down-to-earth, no-BS guy who, by his actions, was teaching me a lot about character and integrity. In our adult lives, he would do much better than I along those lines, and in my old age, I finally told him so.

In Ohio, especially in the winter, my friends and I became absorbed with a few magazines—*Hot Rod* and *Rod & Custom Magazine*, to name a couple. The beautiful customized cars of California were the subject of 90 percent of the articles in these magazines. The work done on car bodies and engines was the main topic of the day, both in the magazines and among most of my friends. Central to that was the theme of drag racing. I knew California was nice and sunny, but it was so far away I probably would never see it, I thought. I didn't suspect then that California would eventually become a big part of my life.

I would work on my car in our Fox Street garage or in Fred Werner's dad's garage. We decided to put a larger engine in my '56 Ford. I would like to say the money for that came from my yard and janitorial work, but Bill bought it for me. We went to the junkyard together to get it. It was the largest Lincoln engine they ever made, I think.

We already had the Ford engine out when Fred climbed up on the front of the car. The hood was off, so he was standing and backing up against the windshield, a foot on each of the mats that covered each front fender. And he had a sledgehammer in his hands. I yelled, "Fred, what are you doing?"

As only Fred could do, he looked at me, paused, and then said matter-of-factly, "You want that engine"—he pointed to the Lincoln engine lying on the floor—"in this space." He pointed to the empty cavity left by the Ford engine we had just removed. "It won't fit. I'm gonna *make* it fit." And he did, in short order. And the firewall looked like it had been recreated with a surgeon's knife rather than the sledgehammer he had used.

After that, I customized the Ford with fifty-two louvers in the hood and with Lakes Plugs, as they were known. (That's what they were called—Lakes, with the *s*.) The Lakes Plugs had caps on the end of a separate exhaust system and, when removed, acted as straight pipes. This allowed efficient air expulsion for the engine, and it was loud. Fred used to say, "It's gotta breathe!" We added hubcaps, different taillights, and different "skirts" and tires. The tires, which were thick and theoretically would help with traction when the Lincoln engine was under power, cost around eleven dollars each. These were for only the rear of the car. The Ford would fly now.

Then I made a mistake and had it painted...purple, or as we called it then, burgundy. Burgundy didn't go well with the blue interior, but I didn't have the money to change it back. It had been a mistake to have it painted, but I learned from it. I found it kind of amazing that nobody in the family was keeping me from doing all this with the car. I'll try to explain my reasoning for this now.

My father once had said to me that if he ever caught me drinking alcohol, he would personally guarantee me a minimum of two weeks in the hospital. I had, to this point, never drunk anything and really didn't intend to—at least in the short term—so I couldn't understand where he was coming from. Years later, I would realize my mother had done a remarkable job of keeping me unaware of my father's earlier drinking days. But I think the family was happy I was spending my time working on my car and not experimenting with alcohol, like many sixteen- to twenty-year-olds.

And so the drag racing continued, but at a more advanced level now, mostly on the streets of Hubbard or in Youngstown. I was never beaten in a drag race on the streets, as we used to say, but going to a real drag strip was a different matter. Because the engine was so big in my Ford, I was put into a class where the big boys played. They brought their cars in on trailers and had more than one mechanic with them, and many of the engines had blowers on them. Blowers were used as a new way to force fuel and air into the engines and made them more powerful. I never won a race on an actual drag strip, but I learned more about speed here during the drag-racing years. I think I could do the quarter mile in around fourteen seconds. This was good on the street but not good at all on the track. To go faster would have taken a lot of money, and I didn't have it.

Names like Art Arfons were appearing. Art was one of the first, if not *the* first, to have a jet-powered dragster. There was a guy out in the Bonneville Salt Flats making speed runs in a vehicle in which he had installed four engines. I think they were Pontiac engines. When I brought these things up to Fred Werner, he said, "Shit, we can do that. All it takes is money." And then we'd look at each other and shrug our shoulders. Fred could have built anything, but we didn't have any money. *You have to have money to do things,* I thought.

Once in a while, Fred's dad would show up in the garage. He called me Willy. He seemed like a great guy but a little worn, probably from working in a steel mill for many years. Most of the time, he was making sure we were using safety blocks under the frames of the cars we were working on, so these cars wouldn't fall on us if we had a tire or two off the car at the time. He died way too early.

AMALGAMATION AND GRADUATION

I wrote the subtitle above to connote a lot of things going on prior to high school graduation, which is not unheard of for most teenagers. The amalgamation: socializing, hot summers, water skiing, stocks, and finally graduation.

Mom said I should learn to dance. While I didn't think I had an interest in it, I was getting interested in girls, and one of the few ways to get close to them, both literally and figuratively, was by dancing. Besides, if Mom said I should learn, I knew it was in my best interests. Dance class was held in the basement of Jack Thiel's parents' house out on West Liberty in Hubbard. Jack's sister and three or four girls gave us lessons all day long, as I remember it. Slow dancing was one thing, but I caught on to the Jitterbug and the Mashed Potato pretty quickly. And then I seemed to be dancing all the time. I think there is something in one of the yearbooks about me dancing. Well, I'm not sure I wanted to be known for my dancing, but in a way, I guess I was. Being a little heavy all the time, I found it easy to lose five pounds on a dance floor in a night.

Some of my friends seemed to enjoy dancing too. Friend, athlete, and high school football star Jimmy LaCivita was one of them. But I still didn't want to be known for dancing.

In my junior year in high school, students had to run for positions in the class if they wanted to be officers, so my high school political life was over. That is, I just wasn't going to run for a position in the class.

So we were dancing, drag racing, and still having fun. Then Fred Werner got a boat—a nice boat, maybe sixteen to eighteen feet long, with a large outboard engine on it. His mom would make us at least twenty ham sandwiches, and we'd take plenty of Coke and Pepsi with us and spend the day on the surrounding lakes, though we were mostly down on the Allegheny River in Pennsylvania. Fred drove, and it was his boat and motor, so I just tried to help with the gas money from my yard mowing and janitorial work. He often took his future wife, Alice, and I had Jo with me.

We had skis, but then Fred came up with a disk we would ride; it was kind of like skis, except the only thing that kept us on it was the water pushing it up against our feet. Weight distribution over this thing became critical, or we would end up in the water. We held a rope from the boat, just as we did when skiing. This disk wasn't a flat piece of plywood but was a beveled, smooth piece of wood, varnished with a glossy finish.

We had already learned how to get speed on the water skis by going outside the wake with the boat in a turn. But when we took the disk outside the wake, we seemed to enter another dimension of speed. That all worked out OK until the day I looked up and saw some fishermen in a very small boat directly in front of me while I approached at Warp 9 speed on the disk. I had only one choice, and that was to bail out, which sent the disk flying—literally. It seemed to go vertical and then seemed to walk on water until it slammed into the side of the fishermen's boat. Not a good deal, but they didn't get crazy mad, and soon we had our disk back and were ready to take on the next event: truck tubes.

We tied these to ropes and rode them wherever they went behind the boat. This seemed more for the leisure class, as there wasn't speed there, as there was when riding the disk.

Fred was obviously making some money in order to afford this boat. I never remember him charging me a dime for all the work he did on my Ford, but maybe I can pay him back before I die. Fred is one of the most honest guys I have ever known in my life. How lucky I've been to know him.

By now I was frequently making phone calls to the Butler Wick stockbrokerage office to get quotes on various companies, mostly IBM—my grandfather's favorite company in the fifties. Bill never told me to do this, but when I did, I would occasionally see him smile. That smile meant everything to me. And then he would ask me what company XYZ was selling for that day. What a difference compared to today. Most every stock price you looked at then was at least twenty-four hours old. There was nothing real-time, unless you went and stood inside a brokerage office, as Bill and I had done when I was about ten years old. And even that was dependent upon how fast the young girls were in going from the ticker-tape machine to posting the price on the chalkboard. None of my friends or their parents talked of the stock market, and there wasn't a word said about it in school. I still wondered why. Of course, Hubbard, Ohio, was not the economic mecca of the world either.

High school graduation came and went. Since Mom was the only one of the four adults in the house to graduate from high school, I could tell the family was feeling good about my graduating from high school. I remember asking Bill one time why he hadn't graduated from school, since he generally seemed in favor of education. He looked at me and smiled. He said, "I'll tell you why I didn't finish school. One day our teacher in sixth grade told us to memorize a poem. She said we were to be able to recite it from memory the next day, if called upon. She called on me the next morning. I rose and said, 'I'm sorry, but I don't know the poem.' And she said, 'Well, Bill Gilmore, you can go home and stay there until you can recite the poem.'" And then Bill smiled at me and said, "So I did." That was it. That had been the end of my grandfather's education. He never went back. But I'd be hard-pressed to tell you of anyone I knew during my whole life who was wiser than he was.

BGSU, ROTC, Flight, and Philosophy

Mom had done all the legwork to send out college applications for me. Mostly I was unaware of what she was doing, but one day, she told me I had been accepted to Bowling Green State University in northwestern Ohio, about a three-hour drive from Hubbard. With the help of that math tutor, I had gotten through the college-prep classes with passing grades—though chemistry was, and still is, a total mystery to me. I was a senior, and Jo was a year behind me, so I wondered what would happen with that relationship.

During a summer visit to Bowling Green (BG), my mother and I ended up in a room where she told me we were going to hear about the Air Force Reserve Officer Training Corps (AFROTC). I signed up for AFROTC at that meeting. This was all a part of the plan to graduate, become an air force officer, and then become an air force pilot. I knew this was significant, but I didn't know how long this road was going to be.

It was 1960, and Bowling Green State University's classes were about to begin. As the four adults and my little brother drove away from Rodger's Quadrangle in my grandfather's green-and-white 1955 Chrysler, I watched until they were out of sight. I crossed the street, went up the stairs in the front of the quadrangle, went into the bathroom on the floor where my room was, locked the door, sat down on a commode, and bawled my eyes out for ten or fifteen minutes. I was a scared little puppy.

The room I lived in was built for two people; it held two desks, two closets, and two chests of drawers. But there were also two sets of bunk beds, and four of us lived there: Doug, Tom, Danny, and me. Doug was the son of a superintendent of schools up in the northeast, and as I said to him months later, I couldn't understand a word he said for at least a couple of weeks, because of his thick New Jersey accent. I don't remember Tom's background, but Danny came from a farming family of eleven kids.

Halfway through the year, Danny and I were the only ones left. The other two seemed to be party animals and liked to drink and smoke. (When I say "smoke," I just mean regular tobacco, not marijuana or anything else.) I was still very worried about my ability to get through the academics, so I was studying as hard as I could. Danny was right next to me at the adjacent desk, night after night and weekend after weekend. Danny was from a town called AI in Fulton County, Ohio. We would ask him time and time again, "How do you spell that?"

And he would say, "A...I?" And then we would all laugh. It was somehow pleasing to know there were towns smaller than Hubbard. Danny was about as honest a guy as Fred Werner, and I liked that. I was lucky to have him as a roommate.

I found the academics difficult. I even flunked American history and had to retake it. My brain seemed to shut down when anyone talked of the past, and I remember I tried to print my notes in class. I had spent a long time perfecting my printing skills at Republic Steel on the drafting tables (more about that later), but college notes really could not be taken while printing. Printing was too slow for me to keep up, especially with this history professor. I needed to open my eyes to history, start writing my notes, and get through the academics. The thoughts of flying military aircraft persisted and motivated me, and ROTC was going well.

I must mention a literature class that I had at BG as well. No matter what I did, my grades were very low in this class. I decided to go see my professor about this. There was no doubt in my mind that this woman was very serious about literature and she wanted her students to be serious about it as well. I mentioned to her that it seemed no matter what I did, I was still having problems with this class. I asked for her guidance. I can't say that I remember any guidance, but I do know that she saw my earnestness to do better. On the next essay assignment she gave us, she left it open-ended. That is you could choose your topic and write about it. My topic was "speed," and I received an A on the paper. It seemed we had a new understanding. I took her more seriously, and I think she took me more seriously. The rest of the class went smoothly.

The Aeronca. It had sixty-five horsepower and a top speed of about ninety-five to a hundred miles per hour. This is the actual aircraft that I soloed in at age nineteen in 1961.

On June 18, 1961, my dad asked if I wanted to go out to a little airfield in West Middlesex, Pennsylvania, about five to ten miles from our house on Fox Street. When we arrived, I noted the broken-down hanger and associated building as we drove in. I saw two airplanes; one was in the hangar, and the other was outside it. A man named Sam Thomas was there, and he had what was called a PA12 airplane, numbered N4111M. Before it was all over, Dad had paid Sam twelve dollars for two thirty-minute flights for me in Sam's airplane. This was a hundred-horsepower airplane. I enjoyed these rides, but boy, were they noisy. Back in those days, nobody wore the headsets that are routinely used today. If you wanted to talk, you had to yell, and most of the time, you heard only about half of what the other guy was saying.

We drove home, and I wondered where this day had come from. Dad was really becoming a part of my life. Bill never would have done this; he would have said it was too expensive and that I likely would never fly for a living. But he *didn't* say that, because he never knew about these first flights. Bill was a product of the Depression and therefore eschewed any spending for anything that by its nature did not provide "value." Like many of his era, for many years Bill only spent money on food, clothing, shelter, and maybe a little more. He provided many things for the family that went beyond food, clothing, and shelter, but the Depression-era experience was a prism through which, I know, he measured things.

Less than a week later, Dad introduced me to a man named John Roche at the same airport. The runway was grass and had the same rolling-hill atmosphere as the rest of the land up in northeast Ohio. Besides being grass, the runway was very wide. John Roche looked like his name sounded; he was close to six feet tall, slender, and mustached, and he wore boots, a leather jacket, and a leather hat with goggles. He was standing next to his big Harley Davidson motorcycle when I met him. Dad seemed to know him, and the next thing I knew— on June 24, 1961—John was instructing me in how to fly an Aeronca Champ airplane, complete with a sixty-five horsepower engine.

John was cool and seemed very understanding as I tried to keep the airplane going straight down the runway. But since this was a tail dragger, a plane that sits on two front wheels and one rear wheel on a swivel, my travel down the runway had a lot of forty-five-degree angles in the ground track. John knew it took a while to get used to anticipating the airplane's reaction to the rudder inputs in order to get it to go straight down the runway, but once we got the airplane to go straight, we focused on pattern work. That is, we stayed close to the field and practiced takeoffs and landings, one after another. Eventually I could land the plane without much input from John Roche, and I thought I was about ready to solo. And then I found out John Roche was not a certified flight instructor.

When I showed up on September 5, 1961, John was standing there with another man. This man talked to me for a while and then said, "Well, let's go for a ride." I wasn't exactly sure what was going on. Once we were airborne, he yelled, "OK, let me see you land this thing." I landed. We did it again and then did it a third time. He then had me pull up next to John, and he got out and said, "OK, now do three more landings by yourself." I did, and then I realized what had just happened. This guy was a certified instructor, and he had trusted John to give me all the required instruction before he ever arrived. We filled my logbook in to show all the work John and I had done, and this certified instructor signed it. I never saw this man before or after that day.

Needless to say, we had saved a lot of money, since up to then, we had never paid for an instructor. I have no idea what that would have cost back in the day. I still remember that John Roche would roll a toothpick around in his mouth during all this. He was cool. Somewhere I got the idea that Dad and he had drunk a few beers or some whiskey together years before. As the years have gone by, I realize more each day that what my father did was truly a gift to me. And the timing was just right too.

Danny and I moved to another dormitory for our sophomore year. This room was built for two, and only the two of us lived there. We seemed to be moving up in the world. We each had a bed, and there were no bunk beds. Our studying continued, and the math courses got tougher, though Dan was better at math than I was. When we got tired of studying, we would wrestle in the small room. The initiation of a match usually started with one of us standing behind the other and smacking the opponent on the back of the head. It is a wonder that one of us didn't die in that room. We would go at it, and soon we would be on the floor, gasping at the fact that, during a takedown, our heads had just missed the corner of one of the two permanent bed frames.

The dorm monitor, an upperclassman paid to maintain order in the dormitory, would often come by and shout, "Will you guys knock that shit off?" The sound of the chairs in our room banging up against our door or our closet doors seemed too much for him. But the wrestling relieved our stress, and then the studying would begin anew.

From our room, you could peer out and see two lanes of fraternity houses, one to the left and one to the right. I would have thought fraternity life would have appealed to me, but I think the whole world was a bit out of focus for me. I was still running scared that I would fail academically and that any dreams about the air force would come to an end. So as an "independent," I would look out at the fraternity houses from our room on the second floor of Conklin Hall.

One night I saw a guy sitting on the windowsill of a fraternity house. He was on the second floor with his feet dangling outside and a guitar in his hands. Outside, two floors below, five or six co-eds looked up, listening to the guitar player. This guy was singing his tail off. I was close enough to him and could see his face pretty well. Similarly, while I sat in the student union one day, a fire truck pulled up and let off a bunch of fraternity people and associated sorority gals. I saw that the driver was the same guitar player. This was Buzzy Miller. I hadn't met him at this point, but it wouldn't be long before I did. Although we would be friends for most of our lives, I decided not to continue my relationship with him when I was in my late sixties. Someday, dear Jason and Jodi, maybe we'll talk about that. But Buzzy and I appreciated each other for a long time, and we laughed most of the time between the BG years and my late sixties—about forty years.

When I met Buzzy in my sophomore year, the meeting was odd. Buzzy asked, "Is your name Gilmore?" (I guess he knew me from ROTC.)

"Yes, it is."

"Hi, my name is Bob Miller, and I've got something here that you might be interested in."

"Really? What is it?"

Bob went on to show me a newspaper clipping about some guy in Pittsburgh who had "flown" a parachute. That is, he had cut holes in a regular parachute in such a way that it actually created some lift and would ascend if pulled by a boat or car. Buzzy wanted to know if I was interested. I said I was, and eventually we talked the ROTC department into giving us a parachute. Buzzy was in charge of cutting holes in it. We eventually got the harness necessary to complete the connection between parachute and intended parasail rider.

One of the full-time AFROTC sergeants, Sergeant Denny, brought out his Chevy Corvair convertible to tow us and see if we could get airborne with it. The first couple of tries did not work, because we were trying to hold on to the rope from the car with a baton, like a water-skiing baton. But as the parachute billowed up and pulled one way, and the Corvair tried to go the other way, we just could not hold on for any length of time. Back to the drawing board we went. We eventually connected the rope directly into our harness so that our arms and hands were free.

Buzzy tossed the coin. I "won." I would go first with the new rig, and we suspected that we just might get airborne. There was a pretty strong wind coming head on to me, and Buzzy was clipping the parachute into the harness when I felt a firm tug in the rearward direction. The parachute had become full bloom and was taking me where the wind wanted me to go: backward. I went down on my back and looked wide-eyed at Buzzy as I moved on down the road. Buzzy started running all out to catch me, but it was fruitless. As I watched him, he became smaller and smaller. I was probably going down the road now at ten to fifteen miles an hour, still on my back, still on the ground. I finally stopped momentarily in a ditch. Buzzy caught up, jumped on top of me, and held on with both arms. Then a new wind came along. The parachute went up, and we went up with it. As we rose about ten feet in the air, I heard Buzzy say he couldn't hold on anymore, and I watched him fall away from me. I was beginning to panic when I realized I was now crossing a paved road, where a truck driver had stopped to analyze what was going on.

I eventually came back down on the ground but resumed the fast ride on my back. Then I thought, *I know how to get out of this harness.* I reached up and pulled on some rings on each shoulder, and finally, the lines holding the parachute to the harness were released. I came to a stop in a field, and the parachute came to a stop a little while later. Everything seemed very quiet now. That was a close call. I suppose I could have died that day. My memory of the truck driver is that he had stopped his truck and was leaning forward with both forearms on the steering wheel, as though to say, "Wow, look at this."

Soon we did things in the correct order, as far as the hookup went, and I was airborne. I flew probably ten to fifteen feet in the air, looking down at Sgt. Denny and the Corvair. Buzzy then did the same. We had done it. And then we laughed, and Sgt. Denny smiled. (He didn't normally.) Eventually we drew a crowd from BG, but soon thereafter, we were on to something else.

We studied, we wrestled, and we parasailed, and I became more and more involved in ROTC. I was on the AFROTC drill team, and this was probably my only activity outside of academics for my first two years. There was something about the discipline of the drill team that I enjoyed. And like dancing, it had a beat to it. There was almost a Zen-like feeling to being in a routine that had been well practiced and well executed. The sound of everyone's feet hitting pavement at the same time was soothing, and the guy stuff going on before, after, and yes—during practice—was a lot of fun. It was a great escape from the constant academic effort as well.

Jo, my girlfriend, was a year behind me, and for a while, I thought she might go to Cornell. She ended up coming to BG, and I was glad. She had ridden on the back of my motor scooters and had been beside me during my drag-racing years. Later she would ride on the back of my Triumph Bonneville motorcycle. She had two roommates at BG, Jean and Sue. Interestingly, Sue's future would, in some ways, be determined by me and by fate.

I should mention here a picture that had an effect on me as I sat in a sophomore ROTC classroom. I was sitting in the second row in my AFROTC uniform, and I had an ROTC book open. As I looked at the picture in the book, I focused intently on a depicted contrail: the contrail of an air force jet high in the sky. The picture wasn't even in color, but I had a very strong thought: *maybe it is possible to become an air force pilot.* It remained much more a question than a statement, however.

About this time, I remember that the ROTC instructor handed out sheets of paper. He said, "I want you to write down a simple goal that you have now." I thought this a little strange but immediately wrote down that my goal was to become the cadet commander in our Bowling Green Air Force ROTC detachment. He collected these and said they would go into a safe. What would happen after that didn't seem clear. For some reason, the goal-writing exercise reminded me somewhat of discussions with my mother. Whether I would achieve this goal would not be determined until my junior year.

I can't say I was buddies with any of my teachers, other than in the first three grades of elementary school, and college didn't change that...until I met a philosophy professor named Dr. Ross. Dr. Colvin Ross was a real instructor, I believed and still believe. He made students think. He challenged traditional thought, traditional society, and traditional education. He really got me thinking about a lot of things. He would say or ask things like, "You know, if you only went to school every other day, you would likely learn just as much as if you went every day." Or, "Do you think Mary was a virgin, or was it more likely that Joseph, a poor shepherd, got her pregnant?" He'd ask, "What is your favorite thing to do?" Then he'd answer for himself, saying, "I like bowling. I really enjoy bowling." Then he'd say, "But you know what? Compared to sex, bowling just isn't in the ballpark."

I had never seen this candor in front of students before. Remember, this was way back in the sixties. No, Dr. Ross wasn't Mr. Studly. He was about five feet six and bald and wore very thick glasses. Eventually I asked him if he would mind if I sat in on other classes he taught, even though I wasn't signed up for them. I thought that if I ever ended up being a teacher, I'd like to be able to use some of his techniques—though not the questions about Mary or bowling.

Dr. Ross had a big influence on my life in some subtle and not-so-subtle ways. Because of him, I became interested in philosophy, to the extent that I have a small statue of Socrates in my backyard today as I write. Ross eventually helped me get through a master's program at BG and later moved and taught at the University of Connecticut. I visited him there in my midforties. He died at age seventy-two of Parkinson's disease. Ross's influence will show up later when I quote from *Thoughts of a Philosophical Fighter Pilot* by Jim Stockdale in the Vietnam Appendix C of this memoir. Here's to ya, Dr. Colvin Ross. And here's to ya, Socrates!

CHAPTER 3

Ages Twenty to Thirty: 1962–1972

Dow Jones Industrial Average
652.1–1,020.02
56.4% Gain

THE JOURNEY TO LIEUTENANT AND GRAD SCHOOL

SOMEHOW I MADE IT TO my junior year at BG. I had a dual major of education and math. The education was not too difficult, while the math was very difficult for me; ROTC was relatively easy. Because of my interests in people, I had thought of doing a psychology or sociology major—those were the only classes where I could sit and listen to a professor speak and then get As or Bs on the tests—but it didn't take long to realize that, with psychology, you couldn't fix people very easily. I learned that these subjects were somewhat gray; that is, sometimes the fixes worked for people, and sometimes they didn't. The fixes that did work, in general, took large amounts of time. I suppose as much as anything I pondered a life dealing with other people's problems. These classes were, in many ways, the direct opposite of the math classes, and I abandoned the notion of a life in psychology or sociology.

My junior year was a watershed of sorts, because it was the first time I decided I would try alcohol. In today's world, I might be shunned by some of my twenty-year-old classmates for abstaining that long. Now I was not quite so afraid of getting through school, and so I was becoming bolder as the months went by. I would never become an alcoholic as my father had, but alcohol would become part of my life, and in some cases, it was not a positive influence.

Danny and I moved off campus in our junior year. As upperclassmen, we sensed that we just might make it through this phase of life. Our room was one of four in the top of a very large, old house also occupied by the owners and their two children, who all lived downstairs. Accompanying us in adjacent rooms upstairs were six other guys, all with their own stories. Our room was smaller than the one we'd had our freshman year, but we still felt cool, because we were no longer tied to the campus. We didn't even have enough space in this room to wrestle. I can't remember how I got back and forth to campus, as I still did not have a car. My Ford had been sold long ago before I came to Bowling Green.

Back in the 1960s or earlier, Studebaker came out with what they called an Avanti, which was the sporty version of a Studebaker, if that was possible. Studebaker was kind of on its way out at the time, and the company actually went out of business in 1966. Skip Fillinger, a friend of mine from ROTC, lived near BG with his parents. In my junior year, he got a little sports car and decided to sell his old Studebaker. I think he actually felt sorry for me when he sold it to me for seventy-five dollars. What a mess that car was. But it ran. I think it was Buzzy who jokingly named it *the Avanti*. We would be sitting in the student union on a Friday, and Buzzy would ask, "Are we taking the Avanti out tonight?" What a riot.

The Avanti was a real piece of crap. Years later, I went to a store and bought a few belts—you know, the kind that go around your waist. The cashier at the store rang them up and nonchalantly said, "That will be a hundred and twenty dollars." I started laughing and then explained that, when I was in college, I had bought a car for a little more than half the cost of these belts. When I think about it now, though, maybe the belts were worth more than the Avanti!

I remember that Skip would usually pick me up in his little MG on many weekends, and we would always end up in Maumee, Ohio, where we would drink beer and dance with the local girls. Skip wore a beer opener on a chain around his neck. Life was beginning to take on that carefree spirit I'd seen in grade school and high school, and I began to relax a little.

Jo's dad, Sam; Jo; and me—a long time ago

Jo's dad, Sam, was always very nice to me, and he got me a summer job at Republic Steel in Youngstown, where he'd worked before and after World War II. He'd done pretty well in the army, becoming a master sergeant. I never knew what he did in the war, and I find it strange that I never asked him about it. Now he was doing very well at Republic Steel also. There were probably about seventy to ninety draftsmen there, all working on developing plans for the sale and placement of steel trusses, steel roofing, or siding for commercial buildings. Probably fifteen to twenty of these men were educated engineers, and they all worked directly for Sam. He proposed that I go there as a mail boy. Similar to at the Mural Room, I was on the low end of the totem pole as far as jobs went. But it was a fun job, and I learned a lot about life, business, money, and movement within hierarchies. Mostly I just had fun. The fun was tempered, however, because of my association with Sam, and I remained on my good behavior.

Most of the time, I could go anywhere in the factory that I wanted, and I spent a lot of time going down into the bowels of the factory to retrieve old drawings. The draftsmen always needed to review old drawings to relate to old customers who had bought products for roofs or siding years ago, sometimes even thirty or forty years ago. There were files stored in buildings as long as a football field, and nobody would be in them except me. They were dusty and full of cobwebs, and I would find myself reflecting on when these drawings had been made, back in the 1940s or earlier. The files also had a musty smell to them. They had been in these drawers for years, baking inside a metal cabinet inside a metal building with no temperature control. Because I worked at Republic Steel in the summer, my memory of these drawing-retrieval trips is of the intense heat in these buildings. Most of the people who had made these drawings were likely dead, I often reflected. I think I earned about a dollar and twenty-five cents an hour on this job—double what I'd made at the Mural Room.

Republic occupied at least three or four buildings, so it was necessary for me to go collect or disburse mail a few times a day at various places within these buildings. The secretaries were all quite a bit older than I was, but I always seemed aware of the women. We would laugh and joke. Of course, because I was dating the boss's daughter, I had to behave myself around them. And morally, I should not have been having any other thoughts, since I was devoted to Jo. This was always difficult for me, I guess. I was still very young, and life waited, in all its forms. Some might say I was too hard on myself, but my mother had given me a rather stringent view of what was right and what was wrong. I would learn years later that to be human was not always an easy thing.

I spent a lot of time on the job getting prints of drawings too. There were different types of machines for this, but one was very large and kind of reminded me of that mangle my mom and Ma used for ironing. An older woman named Kate usually ran this large machine. She was probably near sixty years old, and we sat feeding large drawings into this large machine in order to get copies out the other side. Kate smoked and seemed accustomed to this job, which she had held for probably twenty to thirty years. She never talked of a husband or family. I felt a little sorry for her.

I saw all the men at the drafting tables in somewhat the same light. Some had been there for thirty years or more, and they had a ritual. Work started at 8:00 a.m., so they would be in place behind their desks at 7:55 a.m. At 8:00 sharp, the whistle would blow, and all their heads would go down to start work. Lunch was at noon. At 11:45 a.m. sharp, they would all have their desks cleaned up, and they would stand and talk at their desks until noon, when the whistle would blow, and they would stream out of the office for lunch. Some would stay and eat out of their brown bags, which reminded me of Dr. Ross's remarks about the mundane lives of some of the other professors. He would refer to the possibility of finding them clutching their brown paper bags as they were discovered in shrubs of ivy at the university after suffering a heart attack.

The steel company offered some upward mobility. From draftsman you could be promoted to squad leader, a label I always wondered about; was it chosen because of its familiarity, given how recently we had faced World War II and Korea? Being a squad leader meant that your desk faced a row of five to ten draftsmen. Squad leaders had probably been there longer than the others and probably made a little more money. The chain of command was obvious: draftsman, squad leader, Sam's job, and then the chief of the whole operation. Family as well as workers at Republic often said that Sam would have had the president's job if he'd had a college education. I felt very lucky: I wasn't married, didn't have kids, had little pressure on this job, and was in the process of getting an education. I hoped my path would keep me from that mundane life I first had pondered while a janitor at the Mural Room. Little did I know that I might overdo this thing about avoiding a mundane life.

Before my time was up at Republic Steel, I did rotate to the draftsman position. I sat behind a wonderful man by the name of Jimmy Lipp. He helped me adjust to this new job, took all my questions, and was my key to survival in the new position. Slowly I even developed a decent "printing" technique to go along with the drawings I was preparing. These drawings were made to show customers how the trusses and steel roof panels were to be installed on their buildings and also to show the associated costs of these materials. To put this all in perspective and give you an idea of my prospects for my future as a draftsman, Jimmy once said that he was going to get me a power drill upon which we could mount a three- to five-inch eraser. No, I didn't see a future in this business either.

In my junior year, a surprising thing happened in ROTC. The professor of air science, or PAS, at the university did something different from what many expected. The senior AFROTC class was very small. They had all been to summer camp the previous year and had completed everything except their final academic year. They all knew who among them would be going to flight training and who would not. In my class, we also had just finished our Air Force Officer Qualification Tests (AFOQT) and knew which of us *might* be going to flight school, assuming we got through summer camp and the rest of our junior and senior years of academics. One day the officers, or instructors, came to class and announced that the senior-class cadets were going to be retired; that is, they would no longer compete for positions within the cadet corps. They said that we would vote on who would become the new cadet colonel—the head of the remaining freshman, sophomore, and junior ROTC cadets. Sound familiar?

I was astounded when my peers voted for me. And as in high school, I hadn't even run for the job. I had a good start as the cadet commander, but I must say, after getting the job, I didn't do much to enhance the cadet corps. After all, third-semester calculus needed attention, along with my other three-hundred-level and four-hundred-level math classes.

We were juniors. We had passed the AFOQT, and some of us had been identified as flight candidates. Then there came an opportunity for those of us identified as flight candidates to be enrolled in what was known as the Flight Instruction Program (FIP). We began flying lessons at BG with civilian instructors. The airplane we used was called a Piper Tri-Pacer, and it was a small, single-reciprocating-engine airplane, but at least we were flying off a runway with a hard surface. I thought my grass-runway days were over. Eventually we would take the written and flying tests necessary to get our civilian pilots' licenses. The flight test was not too bad, but I found that the written test was, as usual for me, difficult.

**The Piper Colt or Piper Tri-Pacer had 125 horsepower
and a top speed of about 104 mph; 160-horsepower
models would get to about 140 mph.
I flew one of these via an ROTC Flight Instruction
Program and received my FAA pilot's license
on May 21, 1964. (Photo by Bill Shull)**

During my junior year, an air force officer jumped out of
a balloon from a very high altitude, testing everything that
goes along with something like that. His name was Captain
Joe Kittinger. Kittinger jumped from an altitude of 102,800
feet and accelerated to more than six hundred miles per hour
during the free fall. And then, for some reason, he showed up
at Bowling Green State University, and I got to shake his hand.
Now that is some speed, I thought. My escapades with the parasail at BG made me appreciate what Joe Kittinger had done.
Later our paths would cross in Vietnam, but I would never see
him again personally. He would shoot down a MiG and then

be shot down himself. He spent eleven months as a prisoner of war in Vietnam and eventually retired as a colonel.

Here I am shaking hands with Captain Joe Kittinger. The men behind me were other ROTC members in my class. Colonel Peters, who ran our ROTC detachment, is to the far left.

Regardless of what I was doing, I still thought a lot about cars and speed. A 1932 Ford had been restored in Hubbard and was a real beauty. It had a big Chevy V-8 in it and had a beautiful paint job and leather interior. It came up for sale for $750, but my parents didn't want me to have it while I was in school. They came to equate no car with my finishing school someday. Of course, I had no money and shouldn't have been trying to spend anybody's money on anything but my education at the time. A buddy of mine from Bowling Green ended up buying it and, in less than twenty-four hours, rolled it off the end of a drag strip in Ohio. It was destroyed. I was there and watched it all happen. What a shame.

Around this time, while walking down a hallway in one of the buildings at BG, I saw an ad on a bulletin board that read something like this: "A few men wanted: you will come to the vicinity of Wright-Patterson Air Force Base and take part in an experiment. Studies will be done on how humans react to being enclosed in a capsule for an extended period of time. This study will help determine reactions to this limited environment and help to make recommendations about flights taken on future space flights." It took me about one minute to find a phone. Soon I was at Wright-Patterson with several other guys going through a meet and greet and a fairly lengthy physical. I believe a shrink talked to us as well. I thought all this went well and was excited to be a part of this experiment. Space flight, after all, was right around the corner for a few aviators. I could dream about it, couldn't I? We were told to return home after these physicals. We would hear from them in a few days.

I was at home in Hubbard when the call came. Mom answered the phone and handed it to me, smiling. I was told I had scored among the top candidates during the interview, but I had a problem. The problem was that I'd had a bad reading on the electroencephalograph conducted during the physical. This was a brain-wave test, and the theory was that I might be subject to having a reaction to a high-G environment, such as prematurely blacking out. I felt my knees crumbling. I feared the air force would be notified—I might lose my pilot-training slot. That never happened, but I worried about the meaning of this electroencephalograph for years.

In the summer between my junior and senior years, I was required to go to summer camp, where ROTC students went through a process very similar to the one enlisted people go through in basic training. This was a high-pressure, demanding, and time-compressed environment designed to see how students would perform and then measured against standards developed by the military. The young officer candidates were competitive, yet there remained the remnants of personalities associated with a bunch of college guys. My only example of this will be of a young Tuskegee guy teaching the rest of us the words and melody of the song "Oh Nellie, Roll Your Belly Close to Mine." My officer in charge was a real live air force officer and pilot, Captain Bodie. He would be responsible for our training and for ranking us as to how we did during our stay.

I found summer camp to be a little fast-moving for me. There seemed to be no time to get to know the others, and I guess I always tended to hang back to get the lay of the land before committing myself to many endeavors. I wanted to be in the upper half of the class, since that was necessary to become a distinguished military grad at BG, but I can't say I overdid it here. In the end, I was in the top half of the class, but had I been ranked one notch lower, I would not have been. Even though there weren't any heavy academics, I learned that I needed to speak up a little sooner in this business, or I would likely fall by the wayside in the US Air Force.

Like enlisted troops going through boot camp, we got up very early in the morning; went to bed very late at night; did a lot of exercise, including some marching; and worked to keep our living facility in immaculate condition. The hanger spacing in the lockers was precise, as was the layout of our foot-lockers. Sometimes we didn't even sleep in our bunks, so they would be made up perfectly all the time; instead, we would sleep under the bed. If you did something wrong, the instructor would issue you demerits. Once you collected so many demerits, you spent the weekend marching instead of going downtown with the boys. Yes, I did some weekend marching.

We always had things to memorize. While in line at the chow hall, some of the instructors would walk up behind us and ask us to recite the required memory item of the day. They pressured us twenty-four hours a day to perform both physically and mentally. I think the code of conduct was broken up into at least six parts, and we were responsible for memorizing these one day at a time. If we didn't want to be harassed before breakfast, lunch, or dinner, we learned our memory items for the next day, often by reviewing them with a flashlight at night. I got through it, but I sure didn't set the world on fire.

The origin of this code of conduct was in 1955 and was designed for all of our US services. You can reference it by looking up *The US Fighting Man's Code* published by the Office of Armed Forces Information and Education in November, 1955.

Code of Conduct for the US Fighting Man

1. **I am an American fighting man. I serve in the forces which guard my country and our way of life. I am prepared to give my life in their defense.**
2. **I will never surrender of my own free will. If in command, I will never surrender my men while they still have the means to resist.**

3. If I am captured, I will continue to resist by all means available. I will make every effort to escape and aid others to escape. I will accept neither parole nor special favors from the enemy.

4. If I become a prisoner of war, I will keep faith with my fellow prisoners. I will give no information, or take part in any action which might be harmful to my comrades. If I am senior, I will take command. If not, I will obey the lawful orders of those appointed over me and will back them up in every way.

5. When questioned, should I become a prisoner of war, I am bound to give only name, rank, service number, and date of birth. I will evade answering further questions to the utmost of my ability. I will make no oral or written statements disloyal to my country and its allies or harmful to their cause.

6. I will never forget that I am an American fighting man, responsible for my actions, and dedicated to the principles which made my country free. I will trust in my God and in the United States of America.

(Note: Prior to the Vietnam Conflict, violation of any of the above code elements could result in trial by Courts Martial. After Vietnam, the code allowed some discretion in providing more than just name, rank, serial number or social security number, and date of birth)

I pondered the meaning of each of these items in the code of conduct then and for years to come. I knew this was a tough standard, and I hoped I would measure up to the code's requirements during my time in the service. After Vietnam I remember reading a book about a pilot, an air force academy grad named Lance B. Sijan who upheld these very high standards of the code to the point where he was beaten so badly he lost his life. A Medal of Honor somehow seems not enough for such a man.

Soon summer camp was over, and it was time for my senior year. I had done my job as cadet commander, and our detachment appointed another cadet commander. I was glad that was over; I needed a rest.

Senior year was uneventful, I guess, but graduation and becoming an officer in the air force were fast approaching. I realized around this time that I wasn't going to graduate in four years, because I still had some things to accomplish academically. I would spend another semester at school.

Once my class completed senior ROTC, we went through a commissioning ceremony. The ceremony itself was quite understated. As I remember, we seniors stood in uniform in one of the ROTC classrooms as one of our instructors read aloud, phrase by phrase, our commissioning pledge to officially make us second lieutenants in the US Air Force. The instructors pinned on our brown/gold bars and ushered us out of the classroom, though we were still inside the ROTC building. At this point, I had one of those experiences that would burn itself into my psyche.

When the door opened, the enlisted men who worked within our ROTC department—Sergeant Denny, Sergeant Crepps, and the others we had been around for our four years at BG—stood there. These guys all had at least ten years of service in the air force and were currently employed as noncommissioned officers (NCOs) in the real air force. There they were, standing at attention, with their right arms raised, rendering us brand-new lieutenants a salute. Protocol would require us to salute them before they could lower their arms. What had just happened? Because we had gotten education and an ROTC commission, we were now above them in the chain of command. I had known this would happen someday, but the reality of it all did not sink in until that moment. Of course, the NCOs were enjoying it, because it was tradition that when a lieutenant gives his first-ever salute, he must pay the NCO a dollar. We saluted them all at once, and we dispensed a dollar to each of them.

They were all great guys. I remember Sergeant Denny, the NCO who gave Buzzy and me the parachute. Sergeant Crepps was a big guy, and I remember him breaking into laughter every time he saw Buzzy and me in the ROTC building. I forget the other guys' names, but I can see their faces as if it were yesterday. I probably respected these guys more than they would ever know. I had always had a fair amount of respect for anyone I met, but these guys were special. I had no notion of being superior to them in any way; my mother had drilled that kind of thing out of me before I was old enough to remember.

I graduated in January 1965, still with no air force duties. That would come later. I'd had a lot of motivation to graduate from college, as you can see from my story so far. Mom had set the stage by suggesting long ago that I go to school and leave Hubbard. The yard-mowing, Mural Room, and drugstore-janitor jobs and my time at Republic Steel were all experiences in economics, capitalism, and motivation, among other things. Watching my family work as hard as they did was also a huge motivator for me, whether that occurred at Gilmore's General Store or Alice's Beauty Shop or through Dad's attempts at careers in insurance, radio repair, carpentry, and truck driving. I knew I had to be serious about my approach to higher education. And thinking our family was middle class might have been an exaggeration, but for Hubbard, Ohio, we were middle class. A college degree might help me progress beyond where our family had.

Bill had been doing well with the stock market in the fifties and sixties. Partly because of that and partly because of who he was, he made me a proposition just before my freshman year at Bowling Green. He said he would buy me the car of my choice upon graduation. Imagine that. I spent the majority of my time in college without a car, except for the short time I had the Avanti, and upon graduation, I got a 1964 Corvette with a 365-horsepower engine. I am almost embarrassed by this, but I remember all the students who didn't make it through school because of their lack of effort, discipline, or attitude, and I don't think the promise of a Corvette would have made a difference for them. The Corvette wasn't the reason I made it through school, but it sure was a nice bonus. In short, I was very humbled by this gift from my grandfather, and I still am. Now the challenge was to not kill myself in the Corvette.

Around this time, Dr. Ross sat down with me and said he thought I should go to graduate school. I told him I didn't think that was possible, because my grades weren't that great, and I didn't have any money; that is, I didn't think my parents had the money. He told me he would be my adviser, and he didn't think I would have any problems getting through the curriculum if I could get the money. He went on to tell me that now was the time to do it, before I got wrapped up in the air force or family life. And he said further that, as I went through life, a lot of people would ask if I had a master's degree. "You'll be able to tell them yes, and then the conversation will go on from there," he said. How right he was. I proposed this master's-degree thing at home, and my grandfather forked out the money for me to go. Thank you, Bill.

After I secured a delay from active duty from the air force, the rest was history. I earned a master's degree in education, which would allow me to become a superintendent of a school system sometime in the future. Other than student teaching and a brief visit to see Dr. Ross years later, I would never step foot in a civilian classroom again.

In one of my math classes, I met a guy named Leo. Leo was kind of a wild man, but he was smart enough to get through all those calculus classes with flying colors. I was amazed at the IQ on this guy, but I could tell he was a bit of a party animal. One day he suggested that I needed to get a real place to live while going to grad school. I have no idea why, but I followed along to see where it would end. He took me up to Maumee, Ohio, and introduced me to Jerry, an old man of about forty-four years. (Yes, at the time, I *did* think he was an old man.) Jerry had just been divorced and was looking for someone to share his three-bed, one-bath house with him. He had a bar in the cellar and a pool outside the house. OK.

It turns out this was close to the wildest time of my life. I even tended bar downtown at a place called Brother Baker's.

Well, I poured beer in the upstairs balcony. I accompanied an older gentleman upstairs and poured beer for anybody with money. I noted that most of the time the older man would basically pass out in the corner on weekend nights. I would prop him up on a couple of beer kegs and continue serving the beer until we shut down around two in the morning. This old guy may have been an alcoholic, but I think he might have saved my life and, just as importantly, my flying career.

I had saved some money and decided it would be a good idea to buy a used motorcycle to race on a flat dirt track. I had seen guys do this, and I was mesmerized by it. They came around the corners in a slide, all together and struggling to lead the pack. I knew it was dangerous, but there was that familiar smell of fuel and oil and the sound of loud reciprocating engines.

One night at Brother Baker's, the old guy remained sober all night. After we closed, he told me he wanted to talk to me. So at 2:15 a.m., there we were sitting on some stools downstairs in the very dimly lit bar. He began, "I know you are about to go into the air force, and I know you want to fly. Did you know that my father was the chief racing representative for Champion Spark Plug?" I had heard this part before. He continued, "Do you realize that once you start that flat tracking with that motorcycle and that steel shoe, you will eventually get so beat up that the air force will never let you in the door, let alone allow you to fly their airplanes?"

I was astounded that this guy was sober, but more importantly, he had taken the time to shed some light on the dangers of motorcycle racing. I had been well aware of those dangers but for some reason had not connected the dots to the possibility of them ruining my chances in the air force. *Pretty stupid on my part*, I thought. The next day, I got my down payment back and shed all thoughts of ever doing any real motorcycle flat tracking.

I must pause here to add a few thoughts about my college friend Ken Rock. I met Ken in my last year at BG, and we talked about the usual things guys in their twenties talk about: girls and our futures. I actually introduced him to his first wife, Sue. But I felt it unusual that every time we talked, I would talk about the stock market, and Ken would talk about industry. He was always talking about "furnaces" at some factory. We both seemed to enjoy these business discussions, and it reminded me of the unending discussions my grandfather used to have at the grocery store with a salesman, Bob McKim—slow, deliberate, analytical discussions laced with appreciation for each other and laughter. I once told attorney Sam Rock, Ken's son, that our discussions haven't changed much over the past fifty years, at least the business ones. His daughter, Kendra, is a veterinarian and is almost a replica of her mother, Sue, with a business mind like Ken's.

I'd been with Jo for a long time, though we'd had some on-and-off time (usually because of me). I knew I should marry her, but I seemed destined to take it to the bitter end before I did. While I went to grad school at BG, she went down near Columbus, Ohio, and got a teaching job. I was drinking more, and I had the feeling that she might be giving up on me, so I called her on the phone one evening and asked her to marry me. (I had a lot to learn in life.) We would wait to get married until after I finished school in January 1966.

GOING WEST, LIEUTENANT?

I was not to go to pilot training until June 1966, due to the air force's needs, so I had some time to kill. I worked at Republic Steel again for a while, but eventually I took a trip. We newly commissioned lieutenants were told by the ROTC hierarchy that once we became lieutenants, we could hop rides on air force airplanes if there was space available. By this time, Ma and Bill were living in Arizona, so I decided to try to take a space-available ride to see them. They had been retired for several years now. I put on my uniform, complete with gold bars and name tag, and proceeded to Wright-Patterson Air Force Base to see if I could get a ride.

As I walked into Base Operations, I saw a major looking at me, smiling. A lot of people in any service smile when they see a second lieutenant, because they know how new to the service you are. They also were aware that only God knows what a lieutenant will do next. The major asked if he could help me. I said, "Yes, I'd like to get a ride out to Arizona, if possible—space available."

He looked at a few things and then pointed to a seat and said, "Sit there, Lieutenant!" I did as instructed. Soon a chief master sergeant walked in. The chief had a total of eight stripes on his arm. Chiefs always have the confidence and aura about them that declares them very competent, hardworking, and a force to be reckoned with.

I watched the major I had just spoken to engage the chief in a conversation, and the chief came over to me and said, "Hi, Lieutenant." He was smiling also. He asked, "I hear you are trying to go west, Lieutenant. Is that right?"

"Yes," I said. "I am trying to go to Arizona."

He said, "Follow me." Soon we arrived out on the flight line. The chief walked me over to what looked like a small business jet. The air force called it a T-39, a twin-engine jet with room for a pilot and copilot up front and a decent cabin with room for at least six or seven passengers in the back. It was a very nice plane. *Classy* is a word that comes to mind. The chief opened the door to the aircraft and pointed to a seat inside. He said, "Sit there, Lieutenant."

I smiled, flew up the three or four stairs, and jumped into my seat. I noticed the chief walking around outside like he was checking out the airplane, doing what we call a walk-around or preflight inspection. Soon he was back and took a seat across the aisle from me. About that time, a lieutenant colonel stuck his head around the corner of the passenger compartment, looked straight at me, and said, smiling, "Hi, Lieutenant. I hear you're going west."

I responded that I was and watched as he turned around and proceeded to look over the airplane. He returned, entered the airplane, and took the two or three steps to get into the cockpit. He sat down in the right seat, a seat normally designated for a copilot. I watched as he settled himself in, checking out the way he wore his flight suit and thinking that this probably was a decent job for him, but I was still wondering why he wasn't sitting in the left seat, where a pilot in command would sit.

And then, picture this, another officer stuck his head in the door, looked straight at me, smiled, and said, "Hi, Lieutenant. I hear you are headed west."

I answered in the affirmative, and then I started counting the stars on his shoulders; he had three on each side for a total of six. I had never seen anyone above the rank of colonel thus far in my career. He jumped up into the cockpit after telling me to enjoy the flight and said perhaps we would talk again once airborne. We weren't going to Arizona; we were going somewhere in Nebraska. Well, that was west.

Soon we were airborne, and I figured out that the lieutenant colonel was there to oversee the general. Generals didn't fly that often, so they usually had someone in the right seat to oversee things. Halfway through the flight, I got to go up and talk to the general and the colonel. They seemed interested to know I was eventually going to pilot training and so went into detail about this T-39's instrumentation and performance characteristics. I returned to my seat eventually and felt great about being in the air force.

Soon we were on the ground at Offutt Air Force Base, Nebraska, home of the Strategic Air Command, which is sometimes referred to as SAC. I knew that the Strategic Air Command was a very large military organization responsible for maintaining strategic capabilities around the world. With SAC's bombers, tankers (for fueling aircraft in the air), and missiles, it would be in the middle of any response to any attack by the Soviet Union or anyone else on a worldwide basis.

As we taxied in, I saw a couple of things from the window. First I saw what appeared to be a marching band, and then I saw a few enlisted types rolling out a red carpet. I had no idea that this was the way they prepared for the arrival of a three-star general. Well, the aircraft came to a stop right next to the red carpet, and the chief lowered the aircraft door, through which we were all about to depart. I waited for the general and the rest of the crew to leave. Neither the general nor anyone else left the airplane.

The general stood smiling at me and said, "After you, Lieutenant." Hesitantly, I stepped in front of the general. When my foot hit the red carpet, the band started playing. I couldn't believe this. I looked behind me and saw the general still smiling. As I left the carpet and started heading to Base Operations to see about another flight to Arizona, I looked back at the general and said, "General, this air force stuff is all right!"

I think he laughed out loud. I forget how I got to Arizona from there, and I forget how I got back to Ohio, but I'll never forget the ride with the general. I laugh every time I think of it.

Married and In Pilot Training

In June 1966, Jo and I were married. At the reception, we danced to the song "Barefootin'" with our shoes off. We spent our one-night honeymoon in a fleabag hotel in Youngstown, and within two or three days, we headed to the fine metropolis of Del Rio, Texas, for my pilot training.

When we arrived in Del Rio, we called our parents from a pay phone. It was hot in southwest Texas, but I could hear and see the jets in the air at Laughlin Air Force Base. The sound of them was mesmerizing to me.

I'd saved some money from my odd jobs, and since a couple hundred people had shown up for our wedding reception, we'd received a fair amount of money. We soon purchased a house trailer to live in, because my thoughts were to save the housing allowance given to anyone who did not live on base. The majority of the officers in my pilot-training class would live on base, especially because most were bachelors.

Jo got a job teaching a grade-school class immediately, and I remember one kid in particular taking up 90 percent or her time.

Soon I was deep into pilot training. I remember academics were held in the morning, and flying took place in the afternoon. I think that process was reversed from time to time. We started out flying an airplane known as the T-41, which wasn't that far removed from the small reciprocating-engine airplanes I had flown already back in Ohio. I was surprised our instructors for this part of training were civilian. They all wore tan coveralls and red baseball hats. This instruction was actually conducted at a local civilian field, not on the air base. We trainees would all file off the air force blue bus and walk into the facility, where we were to learn to fly this T-41.

Some of my classmates, maybe three or four, had already been in the air force for a while. They were a little older, and I think they had been navigators; they were all captains in the air force already. They seemed more grounded than the rest of us—no pun intended. That is, they just already knew what this air force thing was all about. Although they seemed more relaxed than the rest of us, one of the captains did not make it through this solo phase with the T-41. I was surprised at that and concerned about my future.

My civilian instructor was Mr. Duncan. He was lean and tanned from the Texas sun. Mr. Duncan was very professional and good at what he did, and he was probably fifty to fifty-five years old. Soon I would solo the T-41. Surprisingly to me, I was the first in my class to do so. With this, I felt like I was on my way. Little did I know what a long road this was going to be.

The T-41's top speed was about 144 mph, and it had about 210 horsepower. My first solo in the T-41 was on July 12, 1966.

Soon after we all soloed in the T-41, we no longer were going off base for any flying activities. A few more guys never did solo and were dismissed from the class. Men who had already spent time in the air force went back to their old jobs, while the others were given some choice of what they wanted to do now in the air force. Our instructors used the term *wash-out* for anyone who did not finish pilot training. It all felt like being a freshman in college again, and I was very concerned about making it through this place.

We were now introduced to the T-37 twin-engine jet, a side-by-side trainer.

The T-37 has a max speed of about 425 mph and two engines, each of which offers about 1,025 pounds of thrust. I first soloed in this plane November 10, 1966. (Photo by Gary Vincent)

I'll pause here to say that horsepower has always intrigued me. My original thought for this book was to provide the horsepower available on each airplane I flew, but I am reminded now that "pounds of thrust," the normal term associated with the force or pressure of a jet engine, cannot be directly compared to "horsepower," the normal term associated with the power of a reciprocating engine.[1] And so as we progress from reciprocating engines to jet engines, I will transition to note the approximate pounds of thrust on each of the engines rather than horsepower.

The T-37. They called it by various names, but most referred to the loud squeal that its engines emitted. Some called it a six-thousand-pound dog whistle, and others called it Tweet or Tweety Bird. We were getting systems training for the T-37's engines, hydraulics, electric system, and such. We studied the operating manual and learned the emergency procedures for the airplane. Simulators helped get us ready too, but they were somewhat rudimentary back then. Little did I know at the time how many hours, days, weeks, months, and years I would spend going through this process: systems training, operating-procedures training, emergency-procedures training, and simulator training. It would become my life for a long, long time.

Some of the other academic classes seemed to involve everything under the sun, including some engineering-type classes involving aero subjects such as lift and drag and some weather courses. I remember that for me it was the usual: working as hard as I could and still getting what amounted to Bs at the most, with a lot of Cs, even though the air force did not use that kind of a grading system. I also remember that some of the pilot trainees in the class already had engineering degrees, especially the Air Force Academy guys. It would drive me crazy that they sat in the classroom bored, as they already knew all this stuff.

After a lot of academics, a lot of systems training, and a lot of simulators, we were going to fly. Before that, we were required to recite all the emergency procedures both generally and specifically. I remember the overarching memory items for coping with an airborne emergency. In case of emergency, take the following steps:

1. Maintain aircraft control.
2. Analyze the situation and take proper action.
3. Land as soon as practical.

These emergency procedures would apply to all the flying I would ever do. The steps were simple and emphasized the most important things in all of flying.

I seldom blame others, but I did not like my first T-37 instructor, and I let it be known, which was not like me. We had been told that changing instructors was possible, and looking back, my naïveté reminds me of Goldie Hawn in the movie *Private Benjamin*. Soon I found myself a "washback," a student who would move to the next class for a host of reasons. This was pretty traumatic for me. I would now have to adjust to being in a different class with different instructors, and I found myself sitting in the new class, watching the instructors talking to their three or four students. One instructor impressed me. He was young, still a first lieutenant, tall, slender, and reserved. I hoped he would become my instructor, and he did.

Soon we were doing everything imaginable in the T-37, including loops, Cuban eights, the split-S, and not only normal spins but also inverted ones. Somewhere in here I received a check ride. I spent hours at home in the trailer going over everything for this ride: entry speeds, entry g-forces, maneuver to be entered next, and on and on and on. It was like flying the tree on Fox Street; I never moved from my chair in the trailer, but I did all these aerobatic maneuvers while sitting there for hours. I think I received one of the highest grades in the class for that ride. So I was on my way again.

This new instructor was Lieutenant Ron Smith, and I felt like he had saved me. Lieutenant Smith would later become Captain Smith working for Delta Airlines. Intuitively, I felt that he was probably one of the finest men I would ever know in this life. I wish I had spent more time with him during and after the air force days.

Eventually we got into instrument flying, learning to fly in the weather, learning to maintain aircraft control in the weather, and becoming aware of how your senses can lead you astray if you are not glued to your instruments. It was a tough business, I thought, but we all persisted.

There were a few parties on the weekends, but most of the time, I was studying: studying academics, studying systems, and studying emergency procedures. It was more exhausting than my early years at BG had been.

Eventually we finished our T-37 flying. We had come a long way from the T-41, and now we were moving on to the T-38—the White Rocket, as it was often called.

The T-38 has a max speed of Mach 1.3, or 858 mph, and had twin engines. It has 2,050 pounds of thrust per engine without the afterburner and 2,900 pounds of thrust per engine with the afterburner. I soloed in this plane March 31, 1967. (Photo by Henk Schuitemaker)

What a beautiful airplane. We did most of the acrobatics that we had done with the T-37, along with formation flying, and we went above Mach 1 at least once. I don't remember doing any spins in the T-38. I remember the first time I made an instructor laugh: he asked why I was shaking the stick so much during one of my first formation flights—my movements were too quick, too often, and too exaggerated to fly formation smoothly—and I responded that I was shaking the stick to shake the shit off it. What else could I say? I was doing the best I could, and it took me a while to settle into formation flying. But hearing the instructor laugh, ironically, made me feel better.

Less than a year before this, most of us had not flown at all or, as in my case, had earned only about twenty to thirty hours of flying time. Now we were flying at speeds of two hundred to five hundred miles per hour or more, in formation, three feet or so from our "leader," and we had all been supersonic at least a few times. This transition from ground pounder to aviator was proceeding very quickly.

Soon we were done with all the requirements associated with the T-38, and it was time to graduate—time to get our silver wings. When I look back on pictures of me receiving my wings, I see I looked pretty slender compared to the heavy guy I had always been. Hell, prior to my coming into the air force, a flight surgeon had demanded I lose nine pounds before I could be commissioned. He said I should weigh no more than 186 pounds, and at the time, I was weighing in at 195. When pilot training was over, I was well under that 186-pound threshold.

In August of '67, many of us, including me got our commercial licenses and instrument ratings, which came mostly from taking a written test and providing an account of our already-accomplished military flying to an arm of the Federal Aviation Agency (FAA).

Most of us wanted to fly fighters and, as requested, put the airplanes we wanted to fly on a dream sheet. Of course, wants and needs are different things, especially in the military, and these assignments were all subject to the air force's needs. At this time, the air force had more of a need for B-52 and KC-135 pilots than anything else. When the list came out regarding aircraft available, one of my classmates divided the number of pilots into the number of engines given to us and came up with something like 6.2 engines per man. So most of our class would be flying "many motors," as we called them. Most wanted one- or two-engine fighters, but only two or three fighters were assigned, as I remember. These were handed out according to where we placed in the class. I ended up where I always seemed to end up, right in the middle of the class, so I was to be a KC-135 pilot.

KC-135s

The KC-135 refueling mission. The picture above was taken at Ramey Air Force Base, where our crew participated in a SAC Bomb Competition. Just to make the competition "inclusive," they gave the KC-135 crews a navigation exercise.

**The top speed for current versions of
the KC-135 is around 580 mph.
The older KC-135s (like the one I flew) were originally
equipped with four Pratt & Whitney J-57-P-59W turbojet
engines, which produced ten thousand pounds of thrust
dry and approximately thirteen thousand pounds of
thrust wet. Wet thrust was achieved through the use of
water injection on takeoff, when the plane injected 670 US
gallons of water into the engines over the course of two
and a half minutes. This water allowed a second set of fuel
injectors to activate without melting the turbine buckets.
The water turned to steam and was ejected out the rear
of the engine, increasing the exhaust mass and thrust.**

I didn't include my usual max-speed description with the older 135, because most information available now is a compendium, illustrating a number of retrofits for the aircraft and the engines. Needless to say, speed ranges of four hundred to five hundred miles per hour were common for the 135; however, heavy fuel loads obviously affected performance, and refueling speeds were usually lower than cruise speeds.

Below I have included some bulleted captions describing some of my jobs, and I hope this helps the reader understand what I was doing at any given time.

Duty Title: copilot, combat-ready jet tanker aircraft, KC-135

- o Twenty-Second Air-Refueling Squadron at Strategic Air Command in March AFB, California
- o Aug 5, 1967, to April 21, 1969

Now I had to go and train for this aircraft. I would eventually be assigned to a refueling squadron at March Air Force Base,

California, just outside of Riverside. First I had to go through the systems, the operating procedures, the emergency procedures, and simulator training for the 135. This was a Boeing 707 that hauled fuel and was used to refuel airborne fighters or bombers on their way to targets anywhere in the world. My initial training would be at Castle Air Force Base near Merced in the central valley of California. I was there for about three months. Because I had taken so long to get through school and had delayed coming on active duty, I was probably about twenty-five by this time. Our house trailer was moved to a park just outside the base at March. Jo got a job teaching.

Our schedules were somewhat like pilot training; we had academics for half of the day and flying for the other half. It was hot in the Central Valley of California, and few buildings had air-conditioning. We students (seemed like we were always students) wore our starched khakis to class most of the time for academics, but with the heat and sweat, I can't say we looked all that great at the end of the day. Unlike in high school, there was little screwing around. This was serious business, and I needed to pay attention. My flight instructor was Major Zeiner, and he had his work cut out for him. The routine was to take a KC-135 airborne with about three copilots. Zeiner would, of course, sit in the left seat, while the three copilots would rotate through the right seat in order to get the required number of landings in to fill out the syllabus for that day. This would usually take several hours, because the KC-135 required such a large traffic pattern, and we did quite a few landings.

The 135 was nothing like a T-38 and was not very responsive to control inputs. Young lieutenants often remarked that the T-38 was the best airplane they would ever fly, and it was ironic that it was flown in training. Now we were in the real air force, and we yearned for a fast mover like the T-38. At Castle, I met a guy named Truman Torquelson—or Tork, as he was known. We did a lot of talking about where this was all leading, and I knew he wanted to fly fighters as well.

Gradually we finished all the required syllabus items and learned the systems of the KC-135, the associated emergency procedures, and all the operating procedures. Starting with the airplanes in pilot training and now in the 135, there were cautions, warnings, and notes in the operating manual that we were responsible for knowing inside and out. Knowledge of these things came at us weekly and sometimes daily in the form of written exams. We always had to write out the memory items for the emergency procedures exactly as they were written in the book. No deviations were allowed, or the instructor would require us to write them again. The cautions, warnings, and notes would appear in question form time and time again. There were hundreds of them.

I'm not sure whether it was before or after this that I was sent to survival school. This entailed a trip to Washington State. An instructor took us out in the woods to learn to survive after a theoretical crash or after being shot down. Capturing, cooking, and eating snakes and other varmints seemed to be the order of the day, but learning to travel light, keeping a source of water, and understanding how long you could function without water or food were the basics of any survival school. Operating with little sleep was a subtext of our experience as well. The instructors were top-notch and challenged us in a number of ways. This was a taxing experience, to say the least. I forget how long we were in the woods, but I believe it was at least a week, maybe two. The rest of the school probably lasted another two to three weeks, and dreams of having a McDonald's hamburger loomed large. And then we were done with survival school. I think it was referred to as Worldwide Survival School, meaning that it didn't focus on any single part of the world. All in all, it was a good school, but I wouldn't want to do it again.

I eventually reported to March AFB, ready to be a copilot in the Strategic Air Command. I had forgotten, but pulling alert was a job required of all B-52 and KC-135 aircrews. Because the United States and the Soviet Union were always trying to anticipate each other's moves, timing was of the essence for us. In the event of an attack by any foreign power, the KC-135s and the B-52s would be "scrambled" to most any part of the world to take appropriate action. In order to be prepared for this, we SAC crews lived in an alert facility for seven days at a time, twenty-four hours a day, in essence waiting for World War III to begin. There were things to keep us occupied while on alert, but looking back on it, I have to shake my head. I wonder if anybody would volunteer to do this nowadays.

The claxon, a loud horn that echoed all over the base when the aircrews were supposed to respond and go to their aircraft, would ring at least once during any seven-day alert period, and the base always timed our response to see if we would meet our timing requirements. We ate in a cafeteria in the alert facility, and we studied in classes regarding our missions. SAC crews were "married" together for their time on alert. You could go to the movies on base, or the BX—the exchange that sold various items—or just about anywhere else on the base. But you went as a crew, in your crew truck. There were four of us: the aircraft commander (the AC), the copilot (the co), the navigator (the nav), and the boom operator (the boom).

Obviously we came to know one another in this alert-facility environment, and sometimes we heard a variety of war stories. I remember one guy who had what looked to be big burn scars on one side of his face. It turns out he'd had a window come open at twenty-five thousand feet and had almost been sucked out of the airplane. Because he had been wearing a seat belt with a shoulder harness, he hadn't gone entirely out the window, but he had obviously been through a traumatic experience and suffered some pain as a result of having his upper body forced into the cold outside air.

Jo had another job teaching in the local area and seemed to adjust to both the area and the teaching job. We both were busy, that's for sure.

When we weren't on alert, we were either in the flight-planning room or simulator or were flying training missions. Flight planning was not automated then, so it took at least half a day to do everything necessary for a SAC flight. The four of us had specific duties. I worked at it all, but the "many motors" did not impress me; that is, I just did not get enthused about flying around in an airplane that did not routinely "get on its back."

On one of my first training missions, I remember sitting back by the navigator when the boys up front were practicing some forty-five-degree banked turns. The nav was a little older and grabbed on to his table for dear life, as if we were not going to live through it. But I yearned to be upside down in a T-38 or fighter. How would I ever get there? I looked at the AC and the nav, who were middle-aged men—good men with families—and wondered how they felt about these jobs. I didn't want to live that life. Sound familiar? It was like being transported back to the Mural Room and looking at the middle-aged janitors. I was in a different situation now, to be sure, but the feeling was just as bothersome. I would again ask myself if it was possible to avoid a humdrum life.

One way I tried to avoid the humdrum was by going out to a nearby field and learning to fly gliders. Flying with no engine was interesting. I enjoyed learning to fly behind the tow plane, anticipating everything required to get back on the ground without power. I found the quiet of gliding very Zen-like. There was no vibration once I separated from the tow plane, and I experienced total silence except for the sound of the air flowing over the wings. Some chose to listen to music while flying the gliders. I flew what was known as a Schwizer 2-33. In 1968, I did get a glider rating while at March Air Base, near Riverside, California. My last glider flight was on October 13, 1984, out of Fremont, California. My glider hours totaled about twelve. After being at March Air Force Base, I think I flew gliders only one other time, and that was years later. I even took Jim LaCivita, my old high school friend, for a ride.

FIRST AND SECOND LOOKS AT THAILAND AND VIETNAM

Vietnam had been the era's hot spot for a while, and by November 1968, I was introduced to it firsthand. The air force sent our KC-135 crew to Thailand to be a part of the airborne refuelers that would regularly give fuel to fighters striking targets primarily in South Vietnam. We would fly out of Utapao Air Base in southern Thailand, about ninety miles southeast of Bangkok. We stayed in a small house trailer, with the AC and me bunking on one side and the nav and boom on the other. A small bathroom separated the two halves. Jo remained in California.

We had a Thai housemaid who washed our flight suits, underwear, and socks; cleaned our bedsheets; and tidied the whole trailer. She was somewhat typical of the Thais: small, lean, and easygoing with a ready smile. She spoke little English but got her point across if she needed to. I appreciated her and remember buying her a small purse one time, just to show my appreciation for her.

Our trailer was air-conditioned. I suppose I was thanking my lucky stars that I was not in the army—or any of the other branches of service, for that matter. We were living pretty well, although to get a surfer dude in California to trade places with me might have been out of the question. And although I had a huge respect for all the services, I was still very happy I had somehow ended up in the air force.

Our missions out of Thailand were all very similar. We would fly to a point in the sky called an anchor and set up a racetrack orbit. We would stay in that orbit until our fighters showed up to take on their fuel. During refueling, we were required to wear our helmets and parachutes; the rest of the time, we were more relaxed. I remember that boom operators commonly remarked that they had "the only job in the world where you got paid to lie on your stomach and pass gas." Of course, they were referring to the fact that when we refueled any aircraft, the boom operator would be positioned in the rear of the aircraft, lying facedown while he controlled the boom, which he would literally position and insert into the receiving aircraft's refueling receptacle. Most of the pump switches and valves that determined from which tank the fuel would flow were up front and controlled by the AC and the co. The boomer had a small window, from which he viewed the approaching aircraft.

He also was able to talk to the approaching fighter or bomber from beginning to end of the refueling operation. In Thailand the communication between us and the receiver was much more limited. Stateside, sometimes our receivers were refueling for the first time, and in these cases, the boomers could become more animated. I remember the standard calls issued by the boomers, like this: "Slow your rate of closure... up two, down one, forward three...stabilize...contact." *Contact* was a signal for all of us that the two aircraft were now joined and could be separated only by a release by the boom operator, a release toggled by the receiver, or a "brute force disconnect." The brute-force disconnect was frowned upon, however, as it caused some stress on the airplane's physical boom and all the refueling connections on both airplanes.

If the boom operator was fearful of the two airplanes colliding, he would call out on the radio, "Breakaway, breakaway, breakaway." If a breakaway was called, the KC-135 pilots would use max power and climb, while the receiver was obliged to pull power and descend. In my times in the KC-135, I witnessed only two or three breakaways, though I do remember the story of a tanker crew calling in one time to their maintenance folks and telling them they had lost the boom. Maintenance responded, "Roger, understand that the boom is inoperative."

The tanker crew responded, "Negative, we have *lost* the boom. The boom has been torn off the airplane!" That was the only such story I ever heard, and it was really amazing that there weren't more problems during the thousands and thousands of refueling operations that took place in Thailand or stateside.

Well, we spent two months in Thailand, and I found that flying operational missions was much more interesting and efficient than doing stateside SAC operations. Here in Thailand, we had a mission, and we were doing it in fine fashion and felt good about it. There was little baloney.

I was promoted to captain in this relative time frame. This was no big deal because most first lieutenants made promotion the first time they were considered for the rank. Maybe ten percent of those considered did not make it.

We had a navigator who hadn't been on our crew up to this point, a guy named Dave. Dave was different. He didn't much worry about the brass, the bosses, the high rankers. I noted that Dave had been in the air force for about eighteen years and was still a captain. Ordinarily this was impossible. The system in the air force was that after about eleven or twelve years in the service, you would be reviewed for promotion to major. If you failed promotion, you would be considered for promotion for two more years. If you failed to be promoted on the third try, you would be eliminated from the service with no retirement. I asked Dave what the deal was. His response was that at about the eight- or nine-year point in his career, he had gotten into an argument with his squadron commander and had punched the man in the mouth. Ordinarily that would have been it;

his career would have been over, done. Dave knew I wanted to know how he had survived and said he knew a general officer who had looked out for him and had given him special dispensation.

Dave was an absolutely outstanding navigator and a hell of a lot of fun to be around. The first thing he did when he got to Thailand was disappear. He went downtown, and when he returned, we noted that he'd had his hair dyed jet black—not only the hair on his head but his moustache and chest hair.

Soon thereafter, Dave said he wanted to take me to the "Black Hole of Calcutta." No, we weren't in India. Saying something like that was standard fare for Dave, and soon after that, I was downtown with him, literally holding his hand as he took me down an alley so dark I couldn't see five inches in front of me. As we did this, my senses of sound and smell became heightened; I was hearing distant Thai music and smelling the smells associated with a third-world country. There's no punch line here: Dave had taken me on an "orientation ride" in this country so far away from the United States. I watched Dave as he seemed to melt into the crowd. He spoke street Thai fluently, mostly because he had lived in Takhli, Thailand, for a year prior to this and had lived with a Thai woman for almost the entire time. Takhli was a base about 144 miles northwest of Bangkok.

The next day, Dave began my Thai lessons. I would ask for words in English; he would answer in Thai. I jotted the phonetic spelling of the Thai word in my little notebook. Occasionally I would try the words on our housemaid, and she would smile, probably because of my accent or my total annihilation of the pronunciation. Soon I was trying one word at a time on the waitresses at the officers' club. They all seemed to enjoy the back-and-forth of my Thai lessons.

Dave had other influences on me as well. One day, while we were airborne, the AC went to the bathroom. Our fighters had just come off the boom and were now climbing out in front of us on their way to their targets. I watched them intently, as I always seemed to do, and then I heard nav on the interphone. He said, "Co, if I couldn't fly one of those airplanes, and if I was a young man, I don't think I would stay in this man's air force." As I watched the fighters turn and head in another direction, I thought, *Of course I'd love to fly something like that, but maybe this is what I am destined to do, or maybe this is as good as it's going to get for me.* Let's face it: I was twenty-five years old and flying a Boeing 707.

Some in the tanker business said their goal was to be an "LC AC in a KC"—a lieutenant colonel aircraft commander in a KC-135. To progress to a bird colonel would usually mean that you no longer flew. So the ole LC AC in a KC did seem to describe a decent job, but it still seemed humdrum to me.

I remember two other navigators besides Dave in the KC-135 business. One was "Hock," a middle-aged major assigned to our crew. We got along and had a few discussions and a few laughs. He was renowned for putting his hand on chair seats just before one of the wives sat down on it; this probably would be reason enough for elimination from the service today, but back then, he would laugh, and usually the wife experiencing this would jump at first but then laugh too. *You* can decide whether hers was an authentic laugh or not.

Hock also took me out to the flight line on my very first alert day. He said it was all right if we just walked straight to the airplane. My senses told me this was not right, because our airplane had been "cocked" for alert and was parked behind security ropes, with armed guards in a shack near those ropes. Soon we were put facedown on the taxiway by the security people guarding the airplane until we produced appropriate ID. I didn't think this was going to solidify any relationship with my squadron commander, and I doubted it would help Hock, who was probably at the fourteen-year point in his career, either. But I still was a lieutenant, and we lieutenants were allowed a few screw-ups early on, because, well, we were lieutenants. I was really pissed I had allowed a senior officer to get me in hot water; however, I never heard from a soul in the chain of command. I don't know if Hock was as lucky.

The other navigator I remember was Ralph. I forget his last name, but I remember Ralph was a quiet guy, a captain, and always seemed to have a newspaper with him. Whether he was on alert or sitting on his bunk in Thailand, Ralph always seemed to be studying his newspaper, and he was eager to engage anyone on the current events of the day. Some were interested in current events, but most of us were working on our flying careers. I would not see Ralph again for some sixteen years, and when I did see him again, it was in a building in Sunnyvale, California, at the Sunnyvale Satellite Control Facility. As an elevator door closed, I walked by and peered in to see who was on the elevator. I saw a general in the elevator: Ralph. Later I remember verifying that it was him, although I never did look him up. So why am I telling you all this? It's just that, at some point in life, it's interesting to see how you've done and how all these people you've come in contact with along the way have done.

I feel bad that I never sought Ralph out to congratulate him on his achievement in making it to the grade of general. I remember reading once that if I was a lieutenant in the air force, my odds of making it to brigadier general, a one-star general, were half of one percent. That's just the way it was. Good on you, Ralph, wherever you are.

After our two-month stay in Thailand, we came back to March Air Force Base in California. Within a week or two, the AC came to the three of us and asked, "Are you guys interested in going back to Thailand?" We were already sick of the state-side flying, with all its regulations and all the preparations for the next Operational Readiness Inspection, and all the state-side testing, and all the alert duty. The four of us volunteered to go back to Thailand.

I don't remember much about our second tour in Thailand, but my Thai improved a little, and I noted that the facilities had improved significantly. Our rooms hadn't changed, but the officers' club had gone from a small place with a screen door and a fan overhead to a huge club comparable to many in the States. Again I felt it was good to be in the air force. Also, I remember what GIs called "water days" in Thailand; this was a Thai celebration that had to do with water. Known as Songkran Festival, it originally celebrated the New Year. Cutting to the chase, during these days, it was fair game to throw water on anyone anywhere, and it seemed that everyone took part in this. And with aviators, it was prone to escalate. It would start in the officers' club with a waitress throwing a glass of water on someone. That would be followed by some-body else throwing a bucket of water, and soon a crewmember would have a fire extinguisher in hand, pumping it as hard as he could in an effort to hit as many people as possible. And on and on it went. It was a great time for anyone with a sense of humor, though of course, the Vietnam War loomed large in the background.

We were logging combat missions on our flights in Thailand, but our flights were generally in low-threat areas. The fighter/bomber story was different. Threat level would evolve for me over the next several years, and as it turns out, my tanker missions were the lowest-threat missions I ever flew in Southeast Asia.

After completing this second two-month temporary duty (TDY) in Thailand, we again arrived back home at March AFB in southern California. On the first day back in our squadron, someone told me I had better go look at the bulletin board. When I did, I saw a notice for several people, including me, saying we had been selected for duty in Southeast Asia. More specifically, I had been selected to become a forward air controller (FAC) in Vietnam. Training would begin soon at Hurlburt Field, near Eglin Air Force Base in northern Florida.

THIRD LOOK AT VIETNAM: THE O-2 AND THE FAC BUSINESS

Jo and I moved to an apartment on the beach near Pensacola, Florida. I would drive thirty miles down the road to Hurlburt Field every day for my FAC training. It was becoming a routine now: get the operating manual and checklists; study systems, operating procedures, and emergency procedures; and go over the warnings, cautions, and notes. Then I'd write the memory items until I knew them cold.

It was easier this time, because I was going to train in a relatively small airplane with two reciprocating engines: one on the front and one on the back. This was the O-2A; the civilian version was known as the Cessna Skymaster. Unlike the civilian version, however, the air force's O-2A was filled with radios so we could communicate to airborne fighters or troops on the ground. Additionally, we could use another radio to talk to our home base or to other tactical centers when we needed to get fighters on scene. Also, unlike the civilian version, this O-2A had two pods—one on each wing—that carried seven white-phosphorous rockets each. We would use these primarily for marking targets for fighters.

We learned all about calling for fighters, talking to troops on the ground, marking targets from the air, and directing fighters on precisely where we wanted their bombs dropped or where to fire their guns. We practiced the briefings we would give fighter pilots regarding where and what the target was, where the friendly troops were, direction of flight for their bombing, direction of flight after their drops, and bailout areas, should they get hit by enemy fire. We practiced marking targets on the ground by diving at the target and firing these rockets off the O-2. We mastered the requirement to clear each pass that each fighter made on each target. If a fighter ever hit a friendly on the ground, it was considered the FAC's fault. Then we learned how to direct artillery fire from the air. I always thought of it as being like a giant pinball machine. We'd talk to an army unit, give them coordinates, and then have them fire on certain targets, and we learned to stay out of the way of the artillery shell coming through the air. Training went by quickly, and soon I was declared a FAC.

The O-2/The FAC business. This was the military version of the Cessna 337 Super Skymaster and had a max speed around 200 mph. It had twin engines with 210 horsepower each and usually carried seven white-phosphorous rockets ("Willy Petes") under each wing in Vietnam. (Photo by Joost de Wit)

Duty Title: squadron forward air controller with Royal Thai Army Voluntary Force in Bien Hoa, South Vietnam

> o Plans and directs air-support strikes using tactical fighter aircraft in support of ground forces; maintains knowledge of fighter delivery tactics, techniques, and ordinance capabilities; maintains combat-ready status in O-2A aircraft; and flies combat missions
> o April 22, 1969, to March 26, 1970

Around this time, I went to jungle-survival school in the Philippines, which everyone headed to participate in Vietnam was required to attend. We received a lot of good training and were supposed to spend a few days out in the jungle in order to demonstrate that we had learned something. Because of a huge typhoon in the area, however, our class escaped the jungle exercise. I was concerned about missing this training, but things were moving quickly, and it was a relief to move on to whatever was coming next.

Jo and I had our house trailer in California moved near Columbus, Ohio, where Jo would live while I was in Vietnam. I then hopped on the big bird filled with other servicemen, all of us on our way to Southeast Asia. While I was gone, she finished a master's degree in guidance and counseling at Ohio State.

Once in South Vietnam, we FACs went through an in-country checkout to bring us up to speed on procedures and to familiarize us with the way things would be done. Soon I was on my way to Bien Hoa (Ben Wah), South Vietnam, about eighteen miles east of Saigon, which is now Ho Chi Minh City. This was where my records would be kept and where I would pick up my .38 revolver and AR-15, a semiautomatic rifle I would carry with me the entire time I was in Vietnam as a FAC.

Bien Hoa was a very busy airfield in 1969. If you looked up in the sky, you might see almost any aircraft in the air force inventory at the time. There were a lot of fighters around, a lot of FAC aircraft, many C-130s, and a host of other transport-type aircraft, along with quite a few helicopters. I felt my adrenaline move up a notch.

On the ramp that day, I also saw a scene that would remain with me for the rest of my life: Probably thirty to forty army troops stood grouped together in the middle of the ramp, seemingly waiting to be picked up. These guys were all seventeen to twenty-two years old. We all know what happens when this many young guys get together...but none of that was going on. They were all staring, and they had a somberness about them. Their boots were muddy; there was no talk—nothing that would say they once had been young, vibrant guys. I guess this was the first time I had seen combat troops fresh out of the jungle firsthand. It was a disturbing sight. These guys had been through something, and they needed a rest—a long rest. I hoped they were on their way back to the States, but perhaps they were on their way back into the jungle. I reflected on the seriousness of it all, and I wondered if I might die in Vietnam.

Soon an officer in a jeep arrived to pick me up to take me to my new home in South Vietnam—Bear Cat, as the GIs called it, though it was actually Ben Cat. I was surprised I wasn't flying into Bear Cat and presumed it must be very close. Without looking at a map, I supposed it was thirty to forty miles southwest of Bien Hoa, but now Google says it was just under twenty. After what seemed like an hour of driving, we arrived at a barbed-wire fence. Guards loomed above us in towers, their rifles aimed out into the surrounding perimeter areas. Adrenaline showed up again.

A guard pulled the gate open manually, and we entered the confines of the small base. We drove up the dusty road and parked in front of a very primitive "hooch," or thatched hut. I'd say this hooch was about two thousand or three thousand square feet, and it had wooden siding and the usual corru-gated-steel roofing. We walked down pallets placed atop mud to reach the front door. It was sundown.

As I opened the door, I saw a large room, which was lit by a single light bulb hanging from the ceiling. There were no windows or openings in this room, other than the door through which we had just entered, and the room contained no furniture. Around the room, about eight FACs sat on the floor, their backs to the three walls I was looking at. Below the light in the center of the room was another FAC on bended knee. In front of him was a cage on a swivel. Inside the cage was a rat. A can of lighter fluid sat next to the cage. As my eyes adjusted to the dim room, I saw the FAC in the center strike a match and light the rat on fire. Of course the rat tried to run, but he was on a wheel, so the wheel only rotated around and around. Knowing I would be judged by my reaction, I said something like, "Jesus, how are you guys doin'?" But I will never forget that meeting.

The guy in the center was John. He would remain a performer and character for the entire time I was there in South Vietnam. Again, I knew I was a long way from California and Ohio. It would be a long effort here in Bear Cat, I thought. I needed some rest.

There were only eight or nine of us FACs at Bear Cat. We were on a base with a Thai infantry division, and each day, a Thai pilot would ride in our right seat. In the event that the Thai army unit on the ground ran into trouble and needed air support, we were on call and ready to help. The Thai pilot was there to interpret if an American adviser was not available on the ground, though 90 percent of the time, an American adviser was there.

Our missions were basically of two different types: First, we had preplanned missions where we knew the target to hit and made plans ahead of time to do so. And second, we had immediate air strikes where troops on the ground needed fighter aircraft on scene to help slow or reverse attacking enemy forces. Regardless of the type of mission, there were similarities: Once we pinpointed the target area, we set up communications with ground forces. After we determined the situation on the ground, we would contact arriving fighters. At this point, we just did what we had been taught in Florida. Fighters would come in high, while FACs remained somewhere around fifteen hundred feet above the ground. Our next job was to brief the fighters, giving them target info, positioning of friendly troops and enemy troops, and bailout instructions in the event that they were disabled during the strike. The FAC could specify how many bombs the fighters should drop on each pass as well. If all bombs were to be dropped at once, for example, the call from the FAC often was "one pass, haul ass."

As I mentioned before, the strike began when the FAC marked the target with a white-phosphorous rocket. The billowing white smoke from the rocket made it easy for these air-to-ground fighter pilots to see where they should direct their bombs or strafing fire. Most flights of fighters arrived in pairs or as a four-ship formation. Our job as FACs was to make sure the targets were hit and that no friendlies were hurt in the process. The FAC closely monitored and "cleared" each pass by each fighter to ensure control of the situation. Each pass by the fighters required a "cleared in hot" call from the FAC; otherwise, no drop would occur. The fighters were always tight on fuel, so things had to move along quickly in order to get the strike completed before the fighters went bingo fuel—that is, before the fighters got down to a fuel state where they had only enough fuel to get back to their home base.

This was my life for about eight months at Bear Cat. I was going to be there for only eight months because I had already spent four months in Thailand in the tanker. Adding the eight and the four gave me the twelve months required to have a full year in Southeast Asia. One year was the required amount of time to qualify for a "combat tour." Until you had a year in Southeast Asia, you could be assigned for a year. The other guys all would be doing a full twelve months there at Bear Cat.

The flying became somewhat routine. That is, the air-strikes all followed a somewhat similar pattern, and I will say the threat level there was relatively low. We didn't lose any FACs while I was there, and nobody got shot down out of our small outfit. This was not the case with the FACs stationed up along the demilitarized zone (DMZ) or in other places and times during the war. Fate would treat us Rake FACs well in this respect. Rake was our unit call sign, and I was Rake 25. We Rake FACs even had a little dog...named Rake.

The Rake FACs were the usual combination of young, eager pilots trying to do well and survive combat, and I found their personalities intriguing. There was Len, the guy who longed to fly with the airlines and was always busy cleaning his M-16. He always seemed worried that he might suffer some bad fate, and so he had a case of various explosives under his bed, including hand grenades. I have no idea where he got them. His bed was ten feet away from mine.

John, whom I mentioned earlier, was always up to something. He got newspapers from his small hometown in Georgia, and each week, he would review the newlywed section. One day he decided he would mail letters to some of the new wives and tell them they had been picked as the bride of the year by the FACs of Bear Cat, South Vietnam. Of course, the women would write John these long, glowing letters of appreciation. John's motives were not spurious, but this gave him and the rest of the Rakes periodic respite from the war.

In the hooch, John always had a radio tuned to a local station that featured the *Adventures of Henry the Chicken Hawk*, a favorite program of the GIs in Vietnam. I remember the radio blaring out a four-note theme that made me laugh, because the whole thing made no sense here in the war zone. I guess the program served its purpose as a break from thoughts of when or whether we would go home and what the threat level would be in a month. The program was reminiscent of Robin Williams's presentations in the movie *Good Morning, Vietnam.* Williams's character was based on a guy named Cronauer, who arrived in Saigon in 1965 and did a routine on the armed-forces radio station.

One day John showed up with a clown mask that covered half his face, complete with bald head, some strands of orange hair, and a big red nose. Below the nose, he wore sharp, angular false teeth that stuck out in all directions, and he carried one of those laughing boxes, the kind you would wind up to hear a woman intensely laughing. In his hand, he held a very detailed miniature skeleton head. Our house girl, Lan, was afraid of this skeleton, it seemed. Of course John made a bee-line toward her, and she and John ran around in circles, both inside and outside our hooch. She screamed, but John's laughing box was almost as loud, and John kept this up until they both tired. We all laughed, including Lan.

Then there was Bill. The guy could have been on the cover of *GQ* magazine; he was blond, blue-eyed, tanned from the sun, and a physical specimen, to say the least. He confided to John that in college or high school football, one of the guys would always say, "Bill C., what makes you so mean?" That became our mantra. Even though he usually had a stern look on his face, this usually made him smile. His father had been a general in the air force but had been killed aboard a B-52 in Asia, probably within two years of when I met Bill. After I learned this, Bill's serious look made sense to me. I always wondered what his mother must think: her husband had been killed in Asia, and now her son was at Bear Cat, South Vietnam, controlling a multitude of air-strikes week in and week out from an O-2 aircraft.

At first our only house girl was Lan, a Vietnamese woman between twenty-five and thirty years old. She was blind in one eye, as evidenced by a blue-grayish cast that covered her eye. I'd say she probably weighed eighty pounds, max. She worked hard cleaning our makeshift flight suits, underwear, and socks, and she kept our boots polished. (I say "makeshift flight suits" because we actually wore camouflage fatigues but modified them so we had pockets in various places to accommodate us when airborne.) There were no washers or dryers to help her in these tasks, and we had access to little running water. She got the job done in fine fashion, despite the hardships. All the FACs treated her with respect, and I think we all wondered what would happen to her after this war was over.

After about three months, Momasan, as we called her, showed up. She was at least fifty years old and brought a little girl named Baba (Bayba), who was maybe five to seven years old, with her. Lan and Momasan worked, while Baba did what little girls do: play. We treated them all with respect, and I think we were glad Lan had some help and some company. A while later, Bong showed up to help. To this day, Bong is still the most beautiful eighteen- to twenty-year-old Vietnamese girl I've ever seen. I can't say she caused any real problems, but testosterone did rear its head for a while.

The first time Bong met Bill, I thought her eyes would fall out of her head. She took a room that had a fairly large lock on the inside, which was a good thing. One night, as I was about to fall asleep, I could hear that door being knocked on over and over, and Bong laughed the whole time. I don't know what happened there, and I never heard any rumors; it was just another day and another night in Vietnam.

The Rake FACs were all unique, competitive US Air Force officers and pilots the American people would be proud to know, and the same goes for the enlisted men we had working on our small flight line. They were all very diligent and very young men from across the United States, and like the FACs, the enlisted guys probably numbered fewer than a dozen.

My memoir would not be complete without a story about our outhouse at Bear Cat. We had a rotating task we called honey-bucket duty, and each of us—only our boss was exempt—got a turn. The schedule was posted, and when it was your turn, you had the following duty: Retrieve a drum full of excrement from under the outhouse, pull it out into an open area, and apply a certain amount of fuel. Then you stirred it; the goal here was to make it just right so that, when lit, it would burn as fully as possible. One day I broke up a fight between two of the FACs over an argument regarding honey-bucket duty. Never before had I ever seen two military officers square off on each other, and I never saw it again, but these two were about to get into a fistfight over... shit. Obviously there were more important things to worry about. Then again, you do have to smile at it all, don't you?

We would gather in a makeshift living room almost every night and watch our favorite TV show, *Laugh-In*, on a very small, maybe eight-inch, black-and-white TV. I guess somehow we were getting a TV signal on our wire antenna from Saigon. One night we were all watching *Laugh-In* when we heard a rifle shot. That was too close—too loud. It turned out that Len had fired a shot, by mistake, through the roof of our hooch. Nothing like having a clean M-16. Yes, despite living in Vietnam, we were still living pretty well. I remember some army helo driver blanching at my mention of "watching TV" while stationed in-country.

Besides our little TV, we also had a good shower. It was fed by two five-hundred-gallon fuel tanks that lay on top of the shower, and these tanks were filled with water every couple days by a water truck that seemed to appear out of nowhere. The heat beat down on the water tanks, and our showers were pretty warm. I suppose there was a water heater attached somewhere, but I don't remember ever seeing one. One day we moved to a new place on the little outpost, and the main thing I remember is that we took our shower with us. Somehow the boys had gotten it tied down to a Caterpillar tractor, and I still remember it being taken down that long, dusty road to our new quarters. The pace was kept very slow, as this shower was indeed one of our most prized possessions.

Our boss, a lieutenant colonel, had scoured the whole area for plywood sheeting, so we could make our rooms more habitable. The large plywood sheets he had gotten for us, stacked, amounted to about a twenty-foot-high pile. Then somebody stole it. All of it. The colonel was outraged and investigated the mystery of the missing plywood 24-7. Since he was out at night looking for our plywood and, in one case, had his headlights off, he soon found himself in a large ditch with his command-and-control jeep on its side. I can't say the Rake FACs did much more than smile at this. However, soon the jeep was back in shape, and the colonel finally found the culprits behind the theft of our plywood. It had been the security police. This stuff seemed right out of the TV show *M*A*S*H*, but this was the reality of our life at Bear Cat.

At some point, we became very involved with some army helo types participating in what were known as hunter-killer teams. These teams were composed of a Loach, a very small helicopter with a minigun attached, and a Cobra, a very lethal helicopter for dispensing rockets or some higher-caliber machine-gun fire. The Loach flew at treetop level; if anything overpowered it, the crewmembers would call in the Cobra, which flew at about five hundred to a thousand in a circular pattern around the Loach. If the Cobra got more than he bargained for, he would call us at our traditional fifteen-hundred-feet altitude, and we would call for fighters to handle whatever threat had been discovered.

We enjoyed meeting the Loach pilots, who landed their helos in our backyard, literally. They would shut down and come into our hooch, and we'd have coffee while we talked about what was about to happen. These helo drivers were all warrant officers, and I came to respect them as I had our senior and chief master sergeants. These warrants were all motivated and the epitome of the ideal warrior when it came to servicemen, and most of them had been shot down from two to five times.

Eventually I would get a ride in both the Loach and the Cobra. I don't think I actually ever took the controls of a Loach but did get some stick time in the Cobra, and the response to stick pressure in that Cobra seemed as quick as that experienced in a T-38—though any air force aviator who never flew the Cobra would probably disparage this remark. I never did figure out what that other lever, the collective, did in any of the helicopters. The army guys always laughed at us, because we never knew what to do with the collective. Looking back, the collective still remains somewhat of a mystery.

My ride in the Loach came after I had repeatedly asked for a ride. One day a guy came running into the chow hall and told the warrant officer I was eating with that someone had been fired at with a rocket-propelled grenade (RPG) out on a perimeter road. They wanted him to go check it out. He looked at me and said, "Well, here's your chance to get a ride in a Loach." We gathered up our gear, and soon we were airborne in the Loach. We flew just above ground level. Although I'd been used to looking at terrain from fifteen hundred feet, things appeared very different at ground level, particularly the tunnel entrances. (The Vietnamese used a tunnel system seemingly throughout the whole country, and we were always leery of being near a tunnel.) This warrant officer seemed hell-bent on looking down every hole that existed. It took at least twenty years for me to realize that we approached every hole that day from my side of the helicopter, and he made sure I had my AR-15 pointed in the direction of the holes. I also remember him leaning back awkwardly, so he was completely shielded by my body.

After this harrowing experience, we moved toward a more thickly vegetated area; it wasn't jungle but was close to it. In the middle of our windscreen appeared this sight: an oxcart with a man and two women as passengers. The cart was being pulled by a water buffalo. We moved closer and landed at about their eleven o'clock. The warrant officer had been in contact with another larger helo, and it was landing at about the oxcart's one o'clock. The oxcart passengers pretended we were not there. They looked straight ahead as if nothing was going on, kind of like me playing the piano with Perla looking at me back in the Mural Room days. Then the warrant told me to get out of the helo and motion the passengers to get out of the oxcart. The warrant wanted me to have them move to and then board the other helo. That scenario played out. I reboarded the Loach, and we headed back to my drop-off point. I vowed that this would be my last Loach ride. And it was. All in all, I was gaining new respect for our helo drivers, as well as for anybody else fighting this war on the ground.

I had become sort of friends with one of our US Army advisers, speaking of dumb things I did. One time he asked if I would go out on the ground with him on a mission. I did the manly thing and said yes. About a month later, he asked if I was still interested. I said yes. He said, "I'll pick you up at about 0500." I was there in my fatigues when he picked me up. Soon we were out waiting for a truck to pick us up. There were also quite a few Thai infantry and some US Army personnel waiting with us. Eventually we headed down some rural roads of South Vietnam. Our job was to drop some "inserts" off in the jungle and pick up some guys who had been out in the jungle for a week or two. This would entail driving to a drop-off point and walking through jungle to a waypoint, where we would be picked up by some navy boats. From there we would go to particular geographical points, where we would insert our troops into the jungle and pick up the guys who had been there for a week or so. Then we would run this schedule in reverse, back to the shore, back to the jungle, back to the trucks, and back to our hooch.

Everything went smoothly until we were back in the trucks headed home, and an ambush hit us from both sides of the road. Both mirrors on the truck were blown off, and we stopped, got out, and jumped into a ditch. I let off a few rounds with the ole AR-15, but I could not see much in front of me. It was dark now. Eventually we got home without any casualties. I really don't know how that was possible. I vowed to never go out on the ground with the army again. It was funny—ground guys didn't much want to fly, and the aviators wanted nothing to do with being on the ground. The next time I saw my army buddy, I could tell we both had more respect for each other. Again, I thought, this was a long way from home.

Eventually we got a new boss, another lieutenant colonel. He was a very cool guy. He'd been a fighter pilot, and his routine was to get up very early in the morning and have his coffee before most of the FACs were up. Gradually I began to sit and have coffee with him. I was there for one reason: to hear him talk about fighters.

Around this time, we had an administrative guy named Staff Sergeant Mason. I liked Mason. Compared to most army outfits, the air force did not have near as many enlisted folks. On most days Mason was surrounded by us FACs and our boss, and he always seemed to be doing paperwork regarding the myriad of things requiring administrative detail. One day someone stole a jeep of ours. Nobody had a clue what might have happened to it. About a month later, after we had all pretty much forgotten about our missing jeep, S.Sgt. Mason decided to go for some rest and recuperation up around Bien Hoa. Well, it was not uncommon for guys to sometimes hitch-hike to get a ride from a passing military vehicle on their way to some destination, and Sgt. Mason got a ride and settled into the front right seat of the jeep. In these jeeps, all the pertinent nomenclature was on a small plate riveted to a panel directly in front of the passenger, below the windshield. Serial numbers, type of vehicle, model numbers, and so on were all right there. Of course, since Sgt. Mason had filed all the reports on our missing jeep, he was intimately familiar with all the numbers he now saw staring him in the eyes as he sat in this jeep. And then he engaged the driver about his unit and unit location. Soon we had our jeep back.

The days went by, the airstrike business continued, and the Rake FACs continued on. One day I landed from a mission and continued the ritual that had begun a few months earlier: talking at the end of a mission with this crew chief I had come to know. He was from Cincinnati, and we talked about growing up in Ohio and wondered how things were back there. This day was no different. We stood there near the wing of the airplane I had just parked. As we talked, we moved back a few feet from the tail of the O-2. Eventually I heard the throaty sound of a mortar being launched from a nearby hill, and then I heard the whistle that accompanies some mortars. I heard someone yell, "Incoming," meaning that we were being shelled from off the base. (To this day I get a shot of adrenaline when I hear the word *incoming.*)

Since this was the first time we'd had any close-in fire, we moved slowly at first, but I soon found myself running toward and then entering a small building with a tin roof and thin walls. Inside was a tech sergeant—an E-6, as they are sometimes called. We didn't say anything to each other. As we heard the mortars begin to hit, the tech sergeant got down on the floor and pulled a metal folding chair over his head. I followed suit. From under the chair, I could see the sergeant staring at me with sweat coming off his nose. He probably saw a very similar thing as he looked at me. I wondered what it would be like to die with a metal folding chair on my back. The next round hit very close, shook the ground, and was very loud. We didn't know where the next one would land, but neither of us was going to move.

Within minutes we could hear the crew chiefs talking outside, and there seemed to be no follow-on mortars. Soon we were outside looking for any damage that might have occurred. And then I saw it: a three-foot-by-three-foot crater in the asphalt behind the airplane I had just parked. The crater was exactly where the crew chief and I had been standing when that guy yelled, "Incoming." My life passed before my eyes, and I was thankful to be alive. I always thought that any close calls or worse would come while I was airborne, not while I was on the ground. I was becoming more somber, and for an instant, I thought of those young army guys I'd seen on the ramp at Bien Hoa.

The only other really tough experience for me at Bear Cat started with a normal FAC mission. I was airborne and surveilling our local operating area, and a Thai pilot who flew with me regularly was in the right seat. We got a call from some infantrymen on the ground requesting air (fighters). We soon had fighters on station but were having a tough time getting approval to drop bombs into the specified area. We waited, pressing our request to let these fighters drop their bombs. Time was fleeting, as it always was in these situations, and approval never was forthcoming. The fighters were low on gas, as was often the case, so we went and "put them in" on a preselected, preapproved target several miles from the one we had been working on. In the meantime, dusk turned to darkness.

As we turned toward our little runway, we couldn't see it, because of a power problem at the base. There were no lights of any sort, and that included runway lights. Because of our own low-gas situation, we ended up getting vectored to the runway in the darkness. There was no instrument approach, no instrument-landing system, no Tacan (a system that measures bearing and distance from a ground system), and no Automatic Direction Finder, only a radar controller in a little radar hut.

Since we never used this kind of approach at Bear Cat, we were not proficient at executing something like this, and neither was the controller. He gave us vectors while we turned our lights on and maneuvered left and right in attempts to acquire the runway visually. The first time around, that didn't happen, and now it was dark as the night Dave had taken me to the Black Hole of Calcutta. The second time around, we saw the pavement but had no idea how far down the runway we were. We blew a tire in the process of trying to make sure we didn't go off the end of the runway. I shouldn't have allowed myself to get into that situation, but in my defense, that was the only time the power to the base had been cut off during my eight months at Bear Cat. I shouldn't have allowed my gas to get that low either.

Midway through this time as a FAC, I saw Jo in Hong Kong for six or seven days. I was glad to get away for a while, but my head remained at Bear Cat, and I noted how odd the rest and recuperation felt. I never adjusted to just relaxing in Hong Kong, and upon my return to my base in South Vietnam, I didn't feel rested or recuperated.

The time went by quickly at Bear Cat. As FACs we had done our job of supporting the ground troops of the Thai infantry division that was colocated with us. But somehow I felt that we just were not making a difference in this conflict. Activity and threat levels varied greatly from year to year in Southeast Asia, and it seemed to me that most of our bombings in and around Bear Cat were dedicated more to knocking trees down than to inflicting damage on the enemy. Despite a couple of close calls during my eight months there, I felt that my time had been spent in a relatively low-threat era of the war, and the geographical area seemed low threat also. Meanwhile, FACs in other areas of Vietnam were having a totally different experience.

As the end of my tour neared, I reflected on a number of things. Mostly I was just glad to be going back to the States. I was surprised I had not become close friends with any of the FACs, given the compressed effects of living in close proximity to one another, the pressures of austere living, and the day-to-day efforts conducting airstrikes. I remembered the sadness and loneliness of celebrating Christmas there. A picture of guys wearing their renovated flight suits dancing with brooms, remains in my memory bank. I wondered how Lon, Momasan, Baba, and Bong would make out in the years to come, and I wondered whether I would run across any of our Rake FACs during the rest of my career. I would never see any of them again, other than a brief encounter with Bill during a visit to Nellis AFB years later. He'd become a fighter pilot.

KC-135s, Part 2

Soon I'd be on the big bird back to the States. I'd gotten a new assignment back to KC-135s; this time I was headed to a base on the west end of the island of Puerto Rico: Ramey Air Force Base.

Jo and I sold the house trailer, which she'd had a difficult time in during the Ohio winter. Built in Texas, this trailer just did not have enough heat, and Jo's friend and her husband had taken Jo in for the winter. I was mostly oblivious to this fact, and later I wondered where the hell my mind had been not to know the details of this problem Jo had been having.

I was not proud of this at all. The air force had been a priority for me, since it was my means of making a living, but I had gone overboard. I still feel guilty about not understanding what had been going on with Jo that winter.

Duty Title: squadron copilot/flight examiner (KC-135)

o   Standardization and evaluation division at Ramey Air Force Base in Puerto Rico
o   Evaluates proficiency of other copilots and assists in refueling strategic nuclear bombers, strategic reconnaissance aircraft, and tactical fighter aircraft day or night under all types of weather and at variable rendezvous points
o   Upgraded to aircraft commander (KC-135) near the end of this tour
o   March 27, 1970, to June 15, 1971

Ramey was a beautiful base: manicured, tropical, warm, and green. Generals from all over would come to Ramey to play golf. I never played, but perhaps I should have. The ocean beckoned from the end of the street we lived on, but I seldom saw it, because I chose to work instead. Jo got another job teaching at Ramey.

Well, now I was doing a repeat of most of the activities I had gone through a few years before. I would be requalified as a KC-135 pilot. The operating procedures were familiar, but I still needed to study to come back up to speed on the aircraft. Alert duty was still a part of this SAC position, but it was conducted off the island, in Florida. I had gotten a job as the copilot for the chief of standardization and evaluation (Stan-Eval), and as a consequence, I pulled alert duty only once or twice the whole time I was in Puerto Rico. We would fly a training mission on our way to Florida, do our seven days of alert, and then return to Puerto Rico.

I conducted a few simulator instructor sessions for crews, but most of my activities seemed consumed with office work, such as making sure evaluation paperwork was proper and correct for any higher-headquarter inspections we were vulnerable to at any given time. Careers seemed to depend on performance during any higher-headquarter inspection, so there was always a sense of urgency in getting everything right. Stan-Eval also had responsibilities to get the crew force up to speed on all test material, especially operational procedures. Otherwise, our crew flew training missions like everyone else.

And then, in June 1971, the air force announced that Ramey was going to close. We had been there only since March 1970.

Rumor had it that the assignment personnel were coming to our base from Texas to finalize assignments. This was unusual, and I wondered if a fighter-type aircraft assignment might be possible. The word was that if you volunteered for a second tour in Asia, you stood a decent chance of getting your aircraft of choice. I doubted that, but I was motivated. Vietnam was still going on.

Another KC-135 pilot named Ray and I learned how to play craps at a hotel in Mayaguez, Puerto Rico, and we learned how to smoke cigars. Paul Bast was another guy who sticks out in my mind from all the others at Ramey. Paul was different from the average air force pilot—he seemed to know about the classics in books, in writing, and maybe in movies too. I think his parents were very well educated. Paul had already had a tour in fighters—the F-100, I think. I had always loved the look of that airplane and would have given anything to fly it. For the life of me, I could never figure out how he ended up being assigned to the KC-135 after flying a single-seat fighter. But he did say he thought he was getting assigned to the F-4 soon. He eventually received that assignment and headed to Udorn, Thailand.

FINALLY—THE PHANTOM (RF-4)

Later, the assignment people came to Ramey, and I found the officer in charge of my assignment. I wouldn't let him out of my sight. In the end, surprisingly, he asked if I wanted an F-4 or an RF-4. It would be my choice. I couldn't believe it. The F-4 was used to drop bombs and carry air-to-air missiles in order to shoot down other airplanes (in this case, MiGs). The RF-4 was a version of the F-4 used specifically for reconnaissance; mostly it took pictures. Its primary system for navigation was the Inertial Navigation System (INS). I reasoned that the FAC job was in many ways a recon job, and I had enjoyed the freedom associated with working alone to get the job done. I had liked being in a single aircraft and not responsible for wingmen. I wondered about the guys who had been doing the fighter mission ever since pilot training, and frankly, I wondered about competing with contemporaries who already had four or five years of experience as fighter pilots. I also wasn't interested in being Blue 4, the low man on the totem pole in a flight of four airplanes, the traditional position for the most inexperienced guy. I chose the RF-4.

Training would entail, first, a transition to fast movers. This was a program to take guys like me from the bigger four-engine airplanes to smaller, more maneuverable aircraft that flew their missions closer to the ground. Little did I know of the really low altitude dictates of the RF-4 mission awaiting me. This transition program involved checking out in the T-33, an old single-engine jet. It had a front seat and a back seat, a configuration similar to the RF-4, at least as far as seating was concerned.

I would now go to Myrtle Beach, South Carolina, to check out the T-33.

The T-33 had a max speed of about six hundred miles per hour. It had a single engine with about forty-six hundred pounds of thrust. (Photo by Brent Beck)

The study of operating manuals, emergency procedures, warnings, cautions, and notes and the usual bookwork that came with systems training, ejection-seat training, and other training were all the order of the day—again. I honestly forget what Jo was doing at the time. And I am embarrassed by that. I had a long way to go to get through RF-4 training, and I was on only the first rung of that ladder. I wondered who our T-33 instructors would be. They were not involved with an actual fighter-type airplane, nor were they flying in any of the other ordinance-delivering aircraft. For the most part, I think most of them came from fighter backgrounds and were doing the best they could to handle the job the air force had thrust upon them with the T-33.

The training went smoothly and quickly. Flying near the ground again—faster than had been the case in the O-2, of course—was fun and demanding. The instructors were there to keep us from doing dumb things, to help us stay on course if we deviated, and to see if we were going to master this new type of flying. Thanks to my T-37 and T-38 experience from pilot training, this training held few surprises for me. I would see the T-33 a few more times in my career, although when that happened, like these instructors, I usually wished I was flying something more sophisticated. Soon we were on our way to Shaw AFB in South Carolina, where I would undergo RF-4 Phantom training.

We moved into base housing; this was the first time we had lived on a base. The base was clean and neat, like all bases, and it was nice to be near the place I was training. Each day I would drive down a street called Polifka Drive to my academic classes for the RF-4. During the first day of class, I noted another captain in my class by the name of Karl Polifka and wondered if there was a connection between him and Polifka Drive. I doubted it, for some reason, but a few days later, I asked him. He nonchalantly said, "Oh yeah, that was my dad... they named a street after him." Later I would learn that his dad had been killed in a reconnaissance airplane in Korea in about 1951. Karl must have been pretty young when that happened, perhaps nine or ten. I pondered this and the meaning of his father's death in a reconnaissance airplane for a long, long time.

In our first few days at Shaw, Jo and I needed to get some clothes washed, so we went to one of the typical Laundromats. As we settled into this process, I noticed a tall, blond-haired man doing his laundry. We were on base, and this guy had a flight suit on. As I watched him, I realized I knew him. His name was Roger Behnfeldt, and he'd been in ROTC with me, possibly a year behind me. I didn't know him well, but I remembered where he'd sat in the one ROTC class we'd shared. I walked over and introduced myself. I was intrigued that he was just about to finish his RF-4 training and would be headed to Udorn, Thailand, for a year. We talked awhile and vowed to meet up in Thailand if I ended up there too.

So here we were, in training, with new operating manuals and checklists. We got new warnings, cautions, and notes, as well as new memory items for emergencies. Eventually we moved on to simulators. I had already studied much of the RF-4 operating manual after getting a copy sent to Puerto Rico, so I was very familiar with the training business, and the academics, systems training, and emergency-procedures training moved along quickly.

We began flying the RF-4. We were training to fly low and fast. At first, it was like taking the proverbial drink out of a fire hose. I think the first few flights may have been at 360 knots (414 miles per hour) and certainly no faster than 420 knots (483 miles per hour). Altitudes were low, as our original goal was getting comfortable at five hundred feet above ground level. Before we graduated from this RF-4 training, we would do our five-hundred-foot low-level routes at 540 knots (621 miles per hour). Years later we would train to "comfort levels" below five hundred feet—yeah, who is comfortable going more than five hundred miles an hour at three hundred feet above ground level?

Eventually we got our back seaters, and that position came with a host of names, including Gib (guy in the back seat), Nav (navigator), and RSO (reconnaissance systems officer). Many, if not most, of the RSOs had just gotten out of navigator training, so they were fairly young. My RSO was Steve, a high-IQ guy with all the associated traits that come with that. He tested very easily and communicated well; he was never at a loss for words. He was still a very young lieutenant, but he had graduated first in his navigator class. In those respects, he reminded me of Buzzy. It soon dawned on me how very inexperienced we both were to be flying the RF-4. Slowly and gradually, we started to get familiar with each other and the airplane.

THE RF-4C McDonnell Douglas Phantom II had a max speed of about 1,473 mph or Mach 2.23. It had two General Electric J-79 engines, each of which provided about 11,905 pounds of thrust (about 17,000 pounds of thrust each with afterburner).

I thought the RF-4 was wonderful and still do. It looked and sounded like the combat-fighter airplane it was. It had afterburners. It was as comfortable upside-down as it was right side up and would go as fast as you wanted to go, within reason. Just how fast would it go? An instructor took me out one day, and we plugged in the burners and watched the airspeed increase. We crossed the Mach 2 area, and just a little after, at Mach 2.05, we had a compressor stall in one of the two engines. A compressor stall is what happens when an engine cannot swallow all the air being forced down its throat. The engine belches. Since it is so quiet in the cockpit, especially above the speed of sound, the sound of the compressor stall surprised me. It sounded more like an explosion. Because both engines are fairly close together, the airplane remained very controllable, but I did notice a little lateral movement. The instructor did not get excited, so I took it to be somewhat of a common occurrence at Mach 2. I actually would never have another compressor stall in the RF-4 again, nor would I fly the RF-4 at Mach 2 again.

This business was tactical reconnaissance. I now wore the Tactical Air Command (TAC) patch proudly on my flight suit. Back in the day, the Air Force separated tactical and strategic responsibilities between TAC and SAC. At a very elementary level strategic generally referred to world wide, long range responsibilities while tactical generally referred to a more specific area responsibility at a specific time. Alternatively, to me, these words meant only one thing. Tactical referred to fast, maneuverable fighter type airplanes, while strategic referred to big, heavy, slow aircraft. Our tactical reconnaissance job in the RF-4 was to take pictures wherever and whenever pictures needed to be taken. There was no GPS back in these days—1971—so the basis for getting to the target coordinates was strict adherence to flying magnetic headings for a certain time at a certain speed—almost Wright Brothers stuff. We had an Inertial Navigation System (INS) aboard, which did a good job, but we were always worried about last-minute errors or a total breakdown of that system. The INS actually seemed fairly reliable to me. But we always worked at "heading/ground speed/and time," a method of navigation that the flying community introduced to aspiring aviators almost from day one. They called it dead reckoning.

Planning these missions was rigorous, but young pilots today would probably shake their heads. We literally drew our route of flight on maps, marking our timing criteria, headings, and speeds on the maps at certain checkpoints and turn points. If we followed the headings, times, and speeds religiously, we would cross a target and get the pictures, whether we saw it from the cockpit or not. I will say that in Asia we got some aircraft equipped with a navigation system called LORAN (Long-Range Navigation) that was pretty accurate and helped significantly in the business of getting to a geographical point while flying at very low altitudes, but there weren't many aircraft so equipped.

Soon Steve and I were flying at the more normal 480 knots at five hundred feet on these low-level missions. Our training would last something like six months. I never did enjoy night flights, but we learned to fly at five hundred feet above ground level (AGL) in the RF-4 at night. Of course we would also learn to refuel from the KC-135 day or night. I remember an operations officer who flew with me on my initial night checkout in refueling. I was a little nervous and certainly didn't want to run into the KC-135, nor did I want to have the boom operator call a breakaway on me, nor did I want a brute-force disconnect. I approached the tanker with a lot of caution. It seemed the closer I got to it, the more I felt like I was being pulled into it. And so I kept getting a lot of up-and-down action, 99 percent of which I was causing.

As I tried to settle down, the instructor in the back seat said something that would focus me. The understanding military officer and instructor in my back seat was there to help, of course. He said, "Hey, Gilmore, have you ever seen a monkey try to fuck a football?"

Well, at least he got my attention. I did settle down, and soon I was hooked up to the tanker and taking on my gas. I was glad when the night tanker check was over. I found refueling to be a lot of fun in the end. After a while, we got proficient and could adjust to almost anything going on at the time in order to get our gas. I especially came to love the refueling portion of the mission, because I was so familiar with the tanker, except now I was usually staring up at the little window in the back of the KC-135, through which I could see the boom operator doing his job, lying on his stomach and passing gas.

Once our proficiency in getting the pictures became acceptable, we went through some defensive air combat maneuver training. This would acquaint us with the idea of having a MiG attack us from some rearward position. Instructors would set us up in an area and then attack us in various scenarios. Some attacks were initiated above Mach 1 speeds, some below. We were supposed to get used to picking up these bogies visually coming in to us at high speeds from difficult-to-see positions. Our objectives were to avoid getting shot down by a MiG and to get separation from it. I enjoyed this training, but it was over too soon. I didn't feel proficient in doing most of the defensive maneuvers we were learning, but they needed to get us on our way to Asia. There wasn't a lot of time to be spent in the air-to-air arena on reconnaissance aircrews. The fighter pilots with strictly fighter missions received a lot more training in this area.

Most of us were headed straight to Southeast Asia when training was over. I would meet a guy, Tony Reyna, at Shaw, and he would play a big part in my RF-4 days and would become a lifelong friend. Tony was a captain, like Karl Polifka and I. Tony, Karl, and I were the only ones in our class who had spent a year in Asia previously. Karl had been a Raven

FAC. Being a Raven FAC meant he had been a forward air controller in a covert operation in conjunction with the US Central Intelligence Agency in Laos during the Vietnam War. The Ravens provided direction for most of the air strikes against Communist Pathet Lao targets and People's Army of Vietnam's infiltrators, in support of the Laotian Hmong guerrilla army. Tony had been in the RF-4's back seat in Asia prior to his training at Shaw, back when the air force was still using two pilots in the RF-4.

All three of us had volunteered for a second tour. Jo fixed the three of us dinner a few times at our base house, and we told one another our war stories. We were all enthralled with our RF-4 training and became fast friends. Steve, my back seater, would be assigned stateside but would go to Asia a few years later.

Soon we were in the big bird on our way to Southeast Asia again. My base this time would be Udorn, Thailand; more specifically, I was stationed on the Royal Thai Air Force Base near the city of Udon Thani in northern Thailand, about 350 driving miles northeast of Bangkok. This was a large airfield that housed four fighter squadrons and our Fourteenth Tactical Reconnaissance Squadron. The squadrons mentioned here were part of the larger organizational structure, the 432nd Tactical Reconnaissance Wing. There were other outfits on the field, but I was mostly blind to them. Air America was based there, largely supporting Laos, I think.

CHAPTER 4

Ages Thirty to Forty: 1972–1982

Dow Jones Industrial Average
1,020.02–1,046.54
2.6% Gain

FOURTH AND FINAL LOOK AT VIETNAM

MY MEMORIES OF UDORN, THAILAND, begin in April 1972 with a ride in an air force blue bus that brought several of us *crew dogs* to the side of the base where we would be housed and fed for the ensuing year. I knew that eventually I would be paired up with another aviator in order to share a two-man room. I usually got along with anyone I met, but the notion of spending the next year of my life with someone I didn't care for and living in relatively tight quarters was starting to worry me.

The bus stopped, and Tony Rena came up to me and asked, "Hey, why don't we room together?" Things were starting out perfectly. If I'd had to choose, Tony would have been my first choice for a roommate. Let's see…a two-man room again. Sounds like Bowling Green State University. No, not even close.

All the guys in our squadron were housed directly across the street from the officers' club. The rooms were all similar. Walk in the door, and here was what we had: a chair on the right, two lockers close by, two desks, two beds, two chests of drawers, and an air conditioner. It was sparse living conditions but better than most other servicemen had living in or near Asia at the time. Our bathroom and shower were a short distance from our room—a step outside, right turn, twenty steps, and you were there. *Much better than Bear Cat*, I thought. *No rats, no pallets, and no outside toilet.*

I wondered what the threat level would be during this year, and I supposed it would not be a lot different from what I had experienced at Bear Cat. I was wrong. Soon after Tony and I started flying combat sorties, things changed drastically. The United States started flying into North Vietnam again, as well as South Vietnam. In a nutshell, the farther north you flew, the greater the threat level became. North Vietnam was divided into six packs, with low numbers in southern North Vietnam and higher numbers in northern North Vietnam. Pack six, the highest-threat area, was around Hanoi, the capital of North Vietnam. MiGs, surface-to-air missiles (SAMs), the SA-2 in particular, and antiaircraft artillery (AAA or triple A) were the standard threats in the north, although the North Vietnamese seldom used SAMs and MiGs on the same day. The lethality and numbers of these weapons increased the farther north you went until you got to Hanoi.

Within a few weeks, I heard of a tragedy that sticks with me today: Paul Bast, the guy I knew from Ramey AFB in Puerto Rico, had been killed in an F-4 accident. There was something about a fire on both engines, and they never made it through the bailout sequence. What a shame. Paul was a fighter pilot but knew literature, even poetry, and was a bit of an intellectual. *He was a rare individual,* I thought. I have his obituary still and was pleased and unsurprised to learn that Paul had received the Silver Star for action on his first tour to Vietnam while piloting the F-100. The Silver Star is America's third-highest decoration for valor in combat, awarded primarily for gallantry in action against an enemy of the United States.

I met the members of the Fourteenth one by one; some had been there for nearly a year, some had been there for six months, and some had just gotten there. One of the guys was Roger Behnfeldt, the classmate from my ROTC class whom I had seen several months earlier in the Laundromat at Shaw AFB. We talked a little about things; he was more than aware that the war effort was beginning to heat up. There was talk of the possibility of the reconnaissance task, as well as the fighter task, changing to include targets in North Vietnam, something that had not been done in a few years. Roger hadn't changed much. He was the picture of an air force recruiting poster: about six feet tall, blond hair, blue eyes, and slender. A bit like Paul Bast had been.

Although we newbies wouldn't be tasked to go north in these first few weeks, we would eventually get our turn. Tony and I listened to the briefings of the men who were going on these early missions. One of these first days, we heard a briefing where the pilot told of how he was going to approach the target area high. This usually meant above ten thousand feet, and maybe even fifteen thousand to twenty thousand, at least for part of the run. On the bus ride back to our hooch, Tony said, in his quiet and unassuming way, that if it were he, he didn't think he would go in high. He said he would probably go in as low as he could, meaning anywhere from tree-top level to five hundred feet above ground level. The radars had a difficult time tracking the low flyers, and so Tony's idea sounded right to me, but I had no experience in this business and just kept listening. The pilot who elected to fly high was shot down, and although he survived, he became a POW. I don't remember what happened to his back seater. This was in 1972, and he was the first of our squadron mates to suffer this consequence—at least, while I was there. I soon began listening more to my roommate and began using his tactics as best as I could. There was no such thing as flying too low on most of these missions into North Vietnam.

NORTH VIETNAM, SOUTH VIETNAM, LAOS, AND CAMBODIA

I suppose I could fill a book about this year flying the RF-4 out of Thailand. Let me just recount a few stories.

First I will tell you about my back seater, Lee VanNamen. Lee was a very young lieutenant, just out of nav school and fresh out of RF-4 school. Again, Lee was very sharp. He made flying a total joy, and he saved my life on more than one occasion. I loved the guy right from the beginning. I tried to get him to talk about his growing-up years just to get to know him better but noticed he didn't seem to want to go there. All I knew was that his dad had developed some patents on some device and seemed to be doing well. I didn't know if Lee had any brothers or sisters. I think his parents lived up in Michigan. I would fly with other navs, but Lee was my primary back seater. My luck continued. With Tony as my roommate and Lee as my back seater, I felt very fortunate.

One day Lee called out a SAM to me that I would not have seen had he not been there. It would have killed me, had I been flying alone. One night he called out an altitude to me when I was busily trying to join up in a night formation. I would have likely hit the ground that night had Lee not been there. He was with me on another day when we were hit by AAA and had to make an emergency landing at another base, just inside Thailand. He helped me get everything done safely, including taking a barrier at a base called Nakhon Phanom, or NKP. He was with me one day when a throttle became disconnected from the linkage that connects the throttle to the engine. This engine was stuck at full power with no way to control it. He rode through this exciting episode with me as we took another barrier, this time at Udorn. What's a barrier? It is a mechanical system used to rapidly decelerate an aircraft as it lands. It is much like the wire that you see carrier pilots take when landing on a carrier. Of course, we were landing on a stable runway, not a pitching, rolling ship.

Lee was so good that I could put my maps away and focus on flying the airplane, regardless of our low altitudes and high speeds. We always got our pictures, and we spent a lot of time flying in North Vietnam. Lee would later become a medical doctor. I knew he was smart.

Somewhere along the line, we were chosen to fly what was called the Atlanta mission. This was a mission where we decided what pictures we were going to take, and we rotated through the areas. One day we would be in Laos, the next

Cambodia, the next South Vietnam, and the next the southern part of North Vietnam. The call sign for anybody associated with these missions was "Atlanta." I have no idea where that came from, but my call sign for these missions was Atlanta 25. Tony's was Atlanta 05. I chose the 25 part because Rake 25 had been my FAC call sign in the Cessna Skymaster (O-2). Our pictures were reviewed there on the base, and fighters would be sent out to hit the targets on our pictures. We felt like we were getting something done in this Atlanta program. Karl Polifka was flying in a similar program that focused on his old stomping grounds, Laos and the Plain of Jars area. He had a "Bullwhip" call sign.

Early in my tour, the air force told me I was going to take an airplane to Taiwan for maintenance. This bothered me, because I was still getting settled into Udorn and figured I had a lot to learn there. I didn't want to interrupt this early phase, but I ended up going anyway. A major flew with me, and I sensed he had some things he wanted to do there. We eventually ended up at Clark Air Base in the Philippines and spent a day by the pool at the officers' club. The major introduced me to a guy named Billy Williams, who was also a major. They seemed to know each other, and I mostly stayed out of the conversation.

Eventually the major and I got back to Udorn, and within a week or so, Billy Williams showed up. He had been assigned as our new squadron-operations officer. Within a month of his arrival, he was shot down over the southern part of North Vietnam. We found out later that he had been killed, and the back seater, Hector Acosta, became a POW. I had flown with Hector just the day before. I would see Hector years later, by coincidence, on the only trip I have ever made to Europe. Hector seemed to be doing fine when I saw him in Europe.

Jimmy Watts and John Pomeroy showed up in our squadron in soaking-wet flight suits one day. They had been shot down and had made it over the water (feet wet, we called it) before bailing out of the RF-4. They had landed in the water, but they were still close to shore.

I'll pause here to explain a little about the survival kit attached to your ejection seat. During a bailout, if everything worked right, you had a one-man rubber raft that would dangle below you and inflate automatically. As I remember the uninflated single man raft was enclosed in part of the survival kit which came out of the airplane with you upon ejection. As the raft fell below you and eventually reached the end of its attached line, a tug from the fall would trigger it to inflate automatically. If that failed you had to blow it up yourself. Because you had some inflation devices under each arm, those were enough to keep you from sinking while you dealt with any raft problems. Getting into the raft was another concern.

Now back to the story. They both got in their rafts, and Jimmy said that, after the Vietnamese started firing at them from the shore, he looked over and saw only a wake behind John's raft—John was paddling so hard someone could have water-skied behind that raft if he'd had a way of hooking up to it. Jimmy got the message and started paddling a little faster. They were almost immediately picked up by a rescue team and flown back to Udorn and dropped off. Now, there they stood in the squadron, their flight suits still wet from the ordeal. AT least that is what I thought at the time. Maybe they were just sweating from the ordeal that they had just been through. I will never forget it. John later became a lawyer. I don't know what Jimmy did after Vietnam.

Bill Gauntt and Fran Townsend took off one day on a mission in North Vietnam. They got hit and ended up bailing out but were immediately besieged by Vietnamese. I was told that the Vietnamese killed Fran immediately, while Bill somehow survived and became a POW. A year or so later, I would see Bill Gauntt in San Antonio, Texas, by coincidence. He said he was going for treatment at the local air force hospital. I assumed it was for injuries obtained during his combat ordeal or his treatment as a POW, but he said he had gotten into a bad auto accident once stateside. Go figure. I had flown more than a few missions with Fran and feel sympathy for him and his family to this day. Like others mentioned here, he was so damn young. I still have his obituary too.

Lee, my back seater, eventually became the squadron scheduler, a big job for a young lieutenant. As mission requirements came down from above, the scheduler would match crews to the mission for the following day. In doing this, much had to be considered, and matching crew experience to the likely threat level of the mission was a primary concern. However, as things heated up, there were inevitable mismatches of crew experience and threat level. The squadron commander or operations officer usually loomed around the scheduler's desk late in the day to see what the following day would look like and to get an overview of how the crews were going to be tasked. Of course, if he wanted to change anything, he could, but for the most part, it all went as assigned by the squadron scheduler, Lee, and later Karl.

As the war progressed, our squadron ran into the same problem as others were having. Newly assigned aviators were being required to go into some very high-threat areas with little combat experience. On or about August 18, 1972, a seasoned pilot, Roger Behnfeldt, and a relatively new back seater, Tom, headed to North Vietnam on a mission. The Vietnamese launched missiles at them, their aircraft was hit, and they went down. I am almost sure Tom got out of the aircraft and then became a POW. Roger was listed as missing in action (MIA) for a long time and eventually was declared killed in action (KIA). I will never get over this. Only because of coincidence I became the go-to guy in gathering his things out of his room and sending them back to family. Few in the squadron knew that Roger and I had gone through ROTC together at Bowling Green and both of us were originally from Ohio. What a good man Roger had been. He probably was about my age at the time, maybe a year younger. That would have made him twenty-nine to thirty years old.

Roger's demise made me even more aware of the bar scene at Udorn. Most nights the guys either would be at our squadron table or would be sitting at the bar. Often you'd see men repeatedly sitting in the same seats night after night. And then you'd notice: nobody's in Roger's seat. This was a tough business. We used to console ourselves by joking that our combat pay—sixty-five dollars per month— made it all worthwhile. I have Roger's obituary upstairs, and I think of him all the time. I should have looked his mom and dad up when I got back to the States, but I never did; shame on me.

**Roger Behnfeldt—my friend, classmate, squadron
mate, RF-4 mate, and fellow Ohioan—was lost on
August 19, 1972. The air force recovered his remains
September 24, 1987. A finer man you will not find.**

The same story was going on with the other squadrons.
The guys going after MiGs experienced an interesting time
from 1972 to 1973. The RF-4 was unarmed, so we stayed out
of that business, but the F-4 guys were given some opportunities to become MiG killers. Three US Air Force aces came out
of Vietnam—Richie, DeBellevue, and Feinstein—and I was in
the same brief/debrief room with all of them on numerous
occasions. It was interesting to watch these guys in the briefing room after they had knocked down three or four MiGs.
(Knocking down five would make them aces.)

Lee and I were airborne in North Vietnam and within forty miles or so of Richie when he killed his fifth MiG. Richie's last words over the radio after the engagement were, "I got 'em!" I'll never forget that day. Sometimes you will hear that the US Air Force has only one ace from Vietnam; this is because DeBellevue and Feinstein were both navigators during their MiG kills. In fact, DeBellevue had *six* kills to his name. Both of these men would come back to the States and become pilots.

I previously mentioned my two close calls in the RF-4, but I want to discuss those more specifically here and talk of one more.

Lee and I had finished a mission and were headed back to Udorn on a fairly bright, sunny day. We were up rather high as we approached a descent point. I had told Lee to fly awhile if he wanted to, and he said he'd fly. Soon afterward I said something about starting our descent, and then, because we often flew with "hot interphone mikes," I heard Lee's breathing speed up. At first I thought nothing of it. Then Lee said, "Something weird is going on with this right engine." I asked him what was wrong, and he said, "Look, I can pull the throttle back, but the power on that engine is not decreasing."

I took the airplane back and tried it myself. I could literally go from the idle-power position to full military (mil) power without the thrust on the right engine changing. It remained at mil power, registering 100 percent on the power gauge, regardless of where the throttle was. We pulled the good engine back to idle and flew the remainder of our flight, including approach and touchdown, with the other engine where it was. Upon landing, we took an approach end barrier as we shut the fuel off to the misbehaving engine via a master switch for that engine. It had been an oddball day.

Another day Lee and I were up in the southern portion of North Vietnam. We came into the target area from the sea from the east. We were flying probably around 540 knots. We were right over the area where we wanted pictures when a very loud explosion occurred, and for the first and last time ever, I heard Lee let out a scream of sorts. I immediately pulled off the target and began maneuvering back to the ocean, so we could bail out if necessary. I checked on Lee's status, and he said he was fine, just a little concerned, as the main impact point from the rounds of AAA was very close to his right leg. These rounds had penetrated a lot of steel on the airplane but never made it to the interior of the aircraft. I had a wingman, Dave, and I asked him to take a look at us underneath the airplane. His report went something like this: "Well, it looks like you've got fuel coming out of every fuel tank, and you have a nine-by-nine-inch hole in the right side of the right engine."

I decided to land at Nakhon Phanom (NKP), 365 miles or so northeast of Bangkok. We went down the coast a little before turning west, where we contacted the tower and requested our emergency landing. I wasn't fully confident of our landing gear, so we decided to take an approach end barrier with our arresting hook. This was the same hook the navy had on their F-4s...only the carrier guys knew what they were doing with it. We air force types had never been trained to use them, let alone use them in the middle of an emergency. The hook worked as advertised, and it was all smoother than I thought it would be, kind of like having a giant rubber band hooked to you after landing.

We got towed to a parking spot, and from there, things moved much more quickly than I thought they would. Someone came out and talked to us for a little while, but very soon after, we were jumping into a C-47. We literally jumped inside the open door, still wearing our G-suits and parachute harnesses, carrying our helmets. Not long after that, we were at our squadron, minus our airplane. I failed to track our RF-4 from there and often wondered if it ever flew again. I feel pretty certain it would have. I still have part of the metal from that right engine in my memento collection.

Often we would hear stories of someone feeling that a certain day was the day he was going to get hit by a SAM or AAA or even a MiG. And then he would get hit. These stories always took on a folklore-type aura, but after this day, I knew many of those stories likely were true. From the time I'd awakened that morning until the AAA impacted our plane, I'd felt it coming. Still, it was a surprise in that moment, and thank goodness we were still alive. I don't ever remember talking to Lee in detail about what had happened, but we were both grateful for the way the mission ended.

I'll pause here to reflect on my religious mind-set during this time frame. Although I always remembered the church in Hubbard, Ohio, by this time, I had been largely ignoring it. I came to say that I was still of a spiritual mind-set but avoided academic religion, and I hadn't been to a church in a very long time. In 1972 and 1973, that changed. Because of some close calls, I found myself returning from some missions and going directly to the small chapel on the base to give thanks for my still being alive.

At one point about this time, I remember sitting down and writing my mother a letter. It was because we were flying a "heavy" the next day. A heavy meant you were going to fly into the heart of Hanoi, North Vietnam, where the defenses were the greatest, where there was no terrain to hide in, and where the surface-to-air missile threat and the MiG threat was the greatest. *No terrain to hide in?* By hugging hills and mountainous terrain, we made it difficult for adversaries to see our aircraft on radar. When you got to Hanoi, the terrain flattened out and you became much more vulnerable to be acquired on radar, and therefore much more vulnerable to having a missile launched at you. Whatever the final contents of that letter were, my intent was to just have a last contact with my mother should something happen to me the next day. Nothing bad happened to me that day, but I was always glad that I had reached out to her the night before.

I also remember a "movie" that has replayed in my mind for over forty years that went something like this: I had flown a mission on the same day in the same area as Wally had. After we flew, the air force "blue bread truck" picked six of us up from the flight line to bring us back to our squadron. We called it a bread truck because it looked like the old bread trucks of the day; it had those large windows in the front and two long benches for crewmembers to sit on during trips to and from the flight line. Because of the AAA and SAMs launched at us that day, everything seemed eerily quiet during our ride back to the squadron. Although we all had our iced-down towels around our necks, the Thai sun and heat loomed large. As I glanced around the bread truck, the sweat and solemnness were palpable. Nobody was saying a word. This was very unusual. As the truck rounded the last bend and headed to the squadron, the sun's rays hit Wally directly in the face. For some reason, I watched him as he seemed to look directly into the sun. Then he smiled slowly and said, as if talking to God, or to the sun, "I'm alive!" And then we all smiled and maybe even chuckled. We all felt the same way.

On another mission way up in North Vietnam, I was number two in a four-ship formation. In the RF-4, we flew a lot of single-ship missions—most of them, actually—but the longer the war dragged on, the more we were being required to have an F-4 escort, in case we ran into some difficulty from MiGS or whatever. On some priority targets, having two RF-4s would provide some redundancy in case of an abort on the ground or in the air by the other RF-4. However, the F-4s generally made us more vulnerable, because they were slower than we were, and they never wanted to fly as low as we did. But that was the way it would be on some of these missions.

On this day, I knew we were going into a high-threat area and would all need to be on our toes. I had usually led missions like this but was going to ride the number-two position for the day. A relatively new major would lead. The two F-4s would fly as numbers three and four. Fighters have a way of consuming large amounts of fuel, especially in areas where you are getting SAMs thrown at you, so our leader briefed the fuel situation in detail, and we even had some options. If we got to point x with everyone having y amount of fuel, we would merely head straight to Udorn for our recovery. As it turned out, we were getting SAMs thrown at us in a big way. As you might imagine, afterburners were used that day, and those take a lot of fuel. In the F-4s, the fuel gauge is in the front seat and to the upper right of the instrument panel.

When the leader calls for a fuel check, everyone makes sure he has some spacing on the airplane next to him, takes a look at his fuel gauge, and then reports his fuel. This happens pretty quickly, and once the leader hears from the last man (sometimes known as Blue 4), he can make some decisions regarding how the mission is going to continue. The fuel check, just taken, verified that all of us had enough fuel to go straight to Udorn, so we turned to head home. Several minutes later, number four called in with not enough fuel to go to Udorn and probably not enough to get to a tanker out over the water, and we couldn't land, because we were still so far into North Vietnam. The die was cast for a very bad day.

I immediately jettisoned all my external fuel tanks, which were now dry and only acting as a big drag and fuel consumer on the airplane. At least one other in the flight did the same. We were now headed out to sea, looking and calling for tankers. Two tankers came into sight, and we two RF-4s headed for one, while the two F-4s split from us and headed for the other. With a few miles to go to my tanker, I heard number four say over the radio that one of his engines was winding down, but he still had his tanker in sight. By winding down, he meant that the engine was quitting, because it was not getting any fuel. Soon thereafter he reported that the other engine was winding down, and he said something like, "We'll be jumpin' out soon; see you guys on the ground." The pilot and his backseater would be bailing out; assuming their ejection was successful and rescue would get them out of the water and take them back to Udorn, they would see us on the ground there. Now the other F-4 had his tanker to himself.

My leader and I had so little gas left that we had to get on and off the tanker quickly to take on enough fuel to keep the engines running and then let the other get on the tanker to do the same. We traded places three or four times until we finally had enough fuel to wait for the other to get a good load of gas. My knees have knocked in an airplane only once; it was that day, just before I got my first little bit of gas. This story has been told in a few places, by a few fighter pilots, but most of the time, it is related by secondhand storytellers who have it divorced from reality by a good margin. If that fuel check had been solid, we all should have landed at Udorn without incident. This was a bad day for all of us, though the two crewmembers who bailed out *were* rescued from the water and returned in short order to Udorn.

Each guy in the Fourteenth Tactical Reconnaissance Squadron had a unique personality. We had consecutive commanders named Sid Rogers and Brian Curry, and you would never find two better men. Amid the war and everything it brought to us, both of these officers were models for leadership. Both were quiet, unassuming, understanding, and capable. John Chancellor and Wally Hopkins were two more I came to know through the years. Both of their fathers had flown in War World II. John's twin brother had been a naval aviator and had been killed in an airplane, and Wally's father had been an ace in World War II. John had a huge sense of humor, while Wally was quieter but a master of the one-liner. John started flying FCFs just before I rotated back to the States.

I noticed that Wally enjoyed the movies. On many nights at the club, Wally would stand up near our squadron table and ask, "Hey, does anybody want to go to the movie?" This movie was put on by our air force personnel, and the movies were sometimes old and sometimes not too far out of date. I don't ever remember anyone taking Wally up on his movie offer, except me, on one occasion. (Once again I am reminded of the infantry guys rolling their eyes at the thought of the air force guys...watching movies.)

As I watched the movie with Wally, I thought this was a good way of distancing myself from the alcohol at the club. I expected to see more movies there, but I never did. I knew I was coming to respect Wally, even though I don't think I ever flew with him. Wally eventually ran some VA hospitals for many years and is now retired down in Florida. He regularly rides his bike more than twenty miles a day. John hunted a lot in his retirement years and had his own airplane for a while, an A-36. He settled in Tennessee, the last I knew. His Ole Miss days, his family and local friends, all his hunting buddies, and his hunting dogs remain very important to him.

A guy named Paul Schmidt was our operations officer toward the end of my tour at Udorn. Although we kept the usual professional distance while at Udorn, I would meet up with Paul again, professionally and personally. He would later help me get what I call the best flying job I ever had.

I remember Tony Reyna telling me this story: Tony was in Paul's office one time when a clean RF-4 took off. (*Clean* meant it had no heavy external fuel tanks and was very maneuverable and responsive to throttle movements.) Paul's office had a large picture window that overlooked the flight line, and aircraft taking off were clearly visible from this vantage point. Tony said Paul was watching the RF-4 as it hugged the ground until its speed accelerated, and then the aircraft went almost straight up off the end of the runway. Paul just shook his head at the steep climb angle and asked Tony if he knew who that aviator was. Tony knew it was me but answered in the negative. There was nothing illegal about what I did. This sounds like much ado about nothing, and it is, except that I didn't hear this story until about twenty years later. What a pleasure these FCF flights were—and nobody was shooting at us, for the most part.

I remember another day when several of us were back near our hooch around midday. That was unusual. We were just looking for things to do, and we found something. John Chancellor was sleeping with his head hanging off the side of his bed. His roommate called us all over to take a look. I hate to admit it, but I backed a motorcycle into the room with the exhaust pipe aimed directly at John's ear. Then I fired it up. John awoke like someone in a horror movie. I decided it had been a bad idea and left. John, remarkably, went back to sleep. This was just another day at Udorn.

One early morning before daybreak, Lee VanNamen, my back seater, and I were riding my motorcycle over to the other side of the base for an early go. Lee got out a harmonica and started playing it. I hadn't seen him do that before, but he was playing "Oh! Susanna" and doing a fair job of it. There was a very light rain falling. Soon we would be at the morning briefing and out of the rain. I was enjoying the sound of the harmonica, the sound of the motorcycle, and the misty early morning, even though it was still very dark. It was funny how times like these could feel calming and soothing amid the ongoing war. Our peaceful ride was interrupted by what sounded like a gunshot. I assumed the sound was coming from an approaching storm, and the beam of the small head-light on my motorcycle bounced along the road. We were now about a quarter of a mile or less from the building where we were headed.

Then I saw a man standing in the middle of the road, motioning for us to stop. It was a military guy, and he was telling us to get off the motorcycle and come with him. I shut down the motorcycle and left it by the roadside as we followed him. He took us to a building that was dark inside and helped us wend our way through a bunch of people to where we could sit or on the floor, and then he was gone. It was so dark we couldn't see these people, but we could hear them whispering to one another in low tones as they sat or kneeled on the floor. I have no idea how many people were there.

We later learned that a Viet Cong (VC) or VC sympathizer had come through the barbed wire on the base and was mak-ing his way to our headquarters building in an effort to set off some kind of charge. Our military police had killed the man but were not sure if there were others inside the wire. Eventually we made it to our briefing, although we were a bit late. The intel folks said there were numerous bullet holes in the operations building, but that was all. I suppose we were lucky we hadn't started out a few minutes earlier that day. I never heard Lee play "Oh! Susanna" again.

It was good being a lieutenant or captain, because we made up the main body of crewmembers there. We looked out for one another, and we all loved our job of flying. When lieutenant colonels from the staff came down to fly with us, the guys tried to make them feel welcome, but depending on who it was, we could sometimes be brutal. At a certain point in the war, someone from above decided it would be a good idea to have the crews take a recorder with them and tape all the interphone conversations going on between the crewmembers. What follows is one result of taping cockpit conversations. After most of the crews from the morning missions returned, the guys gathered in the flight-planning room, just BSing about what had gone on that morning.

One navigator showed up in the middle of the crowd and announced, "I've got something you guys might be interested in." There was silence. He walked over to a flight-planning table and placed his recorder on top of it. He pushed the play button, and we learned that the colonel he'd been flying with had suffered a rough morning. Before we took off, we regularly went through what was known as a leak check. During this check near the runway, a crew chief would hook up an interphone from below and check for oil, hydraulic, or fuel leaks, all the while making sure the landing-gear pins had been pulled and that everything underneath the airplane was in good order. The crew chief would report the status of all this to the crew, then sign off, pull the interphone cord, and move on to the next airplane.

On this particular day, as soon as the crew chief plugged in, he hastily told the colonel to shut down the number-two engine. The colonel asked why and was quickly told the engine had sucked the crew chief's T-shirt out of his pocket, and it had gone down the intake of the engine. The colonel immediately shut down the engine. Just as quickly, the crew chief said, "No, shut down the other engine." He said the colonel had shut down the wrong engine. We all listened to this discussion and were glad it hadn't been one of us, even though I don't think any of it was the colonel's fault. Despite my involvement with maintenance, I don't think I ever found out what happened to that T-shirt or that engine.

Combat Sorties in the Bar at Udorn

The aviators of Udorn relieved their tensions in the bar. After being in this environment for a while, eventually, some of your fellow pilots would come over to you and, without hesitation, pick you up and throw you over the bar. Beer bottles, ice, and glasses of whiskey flew. That's just the way it was. One day a relatively new pilot came to me and said he didn't think the guys liked him. I asked why, and he said, "Because I haven't ever been thrown over the bar." It took me about two seconds to take care of that. Funny, isn't it? We all just wanted to be a part of what was going on, even in situations like this. The psychology of it all was interesting, to say the least.

While all this was going on, the volume from the little Thai band and accompanying singer reaching its crescendo, and one would look at the very large picture above the bar that said it all. Depicted were two buzzards sitting on a fence, and they looked as though they were talking to each other. The line in bold print at the bottom read, "Patience, my ass. I want to kill somebody." That just about summed up our attitude, and thoughts of Washington, DC, policy emerged from time to time.

Simultaneously in the Udorn bar, there were "carrier landings" going on, as well as occasional "carrier takeoffs." As if honoring our navy and marine aviator brothers, we would shove five or six tables together and wet them down with beer, water, or anything liquid. Out in the hallway, crewmembers waited for their turns to run, jump, and slide down the table (the carrier). At the end, two stalwart officers held a towel across the table (deck), so they could stop (arrest) the crewmember from hitting the floor (sea). One night this notion turned to carrier takeoffs, and we needed only one or two tables for this. We'd put a chair on top of the table and put a crewmember in the chair (cockpit). Two stalwart officers would then thread the towels through the chair, and another would motion to the crewmember, basically asking if he was ready. When the crewmember gave the sign that he was ready, the two officers with the towel would launch the crewman into the air. Sometimes we slept better after one of these evenings.

I remember some of the higher-ups getting concerned that someone was going to get hurt doing these things in the bar. They appropriately issued each squadron commander a pith helmet and a whistle. If a squadron commander thought one of his crewmembers was endangering himself or others, he was supposed to blow the whistle, point to the offending crewmember, and announce, "Foul!" That was a riot and lasted about twenty-four hours.

I remember a newly elected female officer running the officers' club. Up to this point, someone would often just smash a glass against the wall. Perhaps this was out of order, but considering any of us could die the following morning, it seemed the normal thing to do. Anyway, the new club president called a meeting and announced there would be no more throwing of glasses. The silence was deafening...until about 150 glasses hit the wall at the same time. Perhaps I exaggerate. The new club officer folded up her book and departed.

"Dead Bug" was always interesting. Anybody could call out loudly, "Dead Bug." At that, everybody in the bar would fall on their backs and put their feet and hands up in the air like a dead bug. If someone failed to do this, he had to buy everybody a drink. If someone was sitting on a barstool, sometimes he could push himself over backward, land on the floor, put his feet up, and not lose a drop of whiskey out of the glass in hand. I witnessed Bill, my old FAC friend, do this years later at the bar in the Nellis AFB officers' club. It brought Cirque du Soleil to mind.

The club was another place to be on the evening of the day when someone bagged a MiG. I remember walking up the front stairs of the club late one afternoon. The celebration was already going on, and one of the squadron commander's jeeps was sitting on the carpet inside the club. Obviously a crew from that commander's squadron had killed a MiG. I could hear the noise emanating from farther inside. They were letting a little steam off. Appropriately so, I thought. I also wondered how in the hell they got that jeep up the stairs and into the officers' club.

The life and death of it all was always interspersed with other periodic happenings. Our ops officer, Travis, was a clean-living, career-oriented officer and would later become a full bird colonel. If we'd had a tape recording of him, this is what you would have seen of him on many evenings in the club: He would finish his meal and sit back in his seat with a slight smile on his face. He was from the south and still had a bit of a southern drawl, despite his fourteen or fifteen years in the air force. As one of the Thai waitresses would approach, Travis would say, "Aud [I'd] like some aus [ice] cream." Although Thailand was usually pretty hot, and cooling anything was a problem, Travis would continue. "Aud like some aus cream in a cold bo-uhl [bowl]."

The Thai waitresses were always pretty good, but to this request, they would always say something like this: "We no hab [have] a cold bowl."

Travis would stay on it. "Ah want some aus cream in a cold bo-uhl."

After at least three of these retorts, the waitress would disappear but would reappear shortly with a bowl of ice cream, of course...in a warm bowl. By then, the ice cream would be like soup. Travis would look disappointed, and the rest of us would laugh. And the next evening, we would see the same show again.

We ate a lot of burgers at our club. Travis loved them. He would say, "Aud like a hamburger"; however, the Thai waitresses at the club would maintain that the club had only cheeseburgers. Call it a language problem or flexibility problem, but it demonstrates the things that just happened overseas in a foreign country with the associated language problems. Knowing all this, Travis would always ask for a hamburger. For effect Travis would say, "But I want a hamburger."

The waitress would then become animated and turn up the volume, saying again, "We no hab [have] hamburger, we only hab cheeseburger!" Travis would eventually relent, but we laughed over and over at this act. Eventually Travis would get his...cheeseburger. And the next night you could tune in to the *Ice Cream and Hamburger Show, with Travis.*

We all have certain phrases we like to use. Travis liked "god almighty damn!" Other than that phrase, I never heard him swear. He would go on to have a very successful career, but unfortunately, he would die early back in the States. I forget what the malady was, but he was much too young to die. I always thought it strange that Travis was probably the cleanest-living pilot I had ever known but died so young, in probably his very late fifties or early sixties.

I had vowed to never become an alcoholic, because of what my dad had been through, so often I would call it an early night and walk across the street to my room and hit the sack. Tony stayed up later than I did much of the time. And like most of us, Tony would just keep going until he was exhausted. Often I would be up very early, and sometimes this is what I would see: as I parted the curtains separating our beds from the rest of the room, I would encounter Tony sitting in our only big chair, sound asleep, with a half-eaten cheeseburger in his lap. I would always whisper, "Tony, go to bed!" Tony was a hardworking and wonderful guy. Another air force friend and RF-4 crewmember, Wally Hopkins, came up with the perfect description of Tony: "Tony was a gentle warrior," he said.

FCFs and Maintenance

Part of the reason I tried to get sleep was that, in addition to the usual combat sorties I was flying, I had volunteered for a job flying functional check flights (FCFs). If a mechanic changed an engine or a flight surface like an aileron in the airplane, the plane needed to be test-flown and signed off on by an FCF pilot. It turned out to be a better job than I'd thought. They would give me an RF-4 without any of its three external fuel tanks, which meant the airplane would be light and very responsive. The other interesting thing was that, among many items you had to check on each of these flights, were the "inlet ramps." In order to get these engine-inlet ramps to open on an RF-4, you had to accelerate the airplane to a minimum of 1.6 Mach.

My boyhood dreams regarding speed were being manifested here. Why this speed quest? I will never know. My grandfather Bill used to say we all had peculiarities; I guess the quest for speed was mine. And so I would sometimes fly two combat missions in a day, followed, at dusk, by an FCF. I was even losing weight, for the first time in my life.

I got very involved in the maintenance of our aircraft. Mostly, I just wanted to learn what was going on out there on the flight line. We had a lot of very young enlisted guys who worked very hard, and they, too, were a long way from home. I eventually spent a lot of time in the "expediter" truck with Tech Sergeant Fayne. He was an interesting man and outstanding at what he did. I'm sure in the beginning he thought I was there to evaluate what was going on. Little did he know that he would be my teacher about the things that needed to be done on a flight line. He and a few of the young guys even took me downtown for a good-bye dinner just before I left Udorn. I was very appreciative of that gesture.

One day an SR-71 Blackbird landed at Udorn with some kind of emergency. I was aware of it and heard it probably would be taking off on a certain day. I was out on the flight line and watched as it taxied by and eventually took off. *What a beautiful airplane*, I thought. We were all aware that it could travel in the eighty-thousand-foot altitude arena and Mach 3.0 speed range. I wondered if it could ever be possible for me to fly that airplane.

A Nod to General Charlie Gabriel

Like our squadron commanders and ops officers, we had others who were just outstanding leaders and aviators. When I got to Udorn, our wing commander was a colonel named Charlie Gabriel. He had graduated from West Point and somehow had ended up in the air force. Colonel Gabriel, a leader through and through, had flown in Korea and had two MiG-15 kills to his credit. At Udorn he took his turn flying some of the tough missions and always seemed in control, despite some very tough times in early 1972. I thought he looked and acted like a leader should. He seemed quiet and reserved, traits I admired.

Colonel Gabriel went on to become a four-star general and served as the chief of staff of the US Air Force. In about 2003, he died of Alzheimer's. Imagine that: you command an air force wing in the Vietnam War, which eventually produces the only air force aces out of Vietnam; rise to the rank of four-star general; and earn the position of chief of staff of the air force...and you die not knowing you did any of it.

TIME TO GO HOME

Lee, my back seater, left to go back to the States just a little before I did. I don't remember giving him a proper sendoff, as I should have, but I remember being on the taxiway in an RF-4 waiting for takeoff when the big bird carrying Lee back to the States taxied into position for takeoff. I called out on the radio to the captain flying the large passenger jet. I asked him to take care of Lieutenant VanNamen for us. He acknowledged that he would and then pushed up the throttles of the big jet. I wept as I saw the airplane with Lee in it become airborne. He'd saved my life multiple times, and we'd received the Aircrew of the Quarter award for that last quarter. What a great friend he had been. I wondered if I would ever see him again.

In April 1973, my time was up in Thailand. My thoughts seemed to crystalize around the notion of flying the SR-71. Why not try? I succeeded in having the wing commander write up an endorsement for my application into the SR program. My time at Udorn had been pretty successful, and I now had as much combat time as anyone around. I had gone through a lot of high-speed time, both during combat operations and during all those FCFs. I felt ready for something like the SR-71, even if it was quite a lofty goal. If I couldn't make it into the program, who could? Few, other than the squadron commander and the wing commander, knew I was working on this goal. This SR journey would consume a large part of my days for the next two years or so. I didn't know it at the time, but I was in for a rough ride.

Tony and I met up in the air during our last flight at Udorn. We flew some formation and then landed, knowing our squadron mates would meet us on the flight line to celebrate. Soon thereafter we would be thrown into the green slime, which was also customary for crews after their last flight. (Green slime was a combination of aging water held in a large container and shark dye. The shark dye was included as part of our survival kit, and it had a bright-green color to it.) That night at the club, the band played a little bit of "We gotta get out of this place...if it's the last thing we ever do..." Tony and I *were* going to get out of this place. We had enjoyed our tours, but I think we were ready to leave.

It's funny; you might wonder how you could not want to leave a war zone, but some of us, like Tony, Karl, and many other guys, had joined the air force to do exactly what we had been doing for the past year. My friend and former U2 driver Sid always called it playing *You Bet Your Life*. (This was a game show hosted by Groucho Marx years ago. The show had no correlation to our life at Udorn, but the show title seemed to be an apt metaphor for our day-to-day experience in the war.)

Leaving Udorn was always going to be with mixed emotions. Stateside flying was filled with a lot of regulation and a lot of supervision, and flying in a war was the opposite. Most of us would miss the intensity of the flying experience at Udorn and the camaraderie of our squadron mates. Underlying the whole experience for many of us was the love affair we all had with the RF-4, which we tended to refer to in the feminine. I think all of us in the Fourteenth TRS were in love with that beauty, the RF-4. Again, the whole experience was capped off with the outstanding leadership we had with two successive top-notch squadron commanders, Sid Rogers and

Brian Currie, and a wing commander by the name of Colonel Gabrial.

As my time at Udorn drew to a close, I was trying to make contact with the assignment people in Texas to see what my fate was going to be in my next assignment. At first I mistakenly thought I had a chance to go out to Beale AFB, California, home of the SR-71, for an interview, but soon communications became almost impossible with the assignment people. Our POWs had just been released, and all assignment people were totally committed to getting the POWs their assignments. This was called Operation Homecoming. I knew Operation Homecoming would take a lot of effort, and I backed off on trying to get through to the assignment people. Remember there were no cell phones, no Internet, and no FaceTime—so I waited to be assigned.

Gradually, assignments started coming in for us. Most were going to flying jobs in Europe, in the RF-4. I had been selected for "special career monitoring" and received a notice to that effect. That's why what followed was shocking to me. I was astounded and very disappointed when I got a ground job as a training officer in a basic military training squadron, just outside San Antonio, Texas, at Lackland Air Force Base. *So much for special career monitoring*, I thought.

BASIC MILITARY TRAINING

I forget exactly where we lived in San Antonio, but I guess it was on base. Although I would be able to fly the T-33 "for proficiency," my primary job was to look after the enlisted training instructors (TIs) and the young recruits coming off the streets of America to enlist in the air force. I was assigned to one of twelve squadrons as the officer responsible for its training. The number of trainees was large, and I would be at Lackland from April 7, 1973, until September 11, 1974. During that time, I'd get back into the operating manual for the T-33; study the emergency procedures; and look at the cautions, warnings, and notes again. This was the same old airplane, a single-engine jet I had flown before going to the RF-4.

My main job, however, was not to fly but to train these newly enlisted young men. Well, the majority of training was done by the TIs—those guys who wear those Smokey-the-Bear hats and do a lot of loud talking to the young trainees. I was frustrated beyond belief at first, because I was not in a primary flying job. But soon four things happened. One, I became one of the squadron commanders. Being responsible for all these people made me pay attention to what was going on, and I would, as usual, give the job my all. Two, I had a training superintendent by the name of Senior Master Sergeant Wendy Davis. Wendy had about twenty-two years in the air force; of those, he had spent about twenty years at Lackland in the basic-training business. He really knew what he was doing and had a honed ability to stay ahead of the trainees and TIs, regardless of what was going on. The tough sergeant attitude and exterior evaporated every time he would explain some of the training situations to me. That is, he always communicated everything to me in a down-to-earth, easy-to-understand manner. I knew I had the best training superintendent on the base soon after I met him. I watched him, time and again, walk out of my office and close the outside door as he donned his hat; at that moment, he became Senior Master Sergeant Davis again. Three, I eventually would talk to hundreds of trainees in order to decide their fate. This became interesting to me, as I was generally interested in people, and I did want to do right by them and the air force, even if I wasn't flying every day. Four, I very quickly realized how close I was to the assignment people over at Randolph Air Force Base. Maybe I could start the SR-71 discussion with them again.

It is interesting that the organization of various units in the air force, and other services for that matter, have so many structural similarities. For instance, at Udorn, my reconnaissance squadron was divided into four flights, and I had been a flight commander there. Here, in a ground job, there were four master sergeants, and each was in charge of one-fourth of the squadron's trainees. These master sergeants were *almost* as good as Senior Master Sergeant Davis, and studying each of them was interesting. They all had that military bearing you could see a mile away, and their khaki uniforms were always starched and pressed to a point where I thought their uniforms might break.

I learned several tricks as to how they made their uniforms look so good. Many TIs changed uniforms midday. Most wore sock garters that held their socks up but were attached on the upper end to their shirts, front and rear. Thus, their shirts were always neatly tucked into their pants. Sometimes they sewed their pockets shut so there were no gaps. And they knew all the tricks to get their shoes to shine like mirrors. Sometimes a thicker sole or heel on their shoes or boots would add emphasis to the uniform. In short, they always presented themselves as pristine examples of the training instructors. (The army called its corresponding instructors drill instructors, or DIs.) You likely have seen movies regarding all this.) I found it all to be very interesting, but I still wanted a flying job.

Still, I learned some things at Lackland. Probably the greatest example of something I learned there was the following. One day one of the TIs asked if I wanted to go out and watch him drill some of his recruits. I hadn't been out of the office enough and answered in the affirmative. Soon I was outside in the sun, walking beside this TI as he marched about thirty troops back and forth, back and forth. I immediately noticed one guy who was out of step. Thoughts of the drill team I had been on at BG shot through my brain, and I smiled. I knew the TI was now locked on to this recruit, who continued out of step. Back and forth we went. The TI said to me in a hushed tone, "You'd think that son of a bitch would eventually know he is out of step, but he won't get in step unless I say something." I smiled. Back and forth we continued. The TI cleared his throat and belted out, "Mister, in the third rank and third column, it's you that is out of step; it's not the rest of the world." I watched the guy who had been out of step quickly change his step to match the others.

At certain points in our lives, I think we all have been out of step. We are convinced we are right. We think we know what we are doing. And then we realize we are out of step. To this day, I think about that TI and what he said, especially when I can't figure out why the world doesn't agree with me.

Very soon after I got to Lackland, the phone rang for me. I got on the line, and the officer on the other end said he was an assignments guy at Randolph. He asked, "Where have you been?"

I said something like, "I'm here at Lackland, where you guys sent me."

Then he really pissed me off. He said, "We were looking for you in order to have you go out to Beale AFB and interview for that SR-71 job, but now that you have signed in to the base at Lackland, we are just going to have to let the assignment stand." It all sounded like a bunch of baloney, but that is exactly what he said to me.

I had to control myself to get through all this while I was settling into my job at Lackland. But, as time marched on I did not give up my goals of getting to Beale and the SR-71. I remember a host of things I did. I talked to an old AC LC in a KC I knew, and he said he knew one of these assignment guys and would put in a good word for me. I went over to Randolph and repeated my desire to go to Beale for an interview. I must say I felt like that was a futile effort. I started calling out to Beale AFB, and I would talk to anyone out there who would talk to me. And I called my old RF-4 squadron commander, Sid Rogers. He was working at SAC Headquarters in Nebraska. He knew of my SR-71 interests, and I had flown on his wing in the air, including during his last mission in Thailand, and a few times in the bar at Udorn. A few days later, he suggested I come out to Offutt Air Force Base, where he was. He said to bring my blues. (These are the civilian version of coat and tie, plus name tag, rank, and ribbons.)

Soon I was there at Offutt, sitting in front of Colonel Rogers, who had been promoted since I'd last seen him. He said he wanted to do two things. One, he set up a phone conversation between an SR crewmember at Beale and me. This crewmember was an officer Sid had known in the B-52 business. I talked to this crewmember for just a few minutes. Little did I know the man I had just talked to, Buck Adams, would eventually set the speed record from London to Los Angeles in the SR-71. Years later he would retire as a general. I didn't know what to think, except that I felt I was getting closer to Beale. Then Sid said something like, "Well, are you ready to go downstairs? I've got a guy I want you to talk to."

We went downstairs and talked to another colonel down in the bowels of Offutt Air Force Base. I am embarrassed to say I do not remember that man's name, and I remember very little of the conversation other than his first words after we shook hands and he offered me a seat. He said, "So I hear you want to fly the Sled." (This was how insiders often referred to the SR-71.) Somehow I managed to answer the colonel in very absolute terms, and the next thing I remember, I was flying back to Lackland. I am almost certain the colonel downstairs had, at one time, been an SR-71 crewmember. It had all gone so quickly. Sid Rogers had put in an effort on my behalf, and I appreciated it. I wondered what would happen now.

I continued doing my job at Lackland with the trainees. In its own way, the job there was fascinating, and I found it interesting that the air force, like the other services, had a host of means available to get these young enlistees through basic training. There was no doubt that the training instructors had their work cut out for them. They had to turn a young civilian man or woman from anyplace in the United States into a responsive, responsible, articulate, motivated service member. Sometimes this was impossible, but most of the time, the trainees would get through basic training and move on to productive jobs around the world. We kept records on each trainee, and I spent most of my time talking to trainees when they ran into some difficulty during the training process. I also spent a lot of time talking with the TIs, and of course, discussions with Senior Master Sergeant Davis were part of my daily routine.

I was still concerned that my primary job was not flying, although I continued to fly the T-33 a couple of times a week to maintain flying proficiency. I noticed that, in the upper ranks of Lackland, the key positions were held by rated officers. That gave me some solace. (*Rated* is a word that implies the individual is someone who has wings. Typically, he or she is a pilot or navigator, at least in the world in which I was living.) Lackland had another whole organization devoted to turning out commissioned officers. College grads could apply to this school, and in a matter of a few months, they would be turned into second lieutenants. This was known as officer-training school, or simply OTS, and many called the graduates of this course "ninety-day wonders." On their behalf, however, I will say it was the most direct route to a commission in the service. This ninety-day commissioning effort compared to a four-year devotion at the academies or a much less involved four-year effort in ROTC.

I want to point out two officers who were part of the hierarchy above me at Lackland. One was Tom Richards, a lieutenant colonel. He was another of those *GQ*-cover kind of guys and could have been the best recruiting poster ever for attracting people into the service. He would later become a four-star general. Seeing him here at Lackland gave me hope that my career wasn't over yet—he was doing this ground job, and he wore wings. Few realized he had started out as an enlistee. He had been wounded in Korea and had flown as a Raven FAC in Southeast Asia. Sometime during my Lackland assignment, an ex-Thunderbird demonstration pilot had the job of running the OTS side of the house, and a two-star general (pilot) was running the entire school, both basic training and OTS. He was General Malloy. Both Malloy and the Thunderbird guy were rated. They wore wings and were doing this ground job. Maybe things would work out for me.

Most generals in the air force had what is called an aide, who was present to provide almost anything the general asked for. I saw that job as a possibility to get one's report card—otherwise known as an Officer's Effectiveness Report (OER)—upgraded. Of course, a job like that could also end your career, if you didn't perform for the general.

The Vietnam War was largely over now, and while I felt ill at ease with my ground job, many officers were being thrown out of the service. Harsh as it sounds, once the conflict ceased, there was no longer a need for all the servicemen who had been part of it. I felt lucky to have a job, but I still wanted to fly.

I started talking to General Malloy's aide and soon became aware of the short time remaining before he, the aide, would move on to another assignment. I started actively soliciting this job.

In the meantime, I was still talking to anybody I could about an interview out at Beale regarding the SR-71. In a matter of days, I found myself talking to a Captain Frank Lewis at Beale. Frank had been a POW in Vietnam after being shot down while flying a B-52 over North Vietnam and seemed to be involved in some administrative duties at Beale, but he was not an SR crewmember, nor was he scheduled to be. One thing led to another in this single phone conversation, and he shocked me. He asked, "Why don't you just come out here and spend some time? Can you get your own transportation out here? I'll pick you up at the airport." Of course. I left on my trip to Beale a day or two after our conversation.

I soon realized I was meeting the hierarchy at Beale, one by one, including most of the current SR-71 drivers there at the time. Most of them, like me, were captains. I had previously known none of them. To say this was pretty exciting would be an understatement. Not long after that, I found myself taking a three-day physical. This was the most detailed physical I ever took in my forty-one years of flying, and I was particularly worried about the electroencephalogram, because of my experience in college. But I passed.

One other thing happened at Beale during this short visit. I was introduced to a Captain Lee Ransom. Lee, a current SR-71 pilot, said we were going to take a ride in a T-38. I hadn't been in a T-38 since pilot training some six years prior. He told me I didn't need to worry about procedures; he was just there to take me up, let me fly awhile, and allow me some stick-and-rudder time, and then we would land. I knew what this ride was all about. It would serve as a glimpse for an insider to determine whether I was comfortable flying a high-performance airplane even though I had not flown that particular airplane for years.

The T-38 handled as it always had: like a dream. We got upside down a few times and did a few slow rolls, the kind of thing any pilot loved to do with this kind of high-performance airplane. I didn't hear anything negative from Lee, and intuitively I liked him. I would be surprised if he gave any bad reports on this flying episode.

Upon my return to Lackland, I wasn't exactly sure of what would happen regarding Beale. While I waited, however, I was called to interview as General Malloy's aide—or aide-de-camp, as some called it. There are many high-minded definitions for a general's aide, but I never deluded myself from the reality that the job would largely be working as a gofer for the general.

I remember going to the general's quarters upon his request. I considered it an interview. He motioned to a chair, and I sat down. He had the TV on and was watching a football game, and he had a large stack of papers in front of him. He asked me only one or two questions, resumed watching the ball game, and slowly continued going through some paperwork. After sitting quietly in this room for about forty-five minutes, he basically said I could go. He also said something that indicated I would soon be his aide.

And then I got a call from either Beale AFB or the assignment people at Randolph Air Force Base—I forget which. I would be going to Beale for training in the SR-71. As an aviator himself I knew that the general would not have a problem with me leaving for Beale. I never saw him again after that interview.

The SR-71

The SR-71 had a max speed of around 2,200 mph (approximately Mach 3.3) and two J58 engines, each of which had about 34,000 pounds of thrust with afterburners[2] and 25,000 pounds without them.[3]

Reg and I are pictured above. I loved flying the airplane but hated the politics. I took the airplane to two air shows and flew it operationally, but I am likely the low pilot on the operational totem pole as regards hours flown.

I had started this Beale assignment journey in about March 1972; it was now September 1974. It had been a long journey. I hoped that, going forward, the SR-71 assignment wouldn't have so much uncertainty associated with it.

I was assigned to the First Strategic Reconnaissance Squadron at Beale Air Force Base in California. The duty title for the job stated: "Squadron Aircraft Commander, SR-71: Charged with global recon missions at exceptionally high altitudes and speeds. Intelligence gathered is critical to our national defense posture. An error in judgment or navigation could result in impairing international relations. Officer is assigned to selectively manned unit."

I will skip over some of the political things regarding this assignment that had effects on me from day one until the day I left. I will leave the politics aside and just say that someday maybe we will get a chance to talk about them. Instead, I will highlight some of the more positive aspects of the job just to give you an idea of what I was doing at the time.

Because we wouldn't be flying the SR-71 on a daily basis, we were allowed to check out in the T-38 in order to maintain flying proficiency. Back I went to the books, operating procedures, emergency procedures, warnings, cautions, and notes, and I relearned the important numbers associated with the airplane. We usually flew the T-38 with another SR pilot or staff person. "Acro," or acrobatics, were a normal part of flying the T-38, and eventually we would join up and fly formation with the SR-71 in the traffic pattern at Beale. For most pilots, this alone was a dream come true. It certainly was for me. Watching the SR-71 from a few feet away while in formation was a sight to behold. And seeing the brute power it exhibited while under acceleration from a low approach was something to appreciate.

I traded in my dark-green flight suits for bright-orange ones, given to all SR-71 crew members to wear during T-38 operations and for most day-to-day functions—so much for low-key. I immediately felt like everyone was watching those of us in the orange flight suits.

Eventually I began training for the SR. As with every other airplane checkout in the air force, I was instructed on the systems of the airplane while I began learning emergency procedures and most other details regarding the SR-71. Somewhere along the line, I learned of the Astro-Inertial Navigation System (ANS), a system that looked at stars to figure out where you were. The difference here in training was that I was the only one in class. Amazing. Instructors were very good at teaching the systems to me, but I am not sure I ever got over being the only one in the class. This was quite different from all the other training I'd had. In the KC-135 training classes, it was not unusual to have twenty-five to forty other officers sitting in a class, and the same went for the RF-4, T-41, T-37, and T-38. Even the O-2 classes had a lot of aviators in them.

Soon the simulator training began. I never enjoyed simulators, and I suppose I had a natural aversion to being "evaluated." I should have been over that aversion by this point, but I'm not sure I ever got over it.

As I write, I find myself thinking about another day in the T-38. I was out flying some formation with this staff guy. He was not in the SR system, but his job allowed him the opportunity to fly the T-38. As we flew along at about 2500 feet I was flying a little high on his right wing, and this is what I saw. It looked like his canopy fogged up for a brief second, and then came completely off the airplane. I couldn't believe my eyes, first thinking that maybe he had bailed out. Then I realized he was still in the airplane but now was in a very crouched position. I don't remember the communications situation, but we soon returned to the base and landed uneventfully. I asked my wingman how he was doing. He responded that he was fine but said the back of his neck had been chafed quite a bit from his flight-suit collar reverberating against his neck from the wind coming into the cockpit. *Just another day in aviation,* I thought. No, it was more like another day where you watched fate play its hand. I have always said that aviation is a very humbling experience, usually on a daily basis. And aviation does not care how much experience you have, as it continues to humble you.

The squadron itself was unusually small, compared to others. There were only about nine crews there, and if you had one on vacation, three gone on some temporary duty, two in training somewhere, and one or two out flying the T-38, then there were only one or two left. When I walked into the squadron, it was not unusual for me to be the only one there, outside of an administrative clerk. Compared to an RF-4 squadron, this was a real change. The flight-planning room in an RF-4 squadron routinely had about twenty to thirty guys doing their flight planning and raising hell.

I like to say there was rarified air at Beale, and I'm not talking about the altitudes at which the SR-71 operated. I'm talking about what was going on there and the aircrews involved. All from the First Strategic Reconnaissance Squadron, there were those who had just set the record going from New York to London, others who set the record going from London to Los Angeles. Another crew had recently flown to the Middle East and set some records for the amount of time they were airborne in doing that. There were the crews involved in world records for World Speed on a Closed Course, World Speed on an Open Course, and World Altitude Record. I had just arrived, but because I didn't hold a world record of some sort,

I began to feel like a failure. There was another crew that ended up visiting Zsa Zsa Gabor, the actress, for some related discussion. I thought this was a total fabrication but years later I was convinced this actually had happened. It was all pretty amazing.

I enjoyed the crews there, and they all had a pretty broad background, though I was surprised to see the number of pilots with air training command backgrounds. Some had been T-38 instructors, and at least one had been a T-37 instructor. In total, they had experience in many airplanes, including some who had flown B-52s and various fighters. Some of the older staff people had flown the B-58, an impressive airplane in its own right. One had flown the F-105, a few had been FACs, and one of those guys had flown the 0-1 while a FAC. At least one guy had been a "Wild Weasel," flying the F-4. (Wild Weasels had the mission of going out and "trolling" for surface-to-air missile (SAM) sites and then hopefully destroying them.) This was always a high-risk mission and very respected by all the crews in the air force. Another pilot had flown regularly as a T-38 pilot at Edwards AFB and often flew with Thomas Stafford, the astronaut.

I was lucky to fly some operational missions in the SR-71. My operational flights all originated out of Okinawa, Japan. After I left Beale, crews would also fly out of Mildenhall, England.

On two occasions, I was lucky to fly the SR to air shows. One was to the Strategic Air Command Headquarters at Offutt AFB, Nebraska, and the other was to Barksdale AFB, Louisiana, another SAC base. What a treat to fly into an air show in the SR-71. These were unbelievable experiences.

At an air show at Beale, the USAF Thunderbird demonstration team was present. I remember one of the bosses asking me to talk to a Thunderbird pilot about the SR. I was to meet him early in the morning of their show and talk to him about flying the SR, which this particular pilot had asked to do. We talked for quite a while, and I thought again about the rarified air I was operating in for the time being. I was talking to a Thunderbird pilot about the airplane I was flying. It was an amazing time. I hadn't been that involved with a Thunderbird team member since the time in the RF-4 in Southeast Asia when one of my F-4 escorts was flown by a former Thunderbird.

Speaking of Thunderbirds, we even had a staff colonel at Beale who had been a Thunderbird solo pilot. I flew with him once in the T-38 and remember him doing eight-point rolls. He was the first Air Force Academy grad to fly with the Thunderbirds, as I remember. Just another day, flying in a T-38 with a former Thunderbird, right?

Another colonel working in the staff was Colonel Merl Dethlefsen, with whom I flew in the T-38 several times. He, like others, enjoyed "beating up the pattern"—that is, doing multiple touch-and-goes right there at Beale AFB. I started to feel comfortable with him, despite our rank difference, and remember three things about him. The first was that he seemed very religious, though I can't remember what gave me this impression. As a consequence, he seemed very understated, quiet, and unassuming. I liked him a lot. The second thing I remember is that he often talked about the Air Force Medal of Honor recipients who had come home from Asia at a fairly young age, only to be afflicted with some ailment that caused their early demise. The Medal of Honor is the United States of America's highest military honor, awarded for personal acts of valor above and beyond the call of duty. The medal is awarded by the United States in the name of the US Congress to military personnel. It took a while for me to realize Colonel Dethlefsen was a Medal of Honor recipient himself. He also was fairly young when he got home from Asia. Thirdly, of course you know where this is heading: he died at about fifty-three years of age. I don't know the cause. He was buried at Arlington National Cemetery. I thought he was an exceptionally decent man, and I really enjoyed knowing him.

I heard Rich Graham say in a briefing once that eighty-six pilots had flown the SR-71 operationally over its long history. Rich was a contemporary of mine at Beale AFB and later became the wing commander for all the SR-71 personnel at Beale, with responsibilities that covered assets throughout a large part of the world. He is a gentleman and a down-to-earth kind of guy, and he has written several books on the SR-71. Although I was at the bottom of the SR-71 heap, I did manage to fly a few operational missions. Eighty-six may sound like a large number of pilots, but it is small, considering the number of years the 71 had been flying. To put it in perspective, years later, when I went to work for American Airlines, my seniority number was somewhere in the eight thousands. When I retired from the airlines some sixteen years later, I still had at least four thousand guys and gals in front of me on the seniority list.

About thirty-five years after being stationed at Beale, I met Rich and accompanied him down to the Naval Postgraduate School in Monterey, where I watched him brief a crowd of a few hundred people on the SR. During the course of our visit, we found we had grown up fairly close to each other, as he was from northwestern Pennsylvania. And then the real surprise: we had both hung out at the same drag strip outside of Warren, Ohio, during the hot summer days in the sixties. I couldn't get past the coincidence that he had been trying to go fast as a teenager too.

I went to an air show as a spectator several years after flying the Blackbird, and the SR happened to be on display that day. As usual, the crewmembers who brought it to the air show were behind a rope in front of the SR. The crowd was on the outside of the rope, and folks were asking their usual questions. I was surprised to see Joe Vida was there as a crewmember answering the crowd's questions. He recognized me from a distance and called out to me. Several years had passed since I'd last seen him, and I was surprised he could recognize me. What a great guy. It turns out Joe got more SR-71 time than anyone on the planet— something like 1,393 hours. A relatively short time later, Joe passed away from some physical ailment having nothing to do with airplanes. He was the first of the guys I had known at Beale to pass away. What a shame.

Another SR-71 RSO named George Morgan was a legend at Beale AFB, and I got to fly with him once or twice. We were flying along at Mach 3 up in the northwestern United States, when I heard him transmit, "Moose Jaw Tower, Moose Jaw Tower, Aspen xx." Then I heard a female tower operator directing a couple of Cessna aircraft to land on a certain runway. Then George repeated his call, "Moose Jaw Tower, Moose Jaw Tower, Aspen xx."

The next transmission came from the female tower opera-tor. "Geooorge, is that you?" I guess George knew people from all over the world. I laughed as we continued to scoot along the northern boundary of the United States at Mach 3.

On another occasion with George, I was getting ready to start a descent from eighty thousand feet and called for the descent checklist. We always tried to do these procedures crisply, because we were still flying one mile every two sec-onds. I waited for George. I called for the checklist again. George responded, "I can't."

I asked, "Why?"

George said, "Because I am listening to the Story Lady on the HF radio."

I smiled, and soon George was reading the descent-check items.

On still another occasion, George told me the flight sur-geon on base had asked for a urine sample. That is, the flight surgeon told him before a particular mission that he was to keep urine that he expelled during the mission and turn it in to the flight surgeon after the mission. It had to do with some study the flight surgeon was doing. George dutifully poured a small bottle of apple juice into the sample bottle and took it directly to the flight surgeon. I know of no repercussions from this, but George continued to keep us all entertained. I remember George saying his father had held a job for thirty or forty years doing something he was really not excited about. George said he didn't want to live that way. As a consequence, you never saw George after four o'clock in the afternoon. George always seemed to know that our time on the planet was limited, and he was going to enjoy it, no matter what.

George took me sailing on his boat in the San Francisco Bay Area a few times. On the evening of July 3, in the late 70's we put the anchor down with a lot of other boats around us and planned to sleep on the boat overnight. At about six o'clock in the morning on July 4, I was awakened by the sound of a cannon. Yes, a cannon. Guess whose. George was on the back of the boat, smoke still rising from his cannon, and he was yelling for everyone to wake up. Needless to say, our neighbors anchored nearby were not impressed. But as George would say, "It was the Fourth of July, by god, and we had to start celebrating."

The pilot—and here I stress the word *pilot*—with the most time in the SR-71 is a guy by the name of BC Thomas. (Vida was the navigator with more time than anybody.) BC was the only real test pilot we had at Beale while I was there. He had gone to the official test-pilot school at Edwards Air Base and had graduated in good standing. He was on his way into the SR-71 program as I was on my way out. I'd always wished to know him better and was not surprised to find that he ended up having the most pilot time in the SR ever, with something like 1,217 hours. Again, this was as a pilot. Joe Vida held the record for the most time in the Sled, but he wasn't a pilot.

Toward the end of my time at Beale with about twelve years in the air force I was beginning to wonder about my remaining years left in the service. During this time, the air force was still making it tough to get to the twenty-year retirement point. They were still a little bloated with people after Vietnam, so they instituted a system we referred to as the silver-bullet system, which was designed to cut down on the number of inflated evaluations within the force. Each of the commanders was given only so many top ratings (silver bullets) to hand out to his or her underlings. This was handled via a very strict accounting program, and the air force succeeded in getting rid of people in the service, but there were unintended consequences. I watched this system unfold and knew I was vulnerable to a less-than-sterling (silver bullet) report, especially since I was the new guy on the base.

I doubted I would fail my promotion to major, which was coming up, but for the first time, I felt that fate could play an ugly hand, regardless of my past performance. The system called for only so many one ratings, followed by only so many two ratings, and the rest would get threes. (There may have been four and five ratings, but I simply don't remember.) I knew we were a "selectively manned" unit, which meant our records were all pretty sterling to get in the door, and so many of us were in for a real psychological awakening when this system demanded that many of us would get threes. I began wondering about the Thunderbirds, who were in the same boat. If there were eight or so of them, probably only three of them would receive one ratings, maybe three more would get twos, and the others would get threes. Can you imagine being a Thunderbird and getting a three rating? The U2 drivers were in the same situation. *Everyone* was in the same situation, and the new guys on the base would take the brunt of the negative aspects of this new system. And I was a new guy. I use all this as a prelude to what happened next.

My promotion board would meet soon, and always preparing for the worst, I wondered what I would do if I failed to be promoted. As I mentioned earlier, in the air force (and, I think, in all the other services), if you failed promotion three years in a row, you would be eliminated from the service. This was not the case in the enlisted ranks. It was a tough system, but it was a competitive system and made for a pretty tough officer force. I always used to say I'd take five military officers and pit them against almost any five civilians—and the civilians could name their game. I respected the officer corps, especially of the US Air Force. I continued my thoughts about my future in light of this new system that would affect me in one way or another.

One day, Jo and I took a ride down to Sacramento just to get away from things. We drifted into old-town Sacramento, and while looking at the storefronts there, I noticed a stockbrokerage office. My subconscious was propelling me now, and I walked into the office and asked to speak to one of the office managers. Within fifteen minutes, this manager was taking me and about five of his colleagues to lunch. He told me I could go to their school to prepare for the Series 7 examination, which would make me a fledgling stockbroker within his firm. I could start work there whenever I decided to. *This is one of those few moments that come in a lifetime,* I thought. And now, as an old geezer, I can't help comparing my struggle to get into Beale with how easy this transition would be into the brokerage business. I suppose I just couldn't imagine not flying anymore; it truly had become my addiction. I thanked the gentleman for the lunch, offered to pay for it, and told him I probably would stay in the air force.

A few days later, I made a call to Western Airlines. When I got the office responsible for new hires, the man on the other end of the line asked, "How old are you?"

I said "Thirty-three."

He said, "Ah, our cutoff is thirty-two." That was that. There would be no airline job in my future. I had really never labored over the thoughts of an airline job, which was unusual as an aviator. Most in the flying business were there for one reason: to eventually get a commercial flying job with one of the big commercial carriers.

I guess my turning down the stockbrokerage job meant I was going to go through the evaluation process to see if I would make major. I thought I'd probably make it, because I had filled all the squares along the way, as we used to say. I had more combat time than almost anyone I knew, except Karl Polifka and Tony Reyna. I'd had a dual major in college, and I had a master's degree, thanks to Dr. Ross. I also had completed all professional military education (PME) appropriate to my rank and then some. These courses were divided into three general categories: a junior-grade school known as squadron-officers school (SOS), a midlevel school known as command and staff, and a senior-level school known as the air-war college. SOS was for the captains, command and staff was for the majors and lieutenant colonels, and air-war college was for colonels.

Interestingly, all three could be accomplished by the methods of correspondence, seminar, or in residence. I had finished SOS by correspondence, and later I had gone in residence. While still a captain, I had finished the command and staff by correspondence; in that regard, I knew I was ahead of most of my contemporaries. These schools were all very time-consuming and took some dedication to complete, mostly because with flying, one just didn't have the time for the PME study and paper writing required to get through them. Looking back on this, I realize I generally worked all week with flying preparation, studying, and testing, and then I worked all weekend much of the time on these PME schools. It would have been better for me to spend more time working on my marriage, although Jo had also kept very busy, working everywhere we went in the air force.

I made major and left Beale Air Force Base soon thereafter. It was wonderful having flown the T-38 again and the SR-71, but I can't say the political situation at Beale was good for me. I was sorry to leave these airplanes and many of the crew members and staff I had met. I had in fact become a habu (see glossary).

WAITING FOR THE NEXT ASSIGNMENT

I had one more episode with nonflying possibilities before I got to my next assignment. A high school friend of mine, Al Yanik, had been in the air force for about as long as I had. I forget how I ran into him again—fate, more than anything, I think. Al had become aware that I was looking for a job, and it just so happened he was responsible for some assignments within the air force, although not specifically for pilots or aircrews. He had been in the finance end of things and had handled some assignments for some officers in procurement—that is, assignments where officers would eventually be involved in buying items from the civilian world for use in military operations.

I smile when I think of our conversation. First of all, it felt good to be talking to someone I knew from Hubbard, of all places. And I knew that, while he had the air force's interests at heart, he was taking my interests into account as well. He looked at me, smiled, and said, "I know you, you SOB, and I know you probably still want to fly. But I can give you a job that will allow you to transition into civilian life in fine fashion at the end of your twenty years. You will be involved in procuring products for the air force.

"This will entail an interaction with civilian business, and you will gain a huge insight into the process, including how money is spent, where it is spent, and what products are purchased and by whom. When you are done with the air force, you can go to some of the biggest companies in America and work on the other side of the procurement business, and they pay a real decent salary. I know you probably won't do it, but you should."

I didn't do it.

PHANTOM, PART 2

My next phone call went to an operational RF-4 squadron at Shaw AFB in South Carolina. I really didn't know anybody there and was just calling around looking for a job. I always was aware that no matter what kind of job you wanted in the air force, unless it coincided with the needs of the air force, you wouldn't get it. In the course of this conversation, I asked to speak to the operations officer or the commander, and soon

I was talking to Lieutenant Colonel Paul Schmidt, the squadron commander. I was flabbergasted, because he had been my operations officer in Thailand when I was flying the RF-4 there. He actually sounded glad to talk to me, and when I told him I was looking for a job, he told me to let the assignments people know, and he would make sure I got placed directly in his squadron once the location of assignment was made. This was a breath of fresh air to me.

Soon Jo and I were packing things up for a move back to South Carolina. We had been living pretty conservatively all these years and decided that, if we could, we would buy a house. I took some leave and went to Columbia, South Carolina, to see if I could work out this house deal. I spent a week there, and by the end of the week, I had bought a house for approximately $60,000. For us, that was a large number at the time. We would live in an old neighborhood, and our neighbors would be pretty much hardcore southerners.

I was already familiar with the term *Yankee*, and it did not bother me to occasionally hear the term being bandied about. By now, I was fully aware of the influence of geography, nationally or internationally, on an individual's personality. Our neighbor had a tennis court and told us we could use it any time we cared to. Still, living in the heart of old Columbia, South Carolina, I kept thinking about the patch many fighter pilots proudly wore on their flight suits in Southeast Asia. It read "Yankee Air Pirate," and a skull and cross bones were emblazoned in the middle of the patch. Yankee Air Pirate was a name coined by the North Vietnamese and applied to any US military pilot of the day. I write this not to disparage the South Carolinians but just to reflect on the term *Yankee*.

The drive to Shaw AFB near Sumter, South Carolina, was about thirty to thirty-five miles on a straight, split four-lane highway. Because of this drive, I would receive numerous speeding tickets going to and from work. This was mostly because I was speeding, but having Ohio plates on my little pickup truck did not help me get by any of the South Carolina police either.

Then I met the guys and gals of the Eighteenth Tactical Reconnaissance Squadron. I was a flight commander for a while, and then I spent most of my time as an assistant operations officer. The Eighteenth would end up being the best flying job I would ever have in my life. I was back with my RF-4, and I had some familiarity with the squadron commander. I would soon meet the rest of the crews in the squadron. Most of these guys were very young. Most were academy grads, so most were lieutenants or very young captains. In short, I would have a ball with these guys.

Here I met Lieutenant Traylor, and despite our age difference, we would remain friends for the rest of my life. Kent Traylor was just out of the academy and nav school. He had graduated first in his navigator class and, despite his youth, seemed like he was much older when it came to analyzing situations, people, and the world in general. And he had a huge sense of humor. And then we flew together.

Kent could draw a picture of a map in the front seater's mind through words as you did your 540-knot, five-hundred-feet-above-ground-level, low-level missions. In that respect, he reminded me of my old back seater from Udorn, Lee VanNamen. I was astounded how they both could do this.

Again, it allowed me or whomever he was flying with to put the map to one side and concentrate on the mission at hand. Keeping your eyes out front was always important in flying, but it was even more so in this unforgiving, fast, low-level environment. Kent even drank Scotch, and by that time, I was drinking it too. He had a girlfriend, Carole, whom he had met there. She had a background in nursing but also had a show on TV that related to small children. They made a great couple. Kent's dad had been a lieutenant colonel and pilot in the air force, so Kent had been brought up speaking air force. His mom, Wendy, was something else, and I loved her. I think she was the reason for Kent's sense of humor, as well as other great personality traits.

We got a new operations officer about the time I got there, so I was going to have to be happy being his assistant for a while. If things worked out, I was hoping I could move into his job when he inevitably moved up to the squadron commander's job. The appeal of these jobs was that if you wanted to keep on flying as you made some of the ranks above major, these jobs ensured that you would—keep flying, at least for a while longer. Serving in these jobs also put the probability of promotion in your favor. The associated problem, however, was that everybody wanted these jobs. The competition was pretty fierce, and fate always played into these things.

I had to get requalified in the RF-4, and that brought on the usual flurry of studying. Jo, in the meantime had gotten another teaching job. We were enjoying living in a real house, but I didn't know how this house thing would work with my being in the air force. I thought maybe I could stay awhile in these RF-4 jobs and get some equity in our house at the same time.

Eventually my boss had me go through another checkout program. I was going to first go through the RF-4 instructor course, and then I was to be an air-to-air attack combat maneuver (ACM) instructor in the squadron. There would be two of us. Flying on a daily basis in an air-to-air environment would be the best flying I would ever be involved in.

The term *air to air* is foreign to many civilians, but another term for the same thing is *dogfighting*. If you Google "define dogfighting," you get this response: "A dogfight, or dog fight, is an aerial battle between fighter aircraft, conducted at close range. Dogfighting first appeared during World War I, shortly after the invention of the airplane." The military guys would almost never use the term *dogfight* these days, instead opting for the words *air-to-air encounter* or *air-to-air engagement*.

For me, having this job was very gratifying. I felt I had graduated into another level in the hierarchy of aviation. I feel compelled to define the many stages of aviation, *as I saw them* during my life. All aviators are proud and may be agitated at anyone's attempt to label these things, but I want to give you a glimpse into the aviator world and the hierarchy within, as I saw it:

Stage 1: These are the people who love to talk about aviation, the people who begin taking flight lessons, and the people who solo.

Stage 2: These are the people who fly the small single-engine airplanes known as general-aviation aircraft, or GA for short. These folks have FAA licenses.

Stage 3: These are the people who have learned to fly on instruments in weather. They study and are examined on their ability to understand and fly in weather conditions.

Stage 4: These are the people who have demonstrated an ability to fly airplanes with more than one engine. Once they master this, they take written and flight tests to get their multiengine ratings.

Stage 5: This stage is where an individual has done all the above. Be he or she civilian or military, he or she is ready to go make a living flying. This person may or may not become an instructor.

Stage 6: These pilots transport people, cargo, supplies, or equipment or instruct others in aviation and are now making a living from flying.

Stage 7: These pilots fly aircraft equipped with afterburners or other high-speed aircraft. They experience true three-dimensional flying and high speeds, often above the speed of sound, at this stage. Acrobatics of all types and high-G maneuvering become a part of daily activity at this stage.

Stage 8: These pilots fly fighter aircraft where the associated missions are bombing, firing missiles, or using
associated guns aboard the aircraft. The fighter pilots
in this community are part of a pretty small group.

Stage 9. I reserve this stage for those whose sole mission
is shooting down other airborne aircraft.

Stage 10. Only a few aviators in history have actually
shot another aircraft down. I put them in this category.
Air force pilots Richie, DeBellevue, Feinstein, and Olds
and navy pilot Cunningham and gib Driscoll are in this
category.

This covers the majority of aviation, although there is always
room for more conjecture on the subject. The commercial
guys and gals might say that flying large airliners with all the
new technology in all weather conditions is a tenth-stage job,
and test pilots at Edwards might be considered tenth, or even
eleventh, stagers. And of course the astronaut jobs place high,
possibly higher than any on this hierarchy. I'll let you place
the astronauts, test pilots, and large airliner pilots where you
think they belong. I've also left out the U2 and SR drivers. You
can figure out where they belong too. The helo drivers are
another discussion. I will defer on the subject: helicopters and
the aviators associated with them are a topic all their own.

I find the personalities of those in any stage of aviation
described here very interesting. That is, an aviator is an aviator, and there is a personality trait that seems to go along
with an aviator. What are some words that describe what I am

talking about? Many adjectives and phrases apply: focused, alive, generally proud, and most imbued with a huge sense of humor. These would certainly be some descriptors.

After that explanation, I can get back to discussing my job in South Carolina in an RF-4 reconnaissance squadron, after my SR-71 experience and after the Vietnam War. I was flying in this operational squadron as a major now. As I said, many of the crewmembers were lieutenants fresh out of the academy and recent grads from pilot or navigator training. Our job was much the same as I had in Asia, except no one was shooting at me. Most of our flying was at five hundred feet above ground level (AGL) or lower, at around 480 knots. We wanted the lieutenants to fly this low at 540 knots, but of course, this was peacetime.

Our job was still to get the pictures, and we used to joke that we would "kill 'em with fil-em." The exception to all this was that now I was often flying as an air-to-air attack combat maneuver instructor, and as I have said, this was the best flying job I ever had. How can I explain it?

Reconnaissance F-4s flew alone much of the time. That is, they had no wingman with them (again, most of the time), and the thought was that they might be vulnerable to attack by enemy aircraft. Since the RF-4 had no defensive armament, its only defense from an attacking aircraft was through defensive maneuvering. It was my job to expose these lieutenants to this experience. I found it interesting that, years earlier in training to fly the RF-4, we crewmembers had been given only one introductory flight to experience looking at an attacking aircraft coming at us. That was it. And off to Vietnam we went. Now, the reconnaissance guys were getting a quarterly exposure to this. With twenty to twenty-eight crews in the squadron, I had just about a full-time job doing this for about a year and a half.

I would take two aircraft out over the water off the East Coast to an area sealed off from other aircraft. It was a pretty large area. There I would "attack" them, using very basic attack maneuvers to demonstrate a missile attack or gun attack upon them. Obviously I still had no armament, but the important thing was for the lieutenants to see an aircraft coming at them from a hind quadrant at high speeds, including those above Mach 1. Their job was to initiate one of a few basic defensive maneuvers to escape the threat. It was here that I developed a deeper understanding of the air-to-air environment, and as the days went by, I could feel my sense of timing and proficiency increasing with a daily exposure to this. I felt I was approaching an understanding of what the dedicated air-to-air fighters did regarding this mission, and it was wonderful.

We examined all dimensions and capabilities of the aircraft, as the air-to-air mission is truly a physical and mental effort. High-G maneuvering and spatial awareness were essential to survival, even in this peacetime training environment. Because pilots spent a lot of time going straight up or straight down in this business, it was essential to keep the sky separated from the water. It was a phobia of mine that on a day when the sky color blended with the sea, the lieutenants or I would "recover" in the wrong direction and crash into the water, especially on a hazy or misty day. We had what we call a ten-thousand-foot floor while we were doing this, and if any airplane approached ten thousand feet from above, we would call a "knock it off" and resume the attacks only when stabilized. I can't help saying that someone not used to this would probably puke his or her guts out during the first maneuver—unless one is used to this environment, it is truly foreign. You just can't describe how a four- to five-G pull feels, and the human body seems to want to eject any food in the stomach unless the person is used to this. (It's worth noting that modern fighter pilots likely would scoff at these remarks, as with innovation, crews now fly regularly in a higher G-force regimen.) In a word, the air-to-air mission was *fun*, though I might also describe it as *addicting*.

Before I leave this topic, I want to mention something I will revisit later: throttle movements in fighters versus throttle movements in commercial aircraft. In fighters, when you want to increase or reduce power, you move the throttles at any rate you want (for the most part). In the air-to-air business, going from afterburner to idle power and vice versa is a common experience. In the commercial business, for the most part, this type of rapid throttle movement is just not done. This difference is mostly due to the engineering of the engines, as well as the mission types of the various aircraft. Of course, in the commercial flying business, the fact that you have passengers on board and flight attendants up and about the cabin requires gentle and limited throttle movements as well.

I would have thought the day-to-day RF-4 flying would have been enough for me, but it wasn't, and I learned that a small general-aviation airport there in Columbia had an open-cockpit Stearman biplane sitting in a hanger. I found that about four or five guys owned it together and soon joined their ranks. The cost was reasonable, and I eventually checked out in the open-cockpit machine. The horsepower, I think, was about 220, and the max speed, according to some sources, was 186 miles per hour. Early on, I was flying with an "instructor" at the controls when we hit the top of a tree during take-off from one of the other local airports. We did some damage to the bottom wing, but we made it back to our own airport. So much for instructors, at least on that day.

As I had throughout my life, after I joined the Eighteenth Tactical Reconnaissance Squadron, I found myself analyzing my colleagues' personalities. For brevity I will try to limit my observations to just a few.

Pictured here is Kent Traylor, also known as Trayls or Elephant Man. Trayls, now a colonel, is on the right, and my friend and SR-71 driver Buzz Carpenter is on the left.

First and foremost, there was the Elephant Man, Kent Traylor, or Trayls. He had just graduated from the Air Force Academy and was first in his navigator-training class. It was this caliber of lieutenant that we had in our back seats in the RF-4. Why the name Elephant Man? Early on, Kent, for some reason, had developed a close association to elephants. And he could imitate the sound of an elephant. You never knew when he would begin his elephant calls, but once he started, you also never knew when he would quit.

I shared an office with the squadron-operations officer, and one day, we heard Kent begin his elephant calls out in the hallway. I looked at the ops officer, because I knew he had never witnessed this. I looked at him and asked, "You think he is going to stop, don't you?" He just sat with a quizzical look on his face. *Brrrup, brrrup, brrrrrrrup.* And so on. And on and on and on. At some point, even a military officer in charge of a flying squadron has got to laugh, as did our ops officer. It was a riot. And you never knew when the next elephant act would begin all over again.

Kent was very smart, very social, and the only navigator I knew who operated as superbly as my old navigator, Lee VanNamen. One day I told the ops officer that if he wanted a treat, he should fly with Kent on a low-level route to see how good he was. He did and was as impressed as I was. One question comes quickly: Why didn't Kent go to pilot training after the academy? All you had to do was look at him and see his large prescription glasses to know the answer: he didn't have the eyesight to get into pilot training. But then something great happened. The squadron commander, the operations officer, and I composed a letter to go up the chain of command that basically requested Kent be given a waiver on his eyesight so he could go to pilot training. I never thought it would work, mainly because after about twelve years in the air force, I had never heard of anything like this happening. Before it was all over, however, the Elephant Man received a letter from the surgeon general's office of the US Air Force giving him an eyesight waiver. We were happy but stunned. I have never heard of such a thing happening since.

Kent and I had already become friends, despite our rank and age differences, and we have remained friends ever since. Kent went on to pilot training, graduating first in his class, and then he moved on to the type of flying I had always wanted to do. He flew a single-seat fighter, the F-15, and eventually became an F-15 squadron commander. He continued on to a very great career. Pat and I would attend his retirement ceremony in Colorado years later. He and his twin brother, Scott, were born on my birthday, and to this day, I usually send a happy birthday wish to at least Kent.

His wife, Carole, is quite accomplished in her own right, completing a PhD in the nursing field, learning to play the violin, being a mother and a willing partner totally involved in the frequent moves, and managing a household and other responsibilities associated with being the wife of a career air force officer. And, oh yes, she has the sense of humor to deal with the Elephant Man.

Another young guy in the RF-4 squadron was a mild-mannered and relatively quiet lieutenant by the name of Carl Meade. How can I possibly make it short? Carl wanted to be an engineer. He didn't have the funds to go to school, but those near him told him that maybe the air force would help pay for his education if he joined ROTC. I think this actually did happen to some extent, even though those of my era received no stipend at all. Carl said that when he graduated with a degree in engineering, he thought he likely would be assigned as an engineer. He was not. He was sent to pilot training. Most aspiring aviators would have *paid* for an assignment to pilot training, but this was Carl. As he told me his story, he sounded disappointed that he had gotten an assignment to pilot training and not to engineering. So he went to pilot training, where he ranked very high in his class and was given this RF-4 assignment. He was still a lieutenant when I met him, and I asked what he saw in his future. He said he hoped he would eventually get involved in engineering. As an aviator, I couldn't get over how easily Carl dismissed the fact that he was a very young lieutenant flying such an outstanding jet in the USAF. His love of engineering was obvious and overwhelming. Fast-forward several years.

Carl went to the test-pilot school at Edwards Air Force Base, and surprise, surprise, he graduated very high in his class—high enough, in fact, that he was asked to become an instructor there at Edwards. I remember talking to him about his experience going through his initial test-pilot training. He said he was flying numerous aircraft and that, at that point, he was doing spin tests on A-7s. (These are subsonic fighters and are single-seat aircraft.) He noted that an instructor in another A-7 would fly next to you and be there to assist with commentary on your first takeoff and your first landing. He said his spin tests began on his second flight in the A-7. He was required to take down a lot of written data during the spin, so he could make a report on it, as the school required of him. In the middle of the spin, he was asking himself how he was ever going to land this airplane. This would be only his second landing in the airplane, and he did not have an instructor or anybody else on his wing. All went well. Fast-forward a few more years.

While reading an *Air Force Times*, I was reviewing a list of selections for astronaut pilots and mission specialists. Carl was on both lists. Forward another year or so.

I went to the Cape to watch Carl blast off for a mission into space. He would be one of the first to go untethered on a spacewalk. This would be followed by two more trips into space. I have lost track of Carl, but I remember him being interviewed on TV after one of his journeys. Someone asked a question regarding emergencies on the shuttle, and Carl looked into the camera and said, as only he could, "Well, if there is a fire up there, we can't call nine-one-one, you know!"

While Carl was an astronaut, he had a very old car—so old, in fact, that on cold days, he had to put a bunch of winter clothes on to keep warm, because his car window would not roll up. One day he was stopped by a policeman and frisked because he looked like a drug dealer rather than an astronaut. When the police asked him what he did for a living, he said, "I'm in transportation." Before it was all over, they found that the policeman's wife worked in the astronaut office. Carl finally traded that car in one day after his young son asked when he was going to get rid of it.

There are many more stories regarding the personalities within our Eighteenth Tac Recon Squadron. Russ twirled the ops officer, "Buddha," around his arm like a propeller one day, and I'll never know how he did that. "Hollywood" was a captain in the squadron too. He was complete with extra-wide sunglasses, wavy black hair, and a gold neck chain, and he always wore his flight-suit collar popped up. Of course he had a mustache too. "FSquared" was a rather quiet navigator who, when asked where his stopwatch was, said it was in the dry cleaner's. "Rabi" was another energetic academy grad, pilot, and lieutenant. Joe Matthews could play the guitar and hold court with such things as *The Book of Lists* as a springboard for philosophical discussion. Things like that always seemed to play out around the front desk, where crews received last-minute briefings, where the scheduling board was that told who was flying with whom and what airplane they were going to use, and where crews congregated during times when the weather was just too bad to fly.

"Mastro" liked to quote various leadership sources. This always seemed to come from "offstage," like out in the hallway, away from the front desk. It often seemed pretty loud, despite his otherwise calm demeanor. One such announcement was George Orwell's proclamation that "men sleep peacefully in their beds at night because rough men stand ready to do violence on their behalf." I must say that, because of distractions in the squadron, most of us wondered what the hell Mastro was saying during these soliloquies. Usually, most of us would pause whatever we were doing and try to listen and make sense of it. After talking to Mastro forty years later, I have finally seen the quotes written in black and white and have viewed the sources. He says these were a few quotes among many he had been required to memorize while at the Air Force Academy. I could go on forever. We also had a captain we referred to as the "yeah/no man." If you asked him a simple yes/no question, his answer was often "yeah...no." He later made it into the general ranks. Joe Matthews and another outstanding lieutenant at the time, Curt Osterheld, would both become SR-71 crewmembers years later.

Here among the lieutenants, while flying these air-to-air attack combat-maneuver training sorties, I had the best time of my air force career.

And then we were told the squadron was going to close. The reconnaissance business was getting smaller and smaller, at least as far as manned recon goes. The satellite business seemed to be taking over for us RF-4 drivers. The SR-71 and the U2s were still flying.

BACK TO ASIA AGAIN
As the reality of our squadron's shutting down set in, I contemplated my future in the air force. I felt I was starting to lose interest. I made a call to a guy I knew and asked him about a job at the Air Force Academy. I think I may have tried to get a job as an ROTC professor of air science. I had flown some very good airplanes and was getting too old to even try to get into the air-to-ground bomb-dropping business, let alone the real air-to-air fighter business. I had experienced Mach 3 and eighty thousand feet in the SR-71 and had flown a multitude of Mach 1.6 functional-check flights in the RF-4, as well as hundreds of low-level flights in it. "Staff work" was looming, and the place for that was at the Pentagon. Most of the people who loved flying found it very hard to contemplate staff work, but I heard that, to make general rank, you had to spend some time at the Pentagon.

And then my phone rang. It was a staff officer who worked for a general I had known at Beale AFB when he was a bird colonel. He said he was calling me on this general's behalf and making it known that, in light of my squadron closing down, there was a job waiting for me working for the general at the Pentagon. I was very surprised, but the clock was ticking. After about ten seconds, I told the major on the other end of the phone to thank the general for the thought, but I wasn't interested in the job. And then we hung up. This may have been a big mistake, but I had never planned to spend more than twenty years in the service. I think I was still numb to the notion that my real flying in the air force was ending.

For a while, the assignment people at Randolph AFB in Texas were talking about sending me to an Air National Guard unit as the active-duty instructor flying the RF-4. These were known to be good jobs, but gradually these jobs seemed to evaporate. And gradually, I just waited for an assignment—whatever it was to be. I had spent so much time over the years trying to affect my assignments; I was tired of it all. So I waited.

And soon I was going to Asia again. This time Jo and I would go to Clark Air Base in the Philippines (PI). I would have one of the first accompanied tours to the PI, which meant Jo would go with me. Since it was accompanied, it would be a three-year assignment. I had already spent two full years in Asia; this would make it a total of five. I guess maybe the Pentagon would have been better. Who knows?

Duty Title: chief of operations and plans, Cope Thunder

o 6200 Tactical Fighter Squadron, Pacific Air Forces (PACAF). Clark Air Base, Philippines o   Directs tactical operations and planning activities for PACAF's Cope Thunder combat-readiness training program

o   May 20, 1979, to May 19, 1982

Although I would again check out in the T-33 for proficiency flying, my primary job was as chief of operations for an exercise called Cope Thunder. It was a staff job.

The job in the Philippines was interesting, but as with the job with the basic trainees, my primary job was not flying. The hardcore aviators in the military always considered a successful career one where they spent twenty years with the primary job of flying. Not many pulled this off. Of course, this was almost impossible, but at each interlude in nonflying jobs, one paused and reflected on this continuing metamorphosis. For the more realistic career person, tours at the Pentagon became a stepping-stone to get to the general ranks. Few seemed to make it to those ranks without the crucible of the Pentagon. Even then, few made it.

I proceeded to check out in the T-33 again in order to maintain proficiency in flying. A few interesting things happened in those three years with the T-33. In my life of flying, I lost all lights during a night flight only once. It was while out over the Pacific Ocean, at least fifty miles offshore. The good news was that I had a flashlight with me, and it illuminated my instrument panel well enough to get me back to Clark Field. Another incident in the Philippines was more serious. I forget how many T-33s we had, but I doubt it was more than five, so I had a 20 percent chance of being involved in the following story. A young guy was flying around over land. As he went into a hard turn, he heard what sounded like an explosion. I don't know what his engine instruments looked like, but as he looked around to survey his situation, he noticed that the entire back end of the airplane had departed. It was gone. His only choice was to bail out. He survived it all nicely and lived to tell about it. As I got older, I realized I was spending more time analyzing these percentages, and I often wondered what my chances were of surviving a twenty-year career in the US Air Force.

Another time, higher headquarters visited for an inspection. Part of this involved inspecting the T-33 operation, the airplanes, and the aviators who flew them. I happened to be sitting in the back of a little operations area while the inspectors were reading through some files regarding our T-33 activities. I heard one of the inspectors speaking to another. He said something like, "Wow, here is a guy who was flying the SR-71 a few years ago, and now he's here flying the T-33." I felt the same way. Wow. Such is life, I guess. Before it was all over, he chose to give me a check ride. That went well, but to be honest, check rides were not my forte. As a matter of fact, I disdained them.

COPE THUNDER

How do I boil down three years at Clark Air Base? I was put in charge of a group of guys who were responsible for planning mock-combat scenarios. These scenarios would then be implemented with live aircrews and aircraft from all over the Pacific. The exercises were very similar to those conducted at Nellis Air Force Base in Nevada, including one called "Red

Flag." Cope Thunder and Red Flag had similar, if not identical, objectives. The primary objective of both was to expose aircrews to realistic combat training that would help them survive actual combat, should they find themselves involved in a conflict in the future. Statistics, we were told, showed that, in actual combat, crews were far more likely to be shot down during their first ten missions than at any other time. So if aircrews could experience at least ten missions in Cope Thunder or Red Flag, the hope was that survival rates would increase during actual combat. I feel certain this hope turned into reality as time passed.

History has never been a favorite subject of mine, but Clark Air Base has its place in history, not unlike the Philippines itself. I worked in a building I imagine was probably built sometime during the early 1900s. The officers' club was not far away, with a nearby pool and tennis court readily available. Clark had an aristocratic feel to it, though the ghosts of World War II loomed large about it. The flagpole that stood between our building and the sprawling parade field seemed to scream out about the thousands of US flags that had been raised during World War II and all the years since, as well as about the thousands of troops that had been assembled on that field.

The officers' club was reminiscent of our strong military. It was equipped for a large clientele and handled meetings and parties of almost any sort. A large dance floor was part of the club, and several nights a week, a live orchestra of about twenty pieces played at the club. The music and the orchestra personnel reminded me eerily of the music or movies popular in the 1940s, though they were always very professionally presented. If you are wondering about the cost of something like this, I can tell you it was pretty inexpensive; after all, as in most developing countries, the standard of living for most of the locals was so low that labor of any sort came unbelievably cheap, even for orchestra members. By way of comparison, I can tell you about the cost of playing tennis. I often hired a pro and a couple of ball boys and rented the court for about three dollars an hour—total. The Filipinos were as happy to get this amount as we were to give it, and this standard of living permeated most other activities as well.

The joke among many of the officers was that if they could come back to this life as anything they wanted, it would be as an officer's wife at Clark Air Base. Most officers had a guard for the house at night and a full-time housemaid, and many of their houses included maid's quarters. Many had "sew girls," who would come to the house and measure you for clothes, which they would make on the spot. The point was that the economics of it all were so out of balance that the marketplace was unbelievably cheap to the Americans residing in the Philippines. And most of the wives did not work. Jo, of course, worked full time the whole time we were there, as a teacher for DOD, and then the Assistant to the Area Director for Los Angeles Community College.

My tours in Vietnam, Thailand, and Puerto Rico mimicked this out-of-balance marketplace situation as well, but since the Vietnam War was over, the experience in the Philippines seemed that much more exaggerated to me. The naval bases at Cubi Point and Subic were similarly iconic, beautiful bases, and to say they were manicured would be an understatement.

My job? I would spend much of these three years at a desk on the second floor of a historic Thirteenth Air Force building at the end of the parade field. Five other desks adjoined mine. That is, six desks sat against one another, and one of the six was mine. At each desk sat a unique individual. Given a choice to have cubicles and all that entails, we repeatedly chose this close desk configuration. I was a reconnaissance guy for sure, but my background as a combat veteran, an air-to-air attack instructor in the RF-4, a forward air controller, and even as a KC-135 driver all had a place in the combat-scenario creativity that went into each Cope Thunder exercise. On my left sat an F-4 guy, and to *his* left sat John, a Ground Control Intercept (GCI) controller.

John was the only one at the desks without wings, but he was very familiar with the methods by which one aircraft is vectored to another aircraft, be it for air refueling or for adversarial reasons. John was good at what he did and was good at dealing with the fighter-pilot bravado that existed both around our desks and among the hundreds of fighter pilots who showed up at our Cope Thunder exercises. Vectors from ground- or air-based radar controllers remained a primary means for a fighter pilot to gain either radar or a visual acquisition of airborne targets.

On John's left was Doc. Doc was a fighter pilot but also was serving as an aggressor pilot. (Aggressor pilots, in my opinion, were at the top of the fighter-pilot hierarchy, and Doc exhibited all the traits associated with that category of pilot. The aggressor's sole job was to attack other aircraft and, in the process, mimic tactics of possible foreign adversaries. They were good. They were proficient, and in a war, they could be very deadly.)

Next to Doc sat Kit or Frank, depending on when we are talking about. Kit had been an aggressor pilot and now was only flying the T-33 for proficiency. Frank had been an F-4 pilot. On my right sat one of three guys, also depending on which year we are talking about. All three had been F-4 gibs or weapon system operators. I spent more time with Paul than I did with the other two. We six would figure out who was going to participate in our exercise, what airplanes they would bring with them, and what the air war would look like for each day of the approximately two-week exercise. It was a good job—though once again—flying was not my primary duty.

We used a vast array of aircraft and aircrews in our exercises, and some foreign countries also participated in our Cope Thunders. I still have a T-shirt that had "I love the smell of jet fuel in the morning" printed on the back. That just about said it all. The environment was very reminiscent of my days back at Udorn, Thailand, with multitudes of aircraft, crews, missions, and jet noise.

Colonel Hoppe became our boss. I had a lot of respect for him, because he had been flying for twenty years prior to pinning on his eagles. His most recent job, as I understood it, was as a squadron commander of an A-7 unit, a single-seat fighter unit with a bomb-dropping mission. Rest assured that he had spent a fair amount of time doing a lot of one-versus-one air-to-air setups. (This is when one aircraft attacks another repeatedly for the purpose of helping aircrews learn how to cope with an attacking aircraft in the air.) Colonel Hoppe had a quiet demeanor, and despite any preconceived notions we might have had of fighter pilots, his telltale smile foretold another personality underlying it all. He also looked like a pro football player, and his wide shoulders barely fit into the Volkswagen he drove around Clark Air Base. His office had a doorway that allowed him to look directly out at our six desks. Just having that view kept him apprised of things we were doing in real time. Colonel Hoppe was cool too.

Once, over about a three-day period, he interviewed secretaries. Whoever his selection would be, she eventually would sit out in our open space within a few feet of our desks. Early on, one of my guys put a projector on his desk that projected "foils" up on the wall. We merely used a grease pencil to write down the main points of a briefing and projected it on a wall. Well, when a secretary applicant would walk down our large room and turn into Colonel Hoppe's office for her interview, my guy would project the picture of a hand with its thumb extended on the wall. By rotating the foil, he could make the projection appear as a thumbs-down, a sideways thumb, or a thumbs-up vote. For two days, the best vote registered was a sideways thumb. Colonel Hoppe pretended to not observe the four-foot-high wall projection of a thumb outside his office, but on the third day, someone finally got a thumbs-up. And Colonel Hoppe hired her. And she was great. She put up with our BS, typed like a maniac, and had a giggle going on most of the time. To this day, I wonder if corporations should use this method of hiring, despite all its seeming shortcomings. In our case, it could not have worked out better.

Reflections about my time at Clark Air Base have tended toward the humorous thus far, but I shouldn't forget the training taking place at Cope Thunder. We always had a lot of briefings before the missions, and we held lessons-learned debriefings after the missions. With a few hundred guys involved, we all learned from these. After all, a lot of beautiful aircraft were involved in our exercises, and most of the crews were fighter pilots. They worked and played hard.

One guy named Kevin was an aggressor pilot, like Doc. But Kevin, despite his place in the hierarchy of pilots, was so reserved that he caught my attention. During his visits, he was just a captain in rank. Many years later, I ran into him and found him wearing one star, signifying his rank as a brigadier general. Years after that, he would be a four-star general. *Good for him*, I thought. *One of the good guys made it.* I knew so many officers, and so very few were promoted into the general ranks. Upon further examination of his career, I discovered that he had spent more than ten years as an astronaut and in his early days had been an RF-4 pilot. He'd also graduated number one in his class when he attended the test pilot school. I guess my elaboration on Kevin Chilton goes to the notion that *reserved* aviators can prevail amidst all the hubbub of competition among the fighter-pilot class of aviators. Again, I applaud Kevin Chilton.

Cope Thunder was one of few environments in which a fighter pilot could flourish without actually being in combat. There were the air-to-air scenarios, close air-support scenarios, and the scenarios in which aircraft would be tracked by ground-to-air shoulder-fired missiles. Multiple bomb loads would be simulated, and we integrated some air-refueling missions into some of the missions. Even B-52 crews got involved in some of our exercises. The air force played the biggest part in our exercises, but the navy, the marine corps, and some foreign services participated in our exercises too.

It is very difficult to explain any of these missions to a civilian. That probably sounds arrogant, but the chief thing lacking in any description is the physical exertion required in many of these missions, let alone the mental effort—at least for the fighter type aircraft. Aircraft pulling three, four, and five Gs amid air engagements were common in the fighter business, and high G maneuvering was an inevitable part of Cope Thunder. Here's an unsophisticated metaphor in an attempt to bring adequate description to all this: The movie *Top Gun* was a good advertisement for the navy, and I thought the way it brought civilians into the cockpit was good; however, a movie can't portray the physical effort going on in most fighter cockpits. It's impossible to describe, I think.

Mostly unrelated to these missions were our T-33 missions. We often went out to an area where the GCI controllers would vector us on one another for their practice and ours, even though the T-33 was not capable of the performance of the F-15s, F-16s, F-4s, RF-4s, F-14s, AV8s, T-38s, and other aircraft that participated in Cope Thunder. One day the only two people in the practice area were Colonel Hoppe in one T-33 and I in another. I will just say that when we merged, I was behind him. Twenty minutes later, he was behind me. I'd known he probably was good, but I still was surprised. I thought even more of him after that. And it bugs the crap out of me to this day.

On another day, I was out in the practice area with a pilot named Fred in my back seat. Fred had F-4 experience. I was joining up on another T-33 for some formation flying, and as I came toward the other T-33, I began pulling the power back to slow down for the join up. As I did this, I felt the throttle stop, as if Fred was keeping me from pulling the power back. (The front and rear throttles were joined together functionally.)

The short story is that, in his F-4 days, he always had wanted crisper formation join ups, and it bothered him that most guys pulled power back at the same place I did. I let him know I didn't appreciate what he'd done. We could have had a bigger problem. A few years later, I heard Fred was in another F-4 squadron and had a midair collision. I always wondered if it was because he pressed the join up. I also wondered if he survived.

There were always a multitude of things happening in Cope Thunder; some were good, and some were bad. Our little group worked hard to prepare these exercises. But no matter how hard we worked, things happened that were beyond anyone's control. It was an incredibly busy environment, You had the navy coming from a ship, from Subic Bay, or from Cubi Point. The Thai Air Force might be bringing some aircraft and pilots in while simulated bomb loads were being sorted out. In addition, air battles needed to be balanced or purposely not balanced, KC-135s and B-52s were participating, and forward air control targets were being set up. All this activity kept us all interested in what was going on.

The question always arose as to how much of this needed to be briefed to our higher-ups. In order to handle this, we developed a method, unorthodox as it was. It was called the Lions versus Christians scoreboard. The scoreboard hung on our wall with a grease pencil next to it, and a rag for erasing also hung nearby. When we posted the scoreboard on a daily basis, it turned out that the higher-ups would come by, take a look at the scoreboard, and ask us what had caused the scoring changes that particular day. This kept them involved, and we didn't have to set aside big formal briefings for this. An example might be if, two days before the exercise, the navy pulled out of participation with six to twelve aircraft and aircrews. This would cause a big strain on our small system, and we'd scramble to realign the plans for this missing part of some combat scenario. Something like this would go down as a point for the Lions, because it caused the "Christians"—us planners—to do a lot of work at the last minute. Sometimes I wish I had that scoreboard in my house! (And I think big business might also consider it.)

At a formal affair of ours at Cope Thunder, we all sat down for a dinner. As is the case with most formal military affairs, the formality dissipates as the evening goes on. And eventually the dinner rolls began to fly, and Colonel Hoppe was hit by a high-speed roll. He laughed it off, and of course, all the other officers and their wives continued to have a great time. The next day, Colonel Hoppe walked into work with his left eye swollen closed from the roll hit. Nothing was said. A few months later, we had another formal party. Colonel and Mrs. Hoppe sat down and seemed to be engrossed in going through a bag they had brought with them. They donned goggles as dinner was being served. What a riot.

Some New Zealand fighter pilots showed up at one of our exercises with their A-4s—the same kind of aircraft John McCain was flying when he got shot down. It was also the same type of airplane James Stockdale had flown the day *he* got shot down. Coincidentally, both had flown off the aircraft carrier USS *Oriskany*. Back to the New Zealanders. I spent a lot of time with them, and one of their guys and I became close during this short time frame. Somewhere along the line, he asked if I wanted to fly with them. Of course I did, but the last time

I'd checked, the A-4 had only one seat. They had a two-seater with them, and that would be our bird for the day. He let me fly in formation with them, and I got to see firsthand how an A-4 drops some cement bombs. As a reconnaissance guy, I had been in only two aircraft dropping live bombs, or cement bombs. The other time was in an A-37 in Vietnam one time. I even have a certificate for the A-37 mission, given to me by the squadron. Anyway, before the New Zealanders left, one of them climbed up on the stage at the officers' club, took the microphone, and dedicated a song to me. (We had had a few.) He was good, the orchestra was good, and we had a great time. It was a great day for an aviator.

We had maintenance people attached to us permanently, but each unit also brought some maintenance people too. Our maintenance people were separated from us and worked closer to the flight line, while we remained in our "headquarters" building most of the time, especially during the Cope Thunder planning phase. One time we had some time on our hands and decided to requisition maintenance for a few things. Our formal request to them was for two crystal balls and two magic wands. In a few days, we received a formal response. It read something like this: "Due to increased demand in these uncertain times, we are temporarily out of crystal balls and magic wands. As soon as we can, we will forward them to you."

Our range, Crow Valley, was a huge piece of land dedicated to supporting our bombing combat scenarios. Scouring the Internet reveals that it was over forty-four thousand acres in size. Each day a range officer and supporting personnel would travel to Crow Valley to do several things. We took an audio-visual crew there to tape each airplane as it approached and then dropped bombs on the targets, and we had bomb scores tabulated on each bomb. Although our methods were rudimentary, an individual with a map and a pencil would keep tabs of where each bomb fell on the range. No technology was used in this endeavor, except that we did have a fax-like system to send the scores back to Clark, so they could be used in mission debriefings. Other personnel included those with shoulder-mounted missile launchers, inert of course, but they assessed which aircraft they thought were vulnerable to these weapons while in a combat area. There were other functions being performed, but to be honest, I forget what they were.

Getting to Crow Valley was not easy. We left Clark at about 4:30 in the morning to get to Crow Valley in time for operations to begin. We used a couple of four-wheel vehicles to get there, and our route took us into what seemed like another universe. As we traveled through jungle like areas, we would see the thatched-roof abodes of the local natives. The children, hearing our vehicles, would run to the often muddy road excitedly and yell, "Hey, Joe! Hey, Joe!" As I thought about the Philippines and World War II, I wondered, *Could this be some throwback to the term* GI Joe? Anytime I went to Crow Valley, that scene was the same: kids chasing our vehicles with outstretched hands and bare feet and wearing only a pair of shorts. On my first visit, I saw some in our crew reach into their packs and pull out small Hershey bars, which they would throw to the children as we made our way through the jungle.

On this last portion of our route, there were no cars or motorized vehicles of any kind. We seldom saw any adults on our way to Crow Valley, but if we did, they were usually tending to a water buffalo, back in the trees near their minimal homes. Remember this was 1979 to 1981. But here there were no telephones of any sort, no vehicles, and no real civilization. It was truly amazing. Eventually we would drive through our two adjacent bombing ranges and then begin the ascent to our perch overlooking the Crow Valley, where thousands of acres stretched before us. We could vividly see the two ranges and, separating them, the road we had just driven on. I would not call range-officer duty good duty, but we shared it among my guys primarily.

Colonel Hoppe volunteered to be range officer one day. He knew it was crappy duty, but that was another reason I liked him. We obliged and put him on the schedule. And then the following scenario developed: All went well for Colonel Hoppe until midday. A forward air controller had fighters on station and was briefing them on a particular target on our range. We had many lifelike targets on our range; trucks were among them. The forward air controller briefed the fighters on this truck target. Well, the short story is that the fighters went after a real truck coming through our access road and put a few cement bombs right through somebody's truck. There were no injuries, but there was a change to the scoreboard: another point for the Lions. Someone heard Colonel Hoppe say, "You can take this range-officer job and shove it," or something to that effect.

On another day at the range, a navy flight of two approached the range for a preplanned attack on a couple of targets. Reviewing the tape later, we all would watch as the leader made an approach and an uneventful bombing run on a target. His wingman went high, waiting for the leader to come off the target. Then the wingman rolled inverted and proceeded to do a split-S maneuver toward his target. There was a problem, however: he had started the maneuver too low. As he now approached the target, he was trying to finish the bottom of the split-S. He had the nose up, and to the casual observer, it looked like this was going to be a well-executed maneuver. However, the downward-vector momentum was too great. With the nose up, the aircraft plummeted into the ground at a very high speed and burst into flames. The aircraft and pilot literally disintegrated.

The tape of this terrible incident was used for years at Cope Thunder to remind our fearless fighter pilots of the unforgiving nature of the fighter business. Combat losses were terrible. Peacetime losses were tragic. Fighter pilots can be a loud and haughty bunch, especially the young ones, but the tape of the exploding navy aircraft quieted the Cope Thunder briefing room—with its hundreds of pilots and crews—every time without fail.

One day some navy officers came to me and suggested that we might consider using one of their bombing ranges as an alternative to our own Crow Valley Bombing Range. They mentioned that I would need to get approval from the navy side of the house. This sounded like a creative alternative for our crews, and I was motivated to do this. Soon I found myself talking to some navy commander about the use of two islands off the coast of Subic Bay. The commander said he would approve the use of the small islands under the condition that air force supervisory personnel would observe and coordinate flights on this bombing range. I told him we could do that, but I questioned how we could get to this island overlooking the bombing-range island. He assured me this was no problem. He said that once I gave him the time and the place for the pickup of our personnel, he would have a helicopter pick them up and drop them off. I thought that here was another example of how the navy seemed to move quicker than the air force to accomplish such things.

Well, on the designated day at the designated time, the navy chopper picked me and a few others up to take us to our island. This was different for an aging air force guy, yet it was a pleasant respite.

We hovered over a very small island and finally touched down on top of a very steep peak on top of a hill. I spent some time getting my footing under the helo before I let go. Others did the same. Dust was everywhere. We held our equipment as the helo added power and departed in a huge cloud of dust. I had assumed all along that this island had to be uninhabited, but as the dust began to settle, I thought I could see an outline of a human about twenty yards away from where we stood. When I could finally see, I determined it was a young girl of about ten or twelve years old. In front of her was a Styrofoam cooler. I looked at her intently, wondering what she was doing out there. She reached into the cooler, picked up a bottle, and asked, "You want Coke?" Now *that* should have been a Coke commercial. Of course there was no ice in the cooler, but there was Coke.

I later determined that there was a little village on the other side of this small island, and to this day, I wonder how the residents subsisted out there. The bombing range worked out well for Cope Thunder, but I don't think we used it very often. A picture of that helo ride with the navy and the little "you want Coke" girl will stay in my head forever.

Background noise in our high-intensity work area was always interesting. One guy on our floor kept yelling intermittently, "Book two to Bogotá." And we would laugh. Another guy, upon seeing one of the secretaries, would comment, "Here comes Darlene, the slinky machine." And we would laugh.

Paul, the major who sat on my right for a couple of years, whittled on a piece of bamboo one day. This bamboo was about eighteen inches long. At first he whittled on the end of it, so it looked like a pickle button, a button in an aircraft used to drop ordinance. Relieving stress was a good thing, so nothing was said about the stick—at least, not at first. Paul smoked a lot, and he would monkey around with that stick, and then he would smoke as he worked on a day's combat-scenario plan. (I will digress momentarily to say that Paul was also unique in that he had been to the fighter-weapons school in Nevada, a school all the fighter guys wanted to attend. It was an esteem marker for the fighter guys to indicate that they had attended a graduate-level course on advanced training in weapons and tactics. It included academics and flying in order to inculcate lessons taught at the school. Those who did attend this school proudly wore a patch on their flight suits that indicated that they were a graduate of the school. Not all fighter pilots went to the school, and as a reconnaissance guy, I would never attend.)

Soon Paul's stick began to take on a life of its own. It was a simulated chair adjuster. With tin foil attached, it became a simulated radar site. Sometimes it became a simulated flute. Like I said, the stress relief was a good thing, and when it came to the stick, there were no boundaries. With any unsolvable problems that arose among us someone would eventually yell out "Get the stick; get the stick!"

When I was getting ready to leave for my next assignment, I took the stick downtown and had a local craftsman manufacture a rather formal-looking box. In the rectangular box, he attached the stick on top of a deep-blue felt background. It was then encased in glass. I got an engraver to write the following on a brass metal attachment, which I placed on the front of the glass: IN CASE OF EMERGENCY, BREAK GLASS.

We had a lot of fun in Cope Thunder, but I wanted a primary flying job. With reconnaissance squadrons closing now as a result of all the satellites, my flying options were diminishing, and I was feeling burned out.

Jo and I both worked very hard there at Clark. On weekends and evenings, I worked on a seminar I was taking: the air-war college. This took up nights and weekends for a year or so. Jo continued to work in an education capacity there. I must admit that I should have known more about what she did in this job.

In some ways, the work paid off. At about midnight one night, we awoke to somebody knocking loudly on our door. This was odd. I went to the door and opened it to find Colonel Hoppe and his wife, Bobby, standing there. Well, you don't let your boss stand outside in the dark. They sat down, and they had our attention. Soon Colonel Hoppe asked what time it was. It was something like 12:05, or 0005 in military time. He smiled and said, "Well, you know the promotion list is out effective today, and we just wanted to be the first to announce to you that you have been promoted to lieutenant colonel. Before midnight we were not allowed to tell you."

I had been in the air force now for about sixteen years. Looking back, I had probably given the air force too much of me. Put another way——— "Yes, I was a prostitute for the air force." Mostly, I did whatever they wanted, although they reciprocated by letting me fly some unbelievable airplanes. Let there be no doubt I was appreciative of the promotion, and I loved the airplanes I flew. Soon we would leave Cope Thunder.

For a while, I thought I might be assigned as the full-timer at an Air National Guard unit. These were good jobs, as I would be flying the RF-4 again as an instructor. The day-to-day operations of guard units were focused on flying, unlike a lot of active-duty squadrons, where people seemed to get tied up in red tape. At least, that was my perception. The bases the air force was considering sending me to were in Kentucky and Nebraska. I would have liked the job, but it seemed to evaporate once I mentioned I would clean floors in order to get to any base in northern California. "What about Monterey, California?" the assignment person asked.

I said, "I am ready for that." And I honestly didn't care what I would be doing there. I guess I was done, and I was ready to put in my last four years in the air force and get on with the next thing in life. Pensions came after twenty years in the service, and I'd never thought of spending more than twenty. Viewing this through an economic lens, the thought for me was always--*all I had to do to collect half my pay for the rest of my life was to—retire.* Compared to executives in business or even the police and firefighters, the military pension below the general ranks was not huge. Many officers liked to stay for about twenty-seven years, because at that point, they would receive 75 percent of their pay in retirement, not including flight pay.

CHAPTER 5

Ages Forty to Fifty: 1982–1992

Dow Jones Industrial Average
1,046.54–3,301.11
215.4% Gain

CALIFORNIA DREAMIN'

IT TURNS OUT I WAS being assigned as an operations officer in a small air force detachment at Fort Ord in Monterey, California. I would be a division air-liaison officer to the Seventh Infantry Division. We had about forty enlisted and about six officers, all fighter pilots or fighter back seaters.

Because part of my plan was to retire in Northern California after the air force, we bought a condo situated just north of Pebble Beach, California. I really wasn't sure what I would be doing in four years, but the living in Monterey was especially good for an old, worn-out military aviator and his wife.

Transitioning to Monterey, I noticed that a lot of things in my life were changing. The sound of jets was no longer around. I wasn't studying operations procedures for a new airplane. Twelve-hour days seemed to be a thing of the past, and

I was living in the United States. In essence, for the first time in sixteen years, I had time on my hands. I would have thought that would be a good thing, but I noticed I was drinking more and not spending my spare time in a productive way. For sixteen years, adrenaline had been a part of my system, because of jobs I'd had or airplanes I was flying. Perhaps I was looking, subconsciously, for a new way to produce adrenaline.

With that as a backdrop, I began the process I had used for years to get started in any assignment. I began interviewing the officers and enlisted to see who they were and what they had on their minds. Among the officers were four F-4 guys, one A-7 guy, and one transport guy.

As I looked at the officers, I wondered how they felt about being away from flying. I knew we were not mainstream air force in these jobs, but I had made this decision, and maybe they had too. The A-7 guy made me realize there were some who actually *did* put family above flying. I thought long and hard about that and how I had probably put flying ahead of my wife, although to this day I looked at it as a joint effort to an air force career. Even that statement falls short of any family priority though, and I guess I felt I was doing the best I could from a family perspective...but it wasn't enough.

Probably the most interesting discussion I had with any of the officers was with a man named Chuck Clifton. As I walked into his office, I saw a picture on his wall depicting Robin Olds in flight in an F-4, preparing to shoot down a MiG. To this day, it is my favorite picture of a military-aviation scene. I became animated after seeing the picture on Chuck's wall. I said, "Ah, Robin Olds, Operation BOLO, shooting down a MiG, right?"

Chuck, an aging academy grad and previous F-4 driver smiled calmly and said, "Yes, that is Robin Olds; do you know who was in his back seat that day?"

I had never even thought about it. "No, I have no idea," I said.

In a very down-to-earth manner, Chuck said, "It was me." Chuck was one of those early back-seat pilots in the F-4, and I am sure his efforts had a lot to do with the MiG shot down that day.

I have a picture painted by Keith Ferris hanging in my house today that commemorates that MiG kill. It remains my favorite military-aviation picture epitomizing the "air-to-air battle," among many other things. Chuck and I spent little time together, unfortunately. I think by not nurturing a closer relationship with him, I truly missed the boat. I saw him years later at a restaurant called Nepenthe, south of Carmel. Our conversation was brief, and I wish he knew that my respect for him has only increased with the passage of time.

The officers of our small detachment interfaced with the brigade commanders of the Seventh Infantry Division. In a war, they would help provide close air support to their troops in the field. I interfaced with the division's operations officer. I was used to seeing an air force squadron-operations officer responsible for maybe eighty to a hundred people at a squadron level, though I suppose our wing operations officers would be responsible for maybe a few thousand. This army division ops guy, a lieutenant colonel, was responsible for about sixteen thousand army troops. I was amazed. He had a big job, and it was interesting watching him lead such a large organization. I met with him and his staff once a week.

The forty or so air force enlisted men in our small detachment were young and, as we used to say, full of piss and vinegar. From my view, they really needed more to do in this peacetime setting not far from the beach in Monterey. I didn't have the motivation to push this, and looking back on it, I fell short in this endeavor. These guys were known as ROMADs, which stood for Radio Operator, Maintainer, and Driver. In fact, at least at the time, the ROMAD's primary mission was close air support (CAS). ROMADs can and will move forward with a team, locate and mark targets, and control CAS aircraft on a target.

Three or four ROMADs stick out in my mind. As I interviewed the enlisted guys in the detachment, I found that one had been sent to an undisclosed location outside the United States previously. A request had been sent to have a ROMAD who could speak a foreign language and still perform his ROMAD duties. Before it was all over, he had been shot in the lower torso and had at least one organ removed. This all happened before I was assigned to the unit. When I learned of this situation, I asked the young, tall airman if he had received a Purple Heart for this endeavor. He said he had not even been submitted for it, because it had not been in a wartime situation. The short story is that I got him a Purple Heart and felt very good about it.

One morning I went to work and heard a lot of scuttlebutt about a drug test. Our boss, Jimmy, had authorized a no-notice drug test of the enlisted. I didn't feel good about this. Normally I was a stickler for the rules and regulations within reason, and drugs were a definite no-no from my perspective. Although I felt this way, I still worried about our ROMADs. Sure enough, one of the airmen tested positive for marijuana. I found myself livid over this. That is, I felt the ROMADs should have been advised as to their vulnerability to such a test.

Up to this time, I had never seen anyone tested, let alone subjected to an unannounced testing. I will say also that I had never seen anyone smoking marijuana while in the service. I was surprised at my visceral reaction to this, and I've tried to write the reason for my reaction four times here, but I can't do it. Maybe some kind of protection mechanism regarding the enlisted guys had kicked off within me. Anyway, a legal hearing was held over this, and I got involved in it. The individual involved was an E-5, a staff sergeant.

In the normal course of the hearings that ensued, I was sworn in to testify. I took a very strong stand on behalf of the staff sergeant. I knew that speaking on behalf of someone who had been caught using marijuana might result in some higher-ups casting jaundiced eyes upon me, but I didn't care. For the first time, I didn't care what the higher-ups thought. And I spoke in direct opposition to my boss, Jimmy. I really didn't care about that either. Although dismissal from the air force was a possibility for our E-5, time in the brig or a reduction in rank would be alternative punishments for him. He received none of these but was put on probation for a year or so. I was happy with the outcome, and I think he was too. I often wonder if he stayed in the air force.

Senior Master Sergeant Pettijohn and Master Sergeant Olney were the two management NCOs in our unit. Pettijohn reported directly to me, and Sergeant Olney reported to

Jimmy. They were good, and they were a riot. I had a lot of fun with them, and we got some work done too. I spent a couple of weeks writing a recommendation for Pettijohn. As a result, he won some leadership award for all the organizations like ours in the western United States. I hoped he would become a chief master sergeant. Humor continued. I remember Sergeant Olney saying, "I tell these guys that I want clean, polished shoes; a clean shave; and a clean ass!"

I remember two major exercises that we were in with the Seventh Infantry Division. One was down in central Southern California. A lot of planning went into it. Thousands of infantry troops were involved, and we supplied "air" for the exercise. My experience in Cope Thunder made it easy to create some air-support scenarios to integrate with the army's plan. We had a lot of F-16s that came out of Arizona, I think. This would be one of two times I spent any time in the field with the Seventh Infantry Division. The exercise was only about a week long. As always I gained more respect for the army in general and for the Seventh Infantry Division Operations Officer in particular.

On another occasion, the entire division and our detachment went to Florida for another exercise. We housed our guys in a local motel, complete with swimming pool, until the army demanded that we show up. Because the army usually had so many troops with them, they always required huge lead times, a.k.a. sit-around time, in order to get things in place to bring off one of these exercises. I assured them we would be in place before they were ready to begin. That all went well in the end. Again, it was good to be in the air force.

Another time, we took a trip to Japan. We had another large contingent of army troops and just a few air force personnel.

Partway through this visit, we learned that there would be a troop review by a Japanese three-star general and an air force three-star general. Officers must be in the formation as well, we were told. As we assembled, I heard an army major declare that this was the first formation he had been in in the past fifteen years. Other than during my days at Lackland with the TIs, the same was true for me. (For any civilians, a formation is a group of military personnel who are required to stand by column and rank in a setting for any one of many reasons, including celebrations, funerals, reviews by higher-ups, and such.) All the things we'd learned when we first came into the service applied. We would stand at ease, which meant we could talk and move around, as long as we kept one foot planted in one place in our relative formation. Upon being called to parade rest, there would be no talking, and both feet would remain in place, though spread apart. Upon being called to attention, everything got serious. Our feet were together, and we looked only straight ahead. Our arms were at our sides, our fingers were holding an imaginary roll of coins, and our thumbs were not to protrude.

We were outside during winter in northern Japan, and the generals were late. We did what all GIs do; we passed the time BSing until we received an order of parade rest or attention. Eventually it came: "Attention." It began to rain, and soon the rain turned to snow. And we stood waiting. And someone spoke. I think it was the major standing behind me. It had been snowing for about a minute when the major said, "Give us more, Lord; give us more!" We all laughed to ourselves. It was like being lieutenants or cadets again. It was also representative of the attitude we all took as military officers, which stated that we could handle almost anything that came our way, including the cold, the rain, and the snow.

My last story about Japan will be short. After days of snow and ice, the Japanese decided to open up their *ofuro* (pronounced "o-phu-ru") to us. In essence it was a giant, very hot indoor hot tub. One of the army guys, having no idea what this was, decided to dive in. He really scorched himself doing this. We all sat back and watched as he writhed in pain. He required no medical help, but it was one of those moments where things got very quiet.

Eventually we enjoyed the ofuro and warmed our bones after the incessant cold we had been exposed to for about three or four days.

THE JAPANESE AND DIRTY HARRY

Stateside, at Fort Ord, we were to receive a contingent of Japanese officers, who were going to participate in a small exercise conducted right there in Monterey. Jimmy, my boss, asked me to sponsor them. That is, he wanted me to take care of them, make sure they understood what was going on, and help them with anything along the way. As always, I enjoyed that. Before it was all over, a couple of them approached me and asked if I would take them to "that place down in Carmel that Clint Eastwood owns, that restaurant." I remembered the restaurant, the Hog's Breath, and had been to it many times. I smiled and said, "I'll be glad to take you down there, but don't expect to see him; I've never seen him down there, as many times as I have been there."

We went late on a Monday afternoon, around four o'clock, as I remember. The Hog's Breath has some steps that patrons walk down, which lead to large, open patio arrangement with the enclosed restaurant to the left and a bar enclosed under a roof to the right. There was nobody on the patio except three guys. They sat with their backs to the outside wall of the bar area, facing the open outside patio area. There he was, Dirty Harry—Clint Eastwood himself. He and his two buddies were playing a dice game and drinking beer. As my two Japanese officers and I looked at one another, it was all we could do not to break out in laughter at our fortune. Some would not get a kick out of this, but I always enjoyed this kind of encounter. What can I say? The Japanese officers were appreciative, and so was I. We never approached the trio, but maybe we should have.

Two Years to Go

My two-year assignment was drawing to an end, and I was completing my eighteenth year in the air force. I had two more years to go to retire. My goal remained the same: stay in Northern California, especially since I now had a condo in Monterey. I studied an air force almanac and found a place I'd never known existed called the Sunnyvale Satellite Control Facility. I made some calls. I would be assigned there, about an hour and a half up the freeway. I didn't think I missed flying, but as I look back on it, my personal life was getting pretty distorted, mostly from my own actions. I was drinking more, not communicating with Jo, and doing some things I am not proud of today. Whether this was because I wasn't flying, who knows? Regardless, it is my only excuse.

THE SATELLITE BUSINESS

We rented the condo out to some naval officers who were attending the Naval Postgraduate School in Monterey and made our way to a rental condo in Sunnyvale, about an hour's drive up the road. Soon I would be introduced to my new job as chief of operations and plans at the Sunnyvale Satellite Control Facility. By the sound of the job, I expected to be immersed in the satellite business there, and although that was partially true, for the most part, I'll call it a second-string job. At the time, the air force was changing the way it controlled satellites.

Things were different in this job. I had some air force officers and some enlisted personnel assigned to me, but some civilians also worked in my office. Almost all the civilians had engineering backgrounds, except for a couple of my administrative people. Altogether there were only about fifteen people in this office.

As the name implies, those within the Sunnyvale Satellite Control Facility had jobs somehow working with satellites or supporting the activity therein. Our office was supposedly responsible for assisting in the conversion to a new method of controlling satellites. More specifically, we were supposed to be part of testing a new system. I took the job seriously at first but found we were playing second fiddle to another group in the system. Once I acknowledged this fact to myself, I began looking at retirement more seriously. And I had already been serious about it before. The eight-to-five work schedule was even lighter than what I had imposed upon myself while down at Fort Ord, and I began to feel there was a life outside of work; however, my personal life was still not a healthy one, and

I was destroying my homelife. My life had been consumed by twelve-hour workdays until Fort Ord. Why had I chosen now to distance myself from Jo? The answer to that question would never be resolved, I'm afraid.

While in Sunnyvale, I did learn a few things, of course. I saw a lot of engineers close up and learned how they operated. I saw some of the civilians who had been in place for decades and how they reacted to change. For the most part, they didn't want to change. I saw that bright young and old engineers could live pretty well and be paid well while living in the sun of northern California.

In some ways, I resented that my military brethren and I had sacrificed our lives in places like South Vietnam, Thailand, the Philippines, and so on, while these engineers, including military engineers, were leading a life of relative leisure by comparison. I wouldn't dwell on this thought, but it crossed my mind a few times. Maybe *leisure* is the wrong word, since I know many worked very hard on a variety of projects. Maybe safety had something to do with it. Their environment was so safe. There were no mortars or other incoming fire. They weren't expected to put their life on the line on a daily basis. It is different to put a career on the line than it is to put your life on the line. These words are just coming out of the keyboard right now. I guess this is some of the self-counseling that this writing effort is giving me.

The people in the satellite control center were interesting, as always. Ed, a young captain and Air Force Academy grad, was my man—my go-to guy. He could give any briefing to anybody without fault. He could explain almost anything to anybody. Warren was at the top of my go-to civilian list. Of Japanese descent, he spent a fair amount of time cultivating a relationship with me and finally convinced me I should pay more attention to him. We developed a friendship that still exists today.

REST IN PEACE, MY DEAR MOTHER

Alice, my mother, developed some kind of back problem shortly after she quit working in her beauty shop. She was with Dad out in Arizona, but for some reason, they were coming back to Ohio to see some doctors. Eventually I was told things had turned very serious for her and that I should come home. I did. She had some kind of cancer and would die of it a short time later. She had always smoked, so that did not help anything. I had actually returned to California by the time she died, so back to Ohio I went.

Mom's death had a huge impact on me both then and for the rest of my life. I owed everything to her, including my education, my ability to move beyond Hubbard and to know right from wrong, and my appreciation of hard work. More than anything she had instilled discipline in me, and I am sure it helped me meld into the military-aviation profession. I feel bad that, in my zest to get beyond Hubbard, I also got too far away from her. I owed her, and I really never expressed to her how much she meant to me and how much I loved her. Dad and I spoke little of what had just happened. I must reflect on what she gave up for my brother and me. She had spent twenty-five or thirty years of her life in the basement of our house, in that fluorescent-lit, small, smoke-filled beauty shop. It was not uncommon for me to go downstairs while in high school and view this scene: two women under hair dryers, smoking cigarettes, one woman in a chair smoking a cigarette, and yes, sometimes my mother smoking a cigarette while doing a woman's hair. She had been out of that basement for about three months when she died.

AG Fluent showed up at the funeral home. It felt good to have my old friend there with me. He had been with me at the funeral home when my grandmother died also. Someone would say years later that "life is mostly learning how to deal with loss." Now I would find out how true this was. How I miss my mother. What I have just written does not serve her well enough. To serve her appropriately, I should write an entire book about her and what she meant to me. I know Jack, my brother, feels the same way.

What Now?

In mid-1985 I had about nine months left to go in the air force and accordingly submitted my papers to retire upon completion of my twenty years. I wasn't at all sure what I would do after the air force, but I knew I was pretty well burned-out and had been for at least four years. I reflected that it would have been nice to retire as a bird colonel. But doing that would have required a large investment of time into the future. First, my bird colonel's promotion board wouldn't have met until a few months after my twenty-year point. Assuming I was promoted, I wouldn't have begun wearing the rank until a considerable amount of time after that, and once I assumed the rank, I would owe the air force three more years. Instead of retiring at age forty-four, I would have had to wait until at least age forty-seven or forty-eight. As I suspected at the time, these were critical age differences. Retiring at the twenty-year point would work to my benefit regarding some jobs, especially the airlines. The funny thing is that now that I wasn't working so hard, my officer effectiveness reports (OER's) were pretty good if I do say so myself. I think my chances of making bird colonel were excellent, but I would be retired before the next promotion board cycled.

Very soon after I submitted my retirement papers, I sat in my office reading the *Air Force Times*, a paper that include all the current news of note going on in the air force. As I turned the pages, I came upon an advertisement by American Airlines. It said something like this: "American Airlines is hiring retired military people; if interested, please write or call." Eight years earlier, Western Airlines had told me that age thirty-two was its cutoff point for hiring pilots. Now American was saying they would hire older guys and gals. Most officers who spent twenty years in the military would be forty-two years old. Because of an extra semester in school, another year in grad school, and a delay of six more months in going on active duty, I was forty-four. I wasn't sure I believed what I had just read. I looked away, and then I returned to the advertisement. It was authentic.

Up to this time, I had really thought that maybe I'd hire on to one of the contractors serving the air force, or maybe I would finally try the finance business, my hobby since that cold February day with my grandfather in Hubbard, at the Butler Wick stockbrokerage office. In about twenty seconds, I made a decision. The love of flight still reigned supreme, so I dared to fill out the application in pencil, put it in the mail, and waited. I guess filling the application out in pencil was a sign of rebellion on my part against all mention of "how you *should* do things." No, I was never much of a rebel. But I was among the few aviators who really had *not* pursued the airlines. Military jets were what I had sought and loved, but I was apparently at the end of that road.

AMERICAN AIRLINES INTERVIEWS

American had a hiring process that involved three visits to the company headquarters plus a physical in Dallas-Fort Worth, Texas. Although I hadn't interviewed much for jobs, I was used to being closely scrutinized. As such, I enjoyed the interview process. I remember someone announcing on one of the interviews that there were going to be some psychological tests but that the military people did not need to take them. Well, you can imagine the levity that was kicked off among the military aviators present. We all thought we needed the psychological testing more than anyone. (Not really.) Still, we all laughed out loud.

Then there was the simulator. It, too, was part of the American Airlines interview process. I hated simulators. I still hate simulators. American Airlines still did not know that it had been about five years since I had flown an airplane. I was not eagerly anticipating a simulator ride. It turned out that the simulator operator put us on an ILS (instrument landing system) final approach and then watched to see how well we flew the approach. I felt like I had done OK. In the ensuing interview, the interviewer, a different person from the simulator instructor, asked how I thought I had done. I said that at one point I had gotten a little off the localizer and, if I had to do it again, would try to do better. The interviewer shook his head and said, "Well, the simulator instructor said you did great."

I knew we would be tested physically, so I had been working out quite a bit. We were wired up before we climbed onto the treadmill, and we signed off on papers promising we would not sue them if we had a bad experience on the treadmill. I had been through this before, during SR-71 physicals. Then I asked the attendee, "How long do I have to stay on this thing in order to get an excellent rating?"

She said, "Twenty-three minutes."

I looked at her, and in a rare moment of braggadocio for me, I said, "When I get to twenty-four minutes, shut 'er down." I didn't know they were going to elevate the treadmill throughout the ordeal—so much for swagger. I made it to twenty-four minutes, and she shut 'er down. I was very tired.

Later, a bunch of us were standing in line waiting for our eye exams. I was very concerned about this, since I was now wearing reading glasses. An older, drill-sergeant-type woman would appear in front of us all and shout, "Next," asking for the next guy to enter the testing room. She would disappear behind the door with the each applicant for the flying job. I knew power when I saw power, and this woman had a lot of it. I watched her intently each time she appeared, and finally it was my turn.

I extended the usual pleasantries. She remained like a drill sergeant. She then gave me her directions. "I want you to sit down in this chair, and I want you to look into this eye-testing machine, and I do not want you to move your head."

I said, "Yes, ma'am." As I sat down, I felt her very close to me and assumed she would be adjusting the machine for the test. I looked into the machine and immediately had an uncontrollable knee-jerk reaction. Because the letters were a little blurred, my head snapped back just a little in order to better read the letters. This was totally a physical reaction. As I did this, I felt the woman's hand on the back of my head. I immediately bowed to the power and began profusely apologizing for moving my head. She said nothing. I finished the test not knowing the results but very concerned.

Before the day was over, someone went over the results of all our tests. Someone asked me, "What did you do to our eye-test lady?" *Oh,* I thought, *here is the end of my American Airlines career.* I said something to the effect that I was unaware of anything I had done, and the person said, "She really liked you." *I must have made it through the eye test,* I thought.

I remember a lot of discussion of suit and tie color for these interviews, and I dutifully showed up for the culminating interview in my dark, conservative suit with an appropriately conservative dark-red tie. My turn came, and I walked into the interview room. It was narrow, with a long table in it and a window at one end of the table with bright sun shining in. There were probably six well-dressed men sitting at the table. As I approached, one rose to greet me, while the others remained seated. First question: "Hey, Gil, it's a nice day, isn't it?" I paused, looked out the same window the questioner was looking out of and felt energized.

I said, "Yes, sir. It is a great day."

The second question I remember was this: "Hey, Gil, this is General X, US Air Force; he wants to ask you a question." Whoa, I hadn't expected this, but I had nothing to hide.

The general asked, "Gil, I notice you say you have taken no disabilities through the air force; is that true?" It was true. The general was done and had no more questions.

Third question: "Hey, Gil, did you apply to any other airline for a flying job?" I had not. I knew little about the airline business.

Fourth question: "Hey, Gil, which airplane did you like the most while in the air force?"

I said I'd preferred the F-4, and they asked why.

I answered that I had been in a lot of situations with the F-4, and it seemed the more you asked from it, the more it gave you. At the higher speeds it just seemed to get better and quieter. I knew they probably wondered why I hadn't cited the SR-71, but they never asked. The same individual who had shaken my hand on the way in shook my hand on the way out. I would catch a flight back to California and wait.

The letter came. It was not what I expected. It said that, during the physical, they had found blood in my stool. The real surprise came when they said that if I could get it taken care of and show them the proof it was fixed, I would be hired. Within a few weeks, I had gone back to the air force and asked a doctor to take another look. They found some polyps on my descending colon and took them out. I forwarded this information to American and was hired, pending my retirement.

USAF RETIRED

Young Captain Ed would read much of my retirement-ceremony litany; Warren had a party at his house for me, and I drank way too much. I had been living away from home. Happy times and sad times prevailed. I was on a roller coaster.

Thus ended my twenty years in the air force. Jo and I had moved twelve times during those twenty years, and this did not include my temporary-duty assignments. I had brought a lot of those moves on myself, because of my desire to fly some different airplanes. Looking back, I now realize it was too much moving for anybody, especially when so much of it included combat operations. I was forty-four years old, and it was 1986.

Over my twenty years in the air force, I received the following awards:

o   Distinguished Flying Cross with one oak leaf cluster
o   Meritorious Service Medal with two oak leaf clusters
o   Air Medal with thirty-two oak leaf clusters
o   Air Force Commendation Medal with one oak leaf cluster
o   Distinguished Presidential Unit Citation
o   Air Force Outstanding Unit Award with Valor Device with three oak leaf clusters
o   Combat Readiness Medal
o   National Defense Service Medal
o   Vietnam Service Medal with six bronze service stars
o   Air Force Overseas Long Tour Ribbon
o   Air Force Longevity Service Award Ribbon with four oak leaf clusters
o   Small Arms Expert Marksmanship Ribbon
o   Republic of Vietnam Gallantry Cross with device
o   Republic of Vietnam Campaign Medal

Although they aren't exactly awards or decorations, my favorite uniform accessory was my Command Pilot Wings, which I received after fifteen years and three thousand hours of military flying.

Also during those twenty years, I had flown 474 missions in combat:

o I flew 110 of the 474 missions into North Vietnam and flew the remainder in South Vietnam, Laos, and Cambodia.

o The air force lost track after some 250. Mission count is available by looking at my Form 5 records, which I still have.

I spent twenty-four months in Southeast Asia (not including thirty-six months spent in the Philippines):

o Utapao Air Base, Thailand (four months—KC-135)

o Bear Cat/Long Thang North, South Vietnam (eight months—O-2)

o Udorn, Thailand (twelve months—RF-4C)

The distinction between the awards and decorations of the military and high pay and bonuses of the business world never escaped me. The fact is that a career in the military seldom yields any real money, unless one retires as a general officer. I don't mean to be too harsh on the military, though. I think once military folks are separated from the military, they are often given jobs as a result of proven leadership and management skills learned while in the military. Often these jobs come with commensurate salaries or bonus plans associated with them.

By now you understand my choice of a military profession. The World War II and post–World War II environment I grew up in, my mother's guidance and disciplinary influence, my father's appreciation of the navy, my appreciation for the military, and my love of flight all combined to take me on the military career path.

Interestingly, in the military, an individual's career is evident by looking at his or her uniform. In the civilian world, things are not so evident. It's a statement of the obvious, but in the military, you seldom misread an individual's past performance.

STARTING OVER IN THE AIRLINES

Coming out of the military felt like returning to the States after being in Vietnam. It felt like I was in a different world. I was headed to Dallas-Fort Worth for training. All my classmates were younger than I was by a significant amount. I was just enjoying the freedom for a while. Soon the seriousness of the training became front and center, and I went into that mode I had spent most of my life in, studying operating manuals, learning emergency procedures, preparing for simulator rides, and learning the systems of the Boeing 727. I would not be responsible for managing or leading anybody. The airlines are a place where unions prevail, and so I would go to the bottom of the seniority list and start out as a flight engineer. Thus the subtitle above, *Starting Over.*

There are three crewmembers on the 727; I would be the low-ranking man on the crew. This really didn't bother me. I am sure some military retirees did not join the airlines because of this requirement, however. It didn't even bother me that most of the flight attendants would be making more money than I would for the first two years.

Believe it or not, I made about $18,000 a year for those first two years. American and other airlines had instituted a "B scale" pay system for new hires during this growth phase in the mideighties. Looking back on that, it seems insane. But as aviators often said, someone who truly loves aviation will do it for free. Yes, that was an exaggeration, but it was still not far from the truth. As if this was not enough, the flight engineer sits sideways in the 727. I was reminded of the navigators who sat sideways in the KC-135. Well, we wouldn't be doing any air-to-air attacks in the B-727, nor would we be getting "on our backs" in the 727, so sitting sideways would be different, but at least I would be in the air and wouldn't be going into combat.

The Boeing 727 had a max speed of about Mach .9 and a cruise speed of about 570 mph. It had three engines, each of which had about fourteen thousand pounds of thrust. (Photo by Fergal Goodman)

My first job at American Airlines was as a flight engineer in the Boeing 727. I was an engineer on this airplane for about three years while based at LaGuardia in New York; Dallas-Fort Worth, Texas; and San Jose, Oakland, and San Francisco, California. I never flew this airplane as a pilot.

As with most training, I did not enjoy it. My mediocre performance in training situations remained intact. One way or another, training came to an end, and I was on my way to LaGuardia in New York, though many called it Le Garbage. I had spent years trying to get to California, and now I was on my way to New York. Go figure, as they say. Someone had me believing I wouldn't need a car in New York. Me, without a car? I should have known better. At first I tried to live at the navy shipyard in New York, and I paid about four dollars a night while there. I would ride the subway to get to the airport. That was a real learning experience with late-night subway rides. I learned that, late at night, there were usually more cops on the subway than passengers, and that was a good thing. Soon I decided I needed two things: a car and somewhere else to live.

For whatever reason, I called my brother to see if he had any extra cars around; he usually did. Soon I was driving his Toyota station wagon. It had two peculiarities: it would back-fire while sitting at a red light, and you could not get it stuck in any amount of snow.

I saw a bulletin-board advertisement for a room in a new condo well north of the airport. A twenty-six-year-old copilot for American had just bought it and wanted to rent out a room. His name was Len. With different flying schedules, we seldom saw each other. The exceptions would be on a few Saturday mornings when I awoke to the sound of drums downstairs. He liked to wear a purple wig while he played the drums. We got along well, despite our age difference. He was really young to be a copilot on a 767. He told me that on one of his first flights, he got there early and proceeded to the cockpit to do his preflight inspections. While in the cockpit, he said one of the flight attendants appeared and asked, "Where's the copilot for this flight?" He told her he was the copilot. He said she looked at him, rolled her eyes, and left the cockpit. That is how young he was. I could have easily been his father. He reminded me of an air force lieutenant.

SHEDDING MY AIR FORCE WAYS

I found it incredible to be working for the airlines, but it took a while to shed some of my air force ways. By this I mean that no matter what anybody told me, my brain could not accept the fact that I had so much time off. When the schedules came out, you could see which days you were flying and which days you had off. Working anywhere from fourteen to seventeen days a month seemed so unusual to me that I felt I needed to stay near my beeper in case I was needed to fly. Finally after I spent most of my time near the condo, the phone did ring one day. (We had no cell phones then.) It was American Airlines calling to inform me that they were using one of my upcoming flights to train someone, and I would not be needed for that day. I had another day off. After that I finally adjusted to the fact that this was not the air force, and I had a life separate from work.

While in New York, I got to see New York and the surrounding area. Since I was living within an hour of the US Military Academy, I would also roam around West Point from time to time. Although LaGuardia was my primary base, I also flew out of Kennedy and the airport in Newark, New Jersey. I saw a few plays while in New York and walked the streets of New York to see some of the sights. In a way, I was disconnected from things, as my personal life was in a state of turmoil. I even spent a period of time looking for answers in an easy-to-read version of the Bible.

After a year and a half, I finally moved closer to California. The Dallas/Fort Worth area would be my home for about another six months. By reviewing seniority lists, I determined that at least one person with a lower seniority than mine had gone to San Francisco ahead of me. Seniority in the airlines was every-thing, and I was still near the bottom. I made a phone call to the folks responsible for assignments, and soon I was on my way to California again. My time at Dallas was so short that I barely remember being there.

California Dreamin', Part 2

Being back in California was good. The weather was great, as always. But my personal life still was in turmoil. Eventually I was divorced from Jo. This was difficult, especially since she had been so loyal to me for all those years.

While based in San Francisco, I would often fly out of two other airports, Oakland and San Jose. The schedules were great as far as I was concerned, and slowly my seniority number moved up as retirees left and as the airlines grew. The airlines were really different from a work perspective. I don't ever remember sitting in an office with a supervi-sor or boss. Matter of fact, I know I never did. The captain you flew with was your boss for that flight or that month, but that was it as far as supervision went. Most of the young pilots were driven to prove themselves and so moved on to "bigger equipment"—larger airplane—as soon as their seniority allowed. For me, it was just the opposite. I had moved too many times and disparaged change. In short, for an aviator, I guess I was getting old. I came to say that from now on, I wanted only to stand in the short lines.

About three years after joining the airlines, I moved up from the 727 engineer's job to the copilot's, or first officer's job, as it is known in the airlines. This was aboard the McDonnell-Douglas MD-80. This airplane hauled about 130 passengers or so. I would spend the rest of my time at American Airlines in this airplane. For a host of reasons, I never became a captain in the airline industry. Somewhere along the line, American merged with an airline called Air California, Air Cal for short. With that merger came a merger of seniority lists. Watching business as I had for years, it came as no surprise that things had suddenly changed because of all the Air Cal captains who came over into our ranks. This bothered some. I felt almost no remorse, because I had never pinned any hopes on the airline industry or had any goals of attaining the captain rank in the airline industry.

Before it was all over, I had the number-one seniority number among the copilots in San Francisco. As such, I could choose when I wanted to go on vacation, and more importantly, I could choose which schedule I wanted. Unlike many who chose to maximize their earnings, I generally chose to have as much time off as I could. Toward the end of my time at American, I was generally flying ten days a month, with the rest of the month off. I flew as much out of San Jose as I could but did spend a fair amount of time flying out of Oakland and San Francisco.

**The MD-80 had a max speed of about 575 mph. It had
two engines, each of which offered 18,500 to 21,000
pounds of thrust, depending on the model.[4] The cruise
speed was about 504 mph or about .76 Mach. I ended
up with something like eight thousand hours of flight
time in the MD-80. (Photo by Bryan Snook)**

My last commercial airline flight was in January 2000, and
my official retirement from American was in March 2002.
The guys and gals at American were wonderful. Because of
the seniority system and the union, individual competition
was nonexistent. Sometimes that was good, and other times
it was bad. I had been told by someone in the air force that
I would miss the camaraderie of the military once I retired.
That person was right. In the military, we worked hard and
played hard together. In the airlines, we flew, and then we
went home and had lives separate from the airlines. I guess
it was more the way it was supposed to be and probably

healthier. This analysis in no way takes away from some of the friendships I developed in the airline business. I will write about some of them in the next chapter.

During this decade, I was seeing a dermatologist more and more regarding some skin cancer, mostly on my face. Some of this skin cancer had started demonstrating itself back in the air force years. Jason and Jodi, and everybody else who happens to be reading this, never underestimate the damage the sun can do to you and your kids. Dermatologists say that most sun damage happens when you are a child, and the effects only begin to appear later in life.

**My dad, William J. Gilmore III, after he got his
real estate license. He seemed more content.**

PATRICIA, MOTORCYCLES, AND *SONGBIRD*

Along the way, I found Patricia. She had been a defense
contractor for IBM and Lockheed Martin. She was a
pilot too. Amazingly, she was also from Ohio originally
(Cincinnati). We lived in San Jose for quite a while, and

then we bought a house in Morgan Hill, California, where I sit writing this.

Somewhere in this time frame, I started going back to old roots. I suppose one reason was that I had such a reduced work schedule with the airlines. Motorcycles and airplanes had been a focus early in my life, and I seemed to be headed there again. Pat and I both had motorcycles now, and because of an odd set of circumstances, I bought an airplane, a Cessna 182. Both the motorcycle and the airplane life yielded an abundance of new people for us to know.

Jerry became a motorcycle buddy and then much more than that. I would eventually eat breakfast with him at least once a week for fifteen years or more. Jerry had owned a flower business and had worked pretty hard at it. For a guy with only a high school education, he had done very well for himself. Eventually, just prior to his retirement, he bought a building in Texas, which yielded a pretty good source of income for him. The building housed a Jiffy Lube business at the time. Eventually all three of his grandchildren graduated from college, and Jerry was rightfully very proud of them.

The motorcycle days in my old age were similar in many respects to those of my young days. Still, you had to be careful, or you could lose your life. I was worried about Pat riding her own bike, but all in all, she did very well and seemed to come alive during those days. I like to tell a few stories about her regarding this. One day about six couples decided to go out to the coast on Route 1, the Pacific Coast Highway, in California. There is a stretch of road prior to Route 1 that is a transition point when it comes to temperature. At certain times of the year, temperatures can vary by thirty degrees between the inland areas and the coastal highway.

We all pulled off the road to don our sweatshirts and leather jackets to ready ourselves for the temperature drop we knew was coming along the coast. Pat just sat there. I told her to hurry up and change. She looked at me and said something like, "I'm going like this"—meaning in her leather pants and a cotton T-shirt. By now, I knew it was fruitless to persist. We got on the road, and with the temperature down at least thirty degrees, I knew Pat had to be freezing, but I also knew she would not let on that she was.

About that time, I looked into my rearview mirrors and saw some motorcycles approaching us from behind. We were doing about seventy, and judging by the closure rate, I felt they were probably doing about ninety. It would be interesting to see them come by; there was plenty of room for them in the adjacent passing lane. As they approached, I could tell they were not all going into the passing lane and wondered how this was going to work out. We were already riding in pairs— that is, two by two in one lane. These guys flew between us on some very nice Harleys. A quick look at their bikes told us they were all Hells Angels, and they were all dressed like Pat in leather bottoms and T-shirts. I looked at Pat; she smiled and gave me a thumbs-up. She was "bad," like the Hells Angels; at least, that was the image she liked.

Her bike was a Harley Lo-Rider, mine a Dyna Wide Glide. Both were outfitted with high-performance cams, carburetors, and exhaust pipes. Her license plate read AKA GRIZZ. This stood for also known as Grizz, the name everyone called her in the motorcycle community. Yeah, I know, but it was fun. My plate read 1BADDWG. The abbreviation DWG stood for Dyna Wide Glide, the model of the Harley. The "bad" part of course was in reference to its custom paint job; the aforementioned cam, carb, and pipes; extensive chrome work; small mirrors; custom turn signals; and lowered frame. I often said that my bike was built for a twenty-year-old. But it was cool, very cool. Jason, you and I rode that bike down Route 1 a long time ago. I am very glad we got to do that. I can't believe you spent the day on that very small piece of leather pretending it was a seat. I wish we could have done it more, and Jodi, let there be no doubt, I wish I could have taken you for a ride on it too.

Pat and I flew back to Ohio three different times in our mighty Cessna 182, which we called *Songbird*. This name came from an old TV show called *Sky King*. The star of the show flew an airplane that he called *Songbird*. Pat and I both were very familiar with the old show, and thus our airplane became dubbed *Songbird*. We kept *Songbird* in a hangar I had bought at a place called Frazier Lake Airpark, about twenty-five minutes south of our house. We were one of many members at this private airpark, which had public access. If you were going to own a hangar, it really was ideal. Costs associated were surprisingly minimal.

I was now flying out of and into a lot of grass runways. The idea was not lost on me that flying off of a grass runway is where I had started when I was eighteen or nineteen years old. The grass runway at Frazier Lake was not that different from the one where I first soloed, a few miles from our house in Hubbard, the one just inside the western Pennsylvania border and known as the West Middlesex Airport. Who the hell ever came up with that name, anyway?

On one of our return trips from Ohio, I remember flying across the whole state of Oklahoma at about a thousand feet above the ground. All the way across the state, the clouds looked as if someone had taken a knife and cut across the bottom of them. I was decent at reading clouds and knew we would likely make it the entire way without getting into the clouds. I had made a pact with myself that I wouldn't fly IFR (instrument flight rules) with this airplane and managed to stick by that agreement. I could have flown IFR, having about twelve thousand to thirteen thousand hours of flying time, but I knew very well that flying IFR only once in a while was not smart. Proficiency was always the key to instrument flying.

In the air force and especially in the airlines, we were very proficient at instrument flying, which I came to call "living inside the attitude indicator." (I meant that keeping focused on an instrument called the attitude indicator was the key to good instrument flying. Few did it perfectly, including me.) Pat has kept some of the logbooks detailing our trips in ole *Songbird*, otherwise known as 8797X (or 8797Xray- used to communicate to aviation facilities or other aircraft). 8797X was also the FAA registration number associated with our airplane.

CHAPTER 6

Ages Fifty to Sixty: 1992–2002

**Dow Jones Industrial Average
3,301.11–8,341.63
152.7% Gain**

SOME AIRLINE STORIES

IN 1992 I TURNED FIFTY. This age thing was not a joke anymore.

I flew with Ed more than anyone, partly because of our relative seniorities and partly because we enjoyed flying with each other. Ed was married to a flight attendant, Sherry, and she became a friend as well. Ed was a study, as we used to say in the air force. When we flew, the airlines provided a name sheet, including nicknames, for the crew. Before going out to the airplane, all the crewmembers and flight attendants would download a copy of these names for reference during the flight. Ed's nickname was Fuzzy, but I never got a straight answer from him on where that name came from. His name never appeared on the crew printout as Ed or Edward. Only his nickname appeared. One day a flight attendant came up to the cockpit and sat down. Neither Ed nor I had ever met her. Sitting there at thirty-seven thousand feet, she asked if Fuzzy was his real name. In a very aristocratic manner, he said, "No, my real name is Fuzzard." I sucked in a lot of air for a huge laugh when I noticed Ed with a very straight face. He continued to gaze forward, not looking at the flight attendant. I kept a straight face and slowly let out the air. I looked back at the flight attendant. She looked at me, rolled her eyes, and left the flight deck.

What a riot Ed was. Somewhere along the line, I started chastising him for talking into his kit bag. Kit bags are what you see all airline crews carrying in the terminals. That bag contains all our procedural maps and so on for anywhere we may go. In the cockpit, these kit bags sit at our sides. Ed quite often would talk while looking through his kit bag, and his voice came across as muffled to this old copilot. I felt relieved that I was flying with a friend and could say, "Get your head out of your kit bag, so I can hear you."

Ed had been a B-52 pilot in the air force but had gone to the airlines after his required five years in the service. He knew uniform requirements, including those of the airlines. But I noted that he wore a red baseball jacket most of the time with the airlines. It hung proudly on the cockpit hanger as he flew for years. I had my ideas as to why he did this and wondered how he managed to get away with it. It turns out that he just did it without worrying about it. Some say he used to wear a blue baseball jacket as part of his uniform, until one of the chief pilots saw him and told him not to wear it anymore. Sure to form, from that day until he retired, he wore a red baseball jacket. He loved baseball and had actually given up some try-outs in the major leagues in order to fly with the airlines.

In the MD-80, one of the jobs of the copilot is to handle the air-conditioning system. That is, he or she is the one who controls how hot or cold it is in the airplane. Some captains would merely reach over and adjust the temperature on their own if they weren't happy with it, but most honored the territory and simply asked the copilot to turn up the heat if he was too cold. Ed would do this: he would turn up the collar on his shirt, and then he would fold his arms in such a way that it appeared he was standing in a freezing windstorm in Alaska.

At first, stupidly, I would ask, "Ed, are you cold?"

He always said no. He was a riot. But I wouldn't want him mad at me.

Paul had been an Air Cal captain. I flew with him for only a couple of months but really appreciated him. I have to say that the Air Cal guys could fly the shit out of the airplane, to a man. They seemed to have that sunny California attitude, combined with a barnstormer's ability to fly. I was impressed with them all. Even the Air Cal gate agents were personalities unto themselves, as you would understand if you saw a gate agent giving wholehearted, efficient guidance to passengers amid a maintenance or weather delay. The Air Cal folks did a hell of a great job of it—not to disparage the rest of the pros at the airline.

Guys were guys, and cockpits were like many industrial locker rooms back in the day. That is, there was some pornography stashed in certain hiding places on the flight decks. On day one, I noticed Paul going about the cockpit, pulling out the porn, ripping it up, and distributing it in the wastebasket. On the first day he met you, he would look over the top of his glasses and say, "I have two daughters at home." I knew him to be a principled man, for sure. He wasn't a Bible thumper, but there was no doubt that religion played a big part in his life. I grew to respect him for standing by his principles. And of course he flew the airplane well and was a great captain.

There were a couple of acts that Paul performed. I'll call act one Food Emergency. At thirty-five thousand feet, on autopilot, things would get boring. Suddenly, Paul would sit very upright in his seat and pretend he was making a distress call to an imaginary controller, which he dubbed Flightcom. He would say something like, "Flightcom, Flightcom, come in, Flightcom." Then he would say, "Flightcom, this is American flight one-two-three with an emergency. We have an emergency, Flightcom. Do you read?" Then he would say, "Our emergency is that we have run out of food!" Of course, by now, I would be laughing. And then Paul would go into a correction mode. He would say, "Flightcom, Flightcom, we have located a food source. I have determined that we probably have about two weeks of food remaining." Much like the comedian Bob Newhart, Paul made it seem that there was a real person on the other end of the line. "Are you asking where we found the food source, Flightcom? We have the captain's and the copilot's ties, Flightcom. I say again, we can eat off the captain's and the copilot's ties for about two weeks!" I guess you might not find all this funny, but when you saw it the second or third time, it seemed to take on a life of its own.

The second act of Paul's was what I will call Eat What You Want. The airline goes out of its way to provide food to the crew while airborne most of the time, especially from an old military guy's perspective. For obvious reasons, FAA rules forbade the two pilots from eating the same thing on any given flight. Generally your choices were chicken or steak. Back in the old days, the captain often took the steak, then the preferred meal, while the copilot got the proverbial rubber chicken. As the years went by, this preference gradually turned around. Due to diet and health habits, the chicken became preferred over the steak. Nevertheless, some folks just liked steak or chicken.

Now enter the busy flight attendant into the cockpit with a simple question: "Who wants the chicken, and who wants the steak?" I had always been deferential to rank, so it was very easy for me to defer to the captain's desire for the chicken or the steak. (Besides, I really didn't care.) Either was much better than the C rations I had eaten at Bear Cat, South Vietnam. With all this said, Paul was always gentlemanly and polite. He would tell me to choose whichever meal I preferred. I would throw it back to him and ask him to choose. Without fail, he would turn it back to me, assuring me he wanted me to have what I wanted. Usually I was aware of the growing frustration of the busy flight attendant standing in our midst, and out of respect for her (or him), I would finally choose. Sometimes I chose the chicken; sometimes I chose the steak. In either case, Paul's response was always the same. Whatever I chose, he would act out a rage. With hands over his face, he would say, "That is what I wanted!" And then we would laugh and laugh. I guess you had to be there to appreciate this humor.

Jim was another Air Cal guy. I remember him because he also was different. In the aviation business, there are a lot of large egos—understandably so. How different folks handled their egos was an interesting topic for me. On average, the captain's ego loomed fairly large. In some few cases, you couldn't get into the cockpit until some air was let out of the ego residing therein. Jim was a quiet captain with his ego very much under control. And I enjoyed that about him. He had served as an army enlisted guy in Vietnam and told of a story about someone coming to his unit and asking if anyone had an aviation background. Jim said he'd been up in the equivalent of a Piper Cub a few times and raised his hand. Soon he was a tower operator at a field called An Khe in South Vietnam, a staging area for hundreds of helicopters.

Once out of the army, Jim spent a good deal of his time pursuing his aviation dreams. Eventually he flew a business jet for General Motors, and then he landed a job at Air California. With the merger of American and Air Cal, there we were in the same cockpit. The thing that interested me about Jim was that he paid less than normal attention to the flight attendants. They were met with a lot of silence outside the normal exchange of pleasantries. The cockpit was quieter and more peaceful than usual. He had married for the first time later in life to a beautiful Air Cal gate agent, and they had two great kids. Jim could sniff out a good deal in real estate and eventually moved to a beautiful house in Hawaii. Last I knew, he and the family were still there.

Before closing out the airline stories, let me tell just a few more. Celebrities ride on the airlines from time to time. I can't say very many rode on airplanes I was in, but a few did.

One night in Chicago, Ed and I were sitting at the gate in the airplane, waiting for passengers to board. A light snow was falling, and we would be flying back to San Jose or San Francisco. We had the cockpit lights turned down low, and the cockpit door was open, as was the custom in those days. The lights were on beyond the cockpit door, so a shaft of light from the passenger cabin was evident in our small cockpit. The shaft of light was being interrupted or flickering, thereby announcing that someone was approaching. *Probably a flight attendant*, we thought. Soon a man in a large winter overcoat stood between us as we remained seated. I looked up and saw Milton Berle in the dim lights of our cockpit. Jason and Jodi, I doubt that this name rings any bells for you, but Milton had been a huge star in TV as a comedian. As I looked at him, I had a visceral reaction. I grabbed his arm with both hands and shouted, "Uncle Milty!" This is what many in his industry, and many members of the public, called him. He smiled and asked if we could heat it up a little in the back. That was it, but today it would be like having Jay Leno, Jimmy Fallon, and Jimmy Kimmel walk into the cockpit all at the same time. That's how big Milton Berle was.

On another day, Robert Stack walked into the cockpit and shook our hands. He had been an actor in a TV show called *The Untouchables* and had appeared in about forty movies.

I'll finish this celebrity discussion with Phyllis Diller. She was a comedienne I loved. After we were airborne, a flight attendant walked into the cockpit and announced that we had Phyllis onboard. I made a big fuss about it, thinking that would be the end of it. We were getting close to our destination, maybe Nashville or some other place in the South, when the same flight attendant came through the door and said Phyllis Diller was asking about a certain river she had seen out the window. I searched some maps and told the flight attendant what river I thought it was. A little while later, the same flight attendant called on the phone and said Phyllis had some other question. Again, I found an answer and passed it on to the flight attendant.

Fast-forward now to the gate where we parked. All the passengers got off, then all the crew. For some reason, I lingered, and as I sat there, I heard a voice say, "Hi." It was Phyllis Diller leaning up against the cockpit door with that grin of hers. I couldn't believe it. There is no punch line here other than to say I think I blew it. Looking back on it, I think she was probably bored and would have entertained any discussion I wanted to engage in. For the most part, I just kept looking at her, smiling, and thinking of all the funny lines I had seen her deliver over the years. I think she had been to Vietnam several times with Bob Hope, and for that, I was very appreciative. Yet I never thanked her for that, nor did I say much. I loved the encounter obviously. She used to tell jokes about her husband. Her name for him was Fang. God, she was funny. Thanks, Phyllis, wherever you are! I really blew a great chance to talk to her.

PAIN

As my years at American Airlines flew by, no pun intended, I realized that this job was not going to last forever. I wondered about upgrading to captain for my last couple of years, but then in January 2000, I could not get out of bed. I had a horrendous back pain. It was so painful I remember talking it over with Pat, wondering if somehow I had broken my back. I managed to finally get out of bed and realized my left foot was not working; that is, my left foot was dragging. I couldn't walk like I used to. I could walk, but that left foot was just being dragged along wherever I went. The doctors all said I had some severely ruptured disks in my lower back. An appointment was set up for me to have an operation. And then I saw two more doctors to get their opinions. One told me I might try to wait awhile. He said that, statistically, those who did not get operated on progressed as well as those who did after a two-year period. Two years seemed like a long time, but as another doctor said, "If you can avoid having holes in your body from surgery, you should do so." I waited, and my foot started working again after a few weeks. I went on sick leave.

In the airlines, sick leave can be strung out for a long time. Because I was a senior copilot who had never been sick, I had 180 days of sick leave built up. Because I could hold schedules that flew only ten days a month, those 180 days would last about a year and a half. I felt guilty about it, but my back never did fully recover. I'd say, "I have constant back pain, but it is tolerable." I never went back to work at the airlines, and for six months, I even took disability. I hated that, because it made me feel like a government mooch, which I had disdained all my life. Still do.

I got my picture of the MD-80 with some signatures on it from crewmembers, ordered my retirement gift from American's retirement catalogue (a statue of an eagle with wings spread), finalized some 401(k) items, and retired from the airline business in 2002. If anyone is keeping track, I had spent twenty years in the air force and now sixteen years with American Airlines. My mother used to say that the older one got, the faster time went by, and she was right. God bless you, Mom.

Left to right: **Me; my brother, Jack; and my nephew, Jason, on Jodi's wedding day**

CHAPTER 7

Ages Sixty to Seventy: 2002–2012

Dow Jones Industrial Average
8,341.63–13,104.14
57.1% Gain

STILL FLYIN' *SONGBIRD*

AT THE END OF MARCH 2002, I officially retired from the airlines and never flew a jet again. It was a federal law that commercial airline pilots retire at age sixty, and my sixtieth birthday was that month. The feds changed the mandatory-retirement age to sixty-five a few years after I retired, but I wouldn't have stayed until I turned sixty-five.

My motorcycle sat collecting dust in the garage. I really couldn't ride it now with my bad back. If it had been a stock Harley, I could have ridden it, but because it had been lowered, it had little suspension, and riding it now felt like taking a beating. After three years or so, I sold it. We sold Pat's bike too. When the buyer drove off on Pat's bike, I remember seeing the tears in Pat's eyes.

Old *Songbird* was a different story. We kept flying, although I was concerned about my next physical with the FAA. We had

303

taken 8797X back east many times. We went up to see an old air force squadron commander of mine in Wisconsin, and we visited some of the islands north of Washington. We visited an old friend, Sid Head, in Montana. Sid had been a U2 pilot I had met at Beale AFB. We flew around Mount Rushmore on one of these trips. We loved Lake Tahoe, although its mountains, changing cloud conditions, and elevation challenged anybody flying a small airplane. On two occasions, pilots lost their lives there within one day of our arrival at or departure from Lake Tahoe. We flew to Colorado a few times, once to see my old friend Tony Reyna and another time to see my favorite lieutenant, now my favorite bird colonel, Kent Traylor. He was retiring from the air force. We flew back again to see Kent's daughter, Megan, get married. Colorado was also a challenging place to fly a small airplane with its mountains, high elevations, and changing weather conditions.

On any of these trips, we seldom flew more than four hours a day. People always wonder where you land for gas, food, bathrooms, and overnight accommodations, but there are literally hundreds and hundreds of small airfields spread across the United States. With the technology we have today in the form of the GPS, these are easy to find on a sunny day. Generally I watched and manipulated the GPS, while Pat kept track of us on a real map and used the old VHF omnidirectional radio range (VOR) in our airplane to cross-check our position. VOR is a fairly antiquated method of navigation, but with effort, you can navigate fairly well. We had two VORs in *Songbird*.

As we flew around to all these places, we found that sometimes these small airports had what they called a courtesy car. Because all these little airports ran on small budgets, they knew that if they could provide a car for people to drive to the next little town to get a bite to eat or a motel room, it might help them get people to fly into their location more frequently. There was usually only one courtesy car at these airports, if any. The courtesy cars could aptly be described by a few words we had used as teenagers. They were all shit bangers. They were usually twenty years old at a minimum, few air conditioners were in working order, paint usually had seen better days, and there were usually a few dents and bruises on them to attest to the fact that they had survived a lot of "combat."

We came to love these courtesy cars, mostly because they were free. Well, they were free in the sense that there was no charge to use them, but the underlying assumption to the use of a courtesy car was that the user would put a few gallons of gas into it. We always filled them up, because we were so happy to have a vehicle for a while.

Well, to the story now. At one of these places, we got our courtesy car, and it had a big sign painted on the side that said, "Such and Such County Airport Commission." It also had one of those spotlights on it, like the old police cars, where the controls to point the spotlight were readily available by the driver's left hand. We laughed as we drove this big white boat toward town. As we got into town, a woman in a car going the opposite direction flagged us down. We stopped in the middle of the street, rolled down our window, and listened to her tell us about a dead deer lying in the middle of the road on some avenue. It became clear to us that she thought we were government employees who would take care of this. We giggled as we drove off after telling the woman "we'll get right on it," as Fuzzy would say.

Ever since I was eighteen or nineteen years old, all I really wanted to do was fly for the military, but my second desire was to be able to fly around the country in a small airplane. The military flying had been a blast, as had the commercial airline business. But the small-airplane flying, or GA flying, was also a world unto itself. I had come to say over the years that flying is a humbling profession. Its humbling capability didn't really care if you happened to be in a military airplane, a commercial airplane, or a general-aviation airplane. Nor did it care how experienced you were. I guess my point here is that, after a while, we relaxed while flying *Songbird*, but the notion of how any airplane could humble you was burned into our psyches. We remained cautious.

REFLECTIONS

In flying *Songbird*, we had some time to reflect on things. I guess I spent a lot of time thinking how lucky I had been to have all these aviation experiences. Of the hundreds of things I pondered while flying around in 8797X, I'll pick just a few to reflect on here.

I always wondered about how the Wright brothers' shop could not have been that much different from Fred Werner's garage in Hubbard. My grandfather had been four years old when the Wrights first flew. And as a measure of the tremendous strides made in aviation in Bill's lifetime, I remember sitting in a phone booth, calling my mother to tell her what it was like to bring the SR-71 to an air show while my grandfather was still very much alive.

I always reflected on all the people I had known who had lost their lives in aviation, regardless of the type of airplane or circumstance. One of the first mechanics I had work on 8797X had been a retired air force sergeant. He had flown GA airplanes for a long time, until one day, up in the mountains, he asked a few people if they wanted a ride in his airplane. He took off, made a low turn, clipped a tree, crashed, and burned. Another very precise, clean-living major and air force pilot I had worked with in Sunnyvale retired and built his own airplane. He took off one day and crashed and burned.

The airline accidents, as few as they were, were often horrific, due to the massive loss of life. I must say that I haven't personally known a pilot at the controls of a commercial jet that crashed, but I always think of the many military guys I knew who lost their lives in airplanes, mostly by enemy fire but sometimes by mechanical failures. Paul Bast, the guy I had met back in my KC-135 days, had a double-engine fire in an F-4 and lost his life in Thailand. Billie Williams, my RF-4 operations officer, was shot down and died in Vietnam. His back seater that day, Hector Acosta, survived capture and imprisonment. I had previously flown with Hector on many occasions. Hector was released at the same time as John McCain and most of the other POWs. Dick Elzinga, from my pilot-training class, was a Raven forward air controller and lost his life in Southeast Asia. Roger Behnfledt, a classmate in ROTC at BG and an RF-4 squadron mate, was shot out of the air with a surface-to-air missile in North Vietnam. His back seater survived. Bill Gauntt's airplane was shot down, and the back seater, Fran Townsend, was killed shortly after parachuting to the ground in Vietnam. Both were squadron mates in the RF-4. Many of the fighter pilots I lived with at Udorn were killed, mostly while flying over North Vietnam.

I always wondered if I would lose my life in an airplane or perhaps on a motorcycle. The cockpit of a small airplane is a place where that kind of unlimited philosophical thought often takes place. Books like *Jonathan Livingston Seagull* were born in an aviator's mind, and other aviators have continued to write about the mystery and wonder of aviation. I often thought I would write a book solely about aviation, but this memoir is as close as I will ever get to it.

I forget the actual date, but somewhere in this time frame, I attended a reunion of the Fourteenth Tactical Reconnaissance Squadron with all the RF-4 crewmembers I'd been with at Udorn, Thailand. My big surprise was how little time Lee VanNamen and I spent together at the reunion. Lee was my back seater, with whom I had flown countless missions into all the highest-threat areas in Southeast Asia. Lee had his medical practice set up in Michigan for over twenty years and had a charming wife and two teenage boys. And then he died at an early age. I was devastated. To this day, whenever I look up in the sky and see any cloud formation, the next thing I think of is Lee. And then I wish I could have helped him. Bless you, Lee VanNamen. Without you I would not have survived Vietnam.

I'll turn to the positive side now. A bottom line to most of this flying thing, for me, could be boiled down to one thing: beauty. The beauty of America, and of the world, for that matter, is an amazing thing to see from the air, whether it is seen from my tree perch on Fox Street in Hubbard, Ohio; from the cockpit of a GA airplane; from the Aeronca Champ I flew as a teenager; or from 8797X, which I flew as a fifty-, sixty-, or seventy-year-old geezer. The commercial jets provided a great view of America from thirty-five to thirty-seven thousand feet, while the views from eighty thousand feet and Mach 3 in the SR-71 were unique experiences, to say the least. The treetop-level experiences of low-level flying in the RF-4 at 540 knots and above were another wonder. Just before sunrise, North Vietnam, South Vietnam, Laos, and Cambodia were stunning from the air, despite the war going on there. Sundown or sunrise makes most places look beautiful, I have found. The mountains and the shafts of light are unbelievably alluring at dawn. Gazing at the constantly changing pictures provided by moving across terrain, water, jungle, mountains, or desert served always to mesmerize me through most of my life.

The thought of no longer flying saddened me, but I guess I was glad to be away from the responsibility of ensuring that every flight was conducted safely and without any loss of life. If I'd had a son or daughter who wanted to fly, I would worry about him or her, no doubt. Maybe I would tell him or her what Ma, my grandmother, told me when she knew that I, as a teenager, was headed out to fly the Aeronca Champ. She would say, "Now fly low and slow, honey." She didn't know the dangers of flying low or slow, but I knew she had my best interests at heart.

At the risk of overdramatizing things here, let me give some of the lyrics to a favorite song of mine. I hummed it for years, having no idea what the lyrics were. Quite a while ago, I found out what the song really meant to me. Because of copyright law I am only going to quote a couple verses that stand out to me. I present them in a sequence different than the original song.

William H. Gilmore

From Somewhere Over the Rainbow[†]

Somewhere over the rainbow
Skies are blue,
And the dreams that you dare to dream
Really do come true.

Somewhere over the rainbow
Bluebirds fly.
Birds fly over the rainbow.
Why then, oh why can't I?

As I sit here thinking that I would like to account for more in my sixty- to seventy-year-old decade, I realize that as the flying slowed down, so did my life. In most respects, that was a good thing. So what else did I do during these years?

GETTIN' REALLY OLD

Computers had been around for twenty years, but by the time I retired at sixty in 2002, technology had really started to bloom. I did my best to keep up with it, and I will say my primary motivation regarding technology was to keep up with

---

† "Over the Rainbow" (often referred to as "Somewhere over the Rainbow") is a ballad with music by Harold Arlen and lyrics by E. Y. Harburg. It was written for the movie *The Wizard of Oz* (1939) and was sung by actress Judy Garland in her starring role as Dorothy Gale.

and investigate ways tech could be used to study the movements in the stock market. The stock market had been the background noise to my life, but now that I was really retired, it took on a whole life of its own. I came to spend more and more time on the computer. I still remember typing cd\DOS. I have a difficult time even finding the backslash on the keyboard now. Thank God those days are over. What a crazy time that was. That crackling sound of the first modems still rings in my ears.

As the technology improved and the computers got better, I found myself spending hours and hours on the computer. I began getting headaches, because I'd never gotten the correct eyeglass prescription for the focal distance I needed. Looking back, I'm not sure any eyeglasses would have solved the problem; I was just spending so much time on the computer. This was all from my office in the Morgan Hill, California, house. I came to joke that when I die, if I worked it just right, nobody would even know I had died—that is, if I executed my plan to be interred in one of those mausoleums. My plan was to have a window in it with a computer and a chair. I always said that if I was propped up in a chair in front of my computer, no one looking through the window would know I had passed on.

My old friend Buzzy used to have another plan. He said I would die before him, and he would get me a casket with a window on it up near my face so I could look out, and only then would he bury me. He said he would have *his* casket made with a window on the bottom to frame his ass. He would say that, upon his death, he would have his casket placed on top of mine so I would have to look at his ass through eternity. I guess some people don't like this kind of humor, but I find it absolutely hilarious.

Buzzy continued to surprise me. Early in my sixties, I received a letter and a note from some unexpected sources. The first was a signed letter from President George W. Bush. Buzzy had somehow communicated with the White House and had gone into some kind of detail on the missions I had flown in Asia. I have no idea what or how he had communicated to the White House staff, but I received a very kind letter of recognition from the president, and I was appreciative of it. As for the note, this actually arrived in an envelope. Inside, on a three-by-three-inch piece of paper, was a very appreciative note for my service to the country. It referenced one of the aircraft I had flown while in the service and was signed "Newt Gingrich." Again, I have no idea how Buzzy made this happen. I did write President Bush to thank him, but shame on me, I never wrote back to Newt. I will, one of these days.

I used to do something with my friends that I found they did not appreciate. My effort, from my perspective, was to shock them into enjoying the days they had remaining on this earth. I looked at this game of mine positively, though I found eventually that most others did not take my game in a positive light. That is, I used to find someone's age and compute the number of days that most longevity tables said he or she had left to live. Then I would report to the person the number of days he or she had remaining. I was the only one who seemed to enjoy this experiment. I found it motivating to continue living life to the fullest, to focus on things you wanted to do, and to sift out the things you did not want to do. But again, nobody else looked at this the way I did. When I used to tell Jerry, my breakfast friend, that he only had 3,500 days left, he never liked it. Pat never liked it either. But at least I would laugh. I guess part of it was that I was amazed I was still alive after Southeast Asia and my lifelong fetish for flight and speed.

So I spent the decade in part on the computer and still did some flying. With the collapse of the real estate market, and almost the banking system in 2008, the stock market had a rough time for quite a while. Many got out of the market at the bottom and never returned. These were some really difficult years for most people. I had a lot of anguish as well. I spent a lot of time trying to figure the markets out, but in the end, I survived it fairly well.

I noticed that many people have a vacation place they go to, sometimes every year. I feel like I missed out on this practice, although Pat and I have been going to Lake Tahoe for a few days most years. I always felt envious of my brother's house on the Allegheny River, though. Ken Rock, my old friend from grad school at BG, and his wife would meet us in Tahoe to enjoy his favorite retirement sports, gambling and fishing. Actually, he was the instigator of this yearly pilgrimage. I suppose we've done this for at least five or six years.

When guys retire, they seem to gravitate to coffee shops. Have you noticed? Look around you at any of your local coffee shops, especially in the early morning. There they are, those old geezers. My buddy Jerry and I became part of that crowd and would eat breakfast together for years; at first we did this two or three times a week, but now we meet only on Fridays. This was partly because Pat liked to sleep late, and Jerry's wife was slow to get out the door early too. Amazingly, I would say I have been eating breakfast with Jerry at least once a week for at least fifteen years.

Jerry is a high school graduate who came from very modest roots. He went to a predominantly African-American school and spent some time in an adolescent group called the Sinners. I've told him that, while in grade school, AG, Paul Leach, and I were known as the Wolves, and we had a big patch on the back of each of our jackets that announced our pack name to the world. Anyway, Jerry had become a flower grower, running his own business in California. At some point, it became possible for a farmer in Mexico to plant, raise, harvest, and ship a rose to the United States cheaper than it could be done here. This spelled the end for most flower growers in the United States, at least the small growers. I guess the North American Free Trade Agreement (NAFTA) was part of the undoing of the US-based flower growers as well. The implementation of NAFTA on January 1, 1994, brought the immediate elimination of tariffs on more than half of Mexico's exports to the United States.

Jerry minimized everything and managed to stay in business longer than most. Eventually he sold his business and bought a building in Texas that housed a Jiffy Lube business He then lived off the proceeds in fine fashion. He golfs a few times a week, and most of his golf buddies are professionals—that is, dentists and engineers. He has suffered two heart attacks, more than fifteen years ago. He loves his wife; his son, a battalion chief in the fire department; and his three grandchildren. Jerry and I have had a lot of fun just talking for these fifteen years in the coffee shop and another ten before that when I was still riding motorcycles. I must say I am surprised at how the time has flown. We don't have another twenty years in us. Well, he might.

The phone still plays a role in some retirees' lives. Occasional phone conversations with my old Hubbard friends; AG, Fran, Fred, my brother, Jack; and my military buddies Tony, Wally, Paul, Karl, John, Don, and Kent have served to refresh once in a while. My ole college buddy Ken Rock and I still talk at least once a week. Fuzzy, Dom, and Frank are the primary airline guys that I still converse with, while my local buddies Jerry, Don, Dave and the BBQ gang, and Warren still help me make sense of this stage of life. Jason, I enjoy our conversations, and Jodi, I need to start calling you. You young people don't talk much on the phone, I've noticed. Everyone is texting now, which I appreciate. I wish my brother did the texting thing more.

DON AND DAVE

Another endeavor these years is what I'll call Don and Dave's BBQ. These guys I met through Jerry. They each also have an interesting story. Their father and mother came from Italy, and Don, Dave, and their sister were born right here in California. The father was a hard taskmaster and stayed on his boys to produce. Most of their tasks were associated with farm life, and gradually the father began making a few real estate investments. The father was growing flowers, and the scene of him and the boys riding to San Francisco in predawn hours became a common occurrence. San Fran is where they sold a lot of flowers. With some of this money, the father bought land in a few places, including in what is now known as Silicon Valley. Needless to say, this worked out well. The boys, Don and Dave, continued to raise flowers after the father died and at some point began raising grapes to be harvested for the production of wine. They continue this still. They also continue efforts in commercial real estate and have done remarkably well there.

Years ago, Don and Jerry used to take a break from their day and meet under a tree on a farm where they would share some wine and eat some cheese. Don and Dave owned the farm, and eventually this cheese and wine break morphed into a BBQ. I would meet Don and Dave through Jerry in our earlier Harley-riding days. I remember the day I met Don. As we shook hands, he asked, "What is a nice guy like you doing hanging around these derelicts?"

I started going to the monthly BBQ. At first there were six or seven people there, but now about twenty people come each month. Don and Dave seem to love to cook, and their boys always attend as well. The rest of the guys resemble the customers in the coffee shops described above—they are geezers. And it is a "guys only" affair at these BBQs. Of course there are no lies ever told at these gatherings. I remain fascinated with the personalities, just as I did with my kids on Fox Street, though now I find I am looking at people whose lives have been lived rather than at kids whose lives are about to be lived.

A machinist, a couple of flower growers, a mushroom grower, an insulation guy, a CPA, some grape growers, a realtor, an aviator, and a host of other retirees and small businessmen who show up as friends of the core group are the people at the BBQ. And the core group for the most part is composed of high school graduates. Individually, their successes remind me of those detailed in a book I read once years ago called *The Millionaire Next Door*. The author describes a number of people who have four to six years of work, earning money, and advancing in their chosen field, while the college folks are getting through school. This sometimes turns out better for these "early to work" individuals than the collegiate set. Many of the BBQ guys are multimillionaires.

Jerry told me one time, early on, that high school–educated Don could do anything. Electrical, plumbing, building, well information, business operations, flower growing, grape growing, shower installation, installations of any sort—he was very familiar with and had a working pragmatic knowledge of all these things and more. Dave, I felt, understood all these areas too. Don and Dave's father would not let them watch TV when they were growing up, and to this day, they find the farm their place to be rather than watching TV. They have saved, they have worked, and they have traveled now in their older years. It is especially interesting that they have been so successful when their father came here with so very little. I guess the only reason I spend so much time writing about them is that they and Jerry are among the few social outlets I have here later in life. Besides that, the Vannis' (Don and Dave's) work ethic is a thing of beauty.

I saw Don stand up and give a little speech at his brother's birthday party recently. Entwined within his speech was a metaphor his father used to use about donkeys. The story he told made the point that if it weren't for the hardworking donkey, the people and goods in the wagon would never get up the proverbial hill. I think his point was that their father had instilled in him and his brother the notion that they better always keep pulling that cart, filled with family members and other goods, in order to get up the hill. These kinds of stories were reminiscent of my grandfather's thoughts and values.

TONY, WALLY, AND KARL

The first draft of this manuscript contained some pictures that eventually had to be pulled because of publishing limits. One was a picture of Colonel Karl Polifka as an older man.

Tony Reyna and Wally Hopkins, aviators extraordinaire. *Left*, Colonel Tony Reyna retired in Colorado. *Right*, Wally Hopkins rode his Harley from Florida to Colorado to see Tony and a few sights along the way. We were all lucky to survive the flights into North Vietnam. Tony, at this point (*above*), had just begun to feel the effects of Parkinson's.

Karl, my RF-4 friend, had also been a forward air controller early on, operating mostly in Laos as a Raven FAC. He wrote a book called *Meeting Steve Canyon...and Flying with the CIA in Laos.* After our tour together in the RF-4, Karl flew the B-52 and spent six or seven years in the Pentagon. He is married to Lois, a retired lieutenant colonel from the USAF.

**This was young Tony Reyna. I think he
loved to fly as much as anyone.
This picture was taken at least thirty years prior to the
one above it, where he is standing with Wally. Wally once
referred to Tony as "the Gentle Warrior"—that he was.**

Another picture I had to cut but still relish is one of a P-51. If you Google "Ferocious Frankie," you will see some better pictures than any I could have provided here. I note one description of the beautiful airplane had some text associated with it, as follows: "It now carries the highly distinguishing colours of Wallace E. Hopkins, as 'Ferocious Frankie,' named in honour of his wife, Frankie, coded B7 H of the 374th Fighter Squadron, 361st Fighter Group. Wallace Hopkins was born in Washington, Georgia, and flew a total of 76 combat missions (during WWII) with the 361st where he flew as Operations Officer. He was an ACE credited with 8 victories and 1.5 damaged. His decorations include the Air Medal and Distinguished Flying Cross both with Oak Leaf Clusters and the French Croix de Guerre, one of four awarded to members of the 361st."[5] This Wally Hopkins, who flew Ferocious Frankie in World War II, is the father of the Wally Hopkins, my buddy shown in the picture with Tony Reyna earlier. The younger Wally had been in the Fourteenth Tactical Reconnaissance Squadron in Thailand with us in 1972 and '73 and remains a friend of mine to this day.

CHAPTER 8

Ages Seventy to Seventy-Five: 2012–May 2017

**Dow Jones Industrial Average
13,104.14–20,804 (as of about 11:25 a.m.
Pacific, May 19, 2017)
58.76% Gain**

DEALING WITH AGE AND LOSS

SOMEBODY SAID THAT IF YOU want to get a picture of just where you stand on this age thing, you should take a tape measure and pull it out to the same number of inches as there are years you expect to live. It's been a while since I've looked at the tables, but thinking positively, maybe I will live to be eighty. That leaves me five inches left on the tape measure. Put another way, five times 365 equals 1,825 days left. I know you might think I am sick for looking at it this way, but, what the hell, you have to have some idea of the meaning of time. When we were approaching retirement from American Airlines, my friend Ed Wilds used to say, "We are getting ready for graduation." I use that now in talking about getting to the end of this road. One of these days, we all get to graduate. We just don't know when.

What have I done since turning seventy? I've continued the discussions with those listed in the last chapter. I've been working on my five acres ever since we moved into this house in Morgan Hill. I have farmed out some of the work but still get involved, mostly in weed cutting and some flower planting, and I am chief repairman for waterlines to shrubs, flowers, and yard. I got two bigger and brighter computer monitors within the last year. I joke that having two screens for my desktop computer allows me to lose money quicker in the stock market than I did with one screen. Some days that is true. But really, somebody asked me what I need two screens for, and my response was that if I had ten screens, I would want eleven. I almost bought a third screen last week, in fact.

The stock market remains almost as vibrant as it has always been for me. I have often said that if I were broke, I would still watch the markets. I guess Jack, my brother, feels the same way. I remember years ago that he had a picture of a bum wearing torn plaid pants, a very old top hat, and shoes with holes in the soles and sitting on a park bench reading the *Wall Street Journal*. I have confessed that the market compulsion is probably related to the love I had for my grandfather and his low-key ways of introducing me to the markets.

So that is what I do now—a few friends, a few telephone calls, some market analysis, and a lot of TV watching. I took my last FAA physical in about 2015, but I told the doctor I would not be back for another. I noticed he had two pictures hung outside his office. One was of an NFL football player, one of his patients. The other was of me standing in front of an SR-71. I had no idea he was going to do that. I told my FAA check-ride pilot I would not be back again either. I remained qualified to fly until 2016.

Tom Alison died. He was an SR-71 pilot I was stationed with—a good guy. I talked to Fran Fluent a while back, and he said Janet Cox died in Hubbard. I went to high school with her and actually had one date with her. She died of cancer and lived next to Fran. This seems impossible. Thom Evans, an old RF-4 driver and once U2 pilot, died. One of my best air force friends, Tony Reyna, is fighting a battle against Parkinson's. What a miserable disease. He was a full-bird colonel in the air force, a great pilot, and my roommate when we were in Thailand flying RF-4s. Dan Smelko, an old Hubbard friend, says he has some disease—I forget the name—that is a derivative of Parkinson's, but he says the doctor told him he will not die from it. He shakes a little and worries about whether he will be able to rope and ride horses as he has done for the majority of his life. He left Hubbard at eighteen with a football scholarship to Missoula, Montana, and then never left Montana. He was always so physically fit.

Me? My back still is painful but tolerable. I have small vision impairment in my right eye, but for the most part, I see just fine. A recent update says I need cataract surgery. I am tired all the time now. They say I have sleep apnea, but at my last visit to a sleep doctor, the doctor said I was using the equipment properly and getting good numbers. She said she didn't think that anything else could be done. It's funny; I sleep straight through for seven or seven and a half hours a night, and when I wake up, I feel like I have not slept at all. Many old people have this problem. I take Lipitor, like all my buddies, for cholesterol. You two, Jason and Jodi, will find out more about this about thirty-five years from now. In short, I still feel lucky to be alive and generally enjoy each day.

At American Airlines, I flew a couple of times with a younger captain named Jon Dennis. I saw he had that off-this-planet sense of humor I had always appreciated, but I contained myself, as I still did not know him well. As time went by, I kept hearing from Jon, especially because he had bought a hangar two doors down from mine at Frazier Lake. He had some small glider airplanes strung from the top of his hangar. These were airplanes he had assembled as a kid. He had a small Evinrude outboard engine in there as well. It reminded me of the Mercury engine Grandpa Bill had had for his trips to Canada and the one my Fox Street neighbor Dick Mason had for his little boat. As time went by, I was seeing more and more of Jon. I met his outstanding wife and heard his stories about all his years of flying. He told stories of learning to fly on floats before he learned to fly an airplane with wheels, flying some executives of Intel around in a business jet, and of his eventual job with Air California and American Airlines. I remembered thinking he fit the Air California mold. He could fly the hell out of any airplane he put his hands on.

After Jon retired from American Airlines, he went to work selling one of the modern GA airplanes. As that business wound down, he ended up driving eighteen-wheeler trucks for at least four or five years. I think his dad had driven trucks for a while. Eventually Jon took a job with an FAA reporting organization, reviewing and analyzing commercial airline reports to help decide if changes were needed in the FAA system to enhance safety. He seemed to enjoy this and made some friends there.

Energetic, Jon always seemed to be looking for what was next, so one day I asked if he wanted to join Jerry and me for our Friday breakfasts. He did. From about February or March 2014 until November 2014, Jon would show up for our Friday breakfasts. In the meantime, I watched him at Frazier Lake flying his Cessna 140, a light, 1950s-vintage airplane. I learned more about his humor, writing, and photographic abilities and his stint in the coast guard, where he started as a teenager. He was a real horseman who loved the outdoors. He had two or three horses at his home, just a five-minute drive from my house. We had a few martinis together and visited each other at our homes. And then I got a call from his wife one morning in November 2014. She told me he had taken a granddaughter flying the day before and hadn't returned home. Jon and his granddaughter had perished in a plane crash. The cause is undetermined, at least at this point. Life is tough as you get older. I am missing Jon and going through the frustrations of not being able to fix everything for his wife and family.

I think about the flying time Jon had, something like twenty thousand to twenty-four thousand hours, and five thousand hours of that was in small tail-wheel aircraft. I know very few pilots with that kind and variety of flying time, and I have known a lot of aviators. This was a lot of flying time for anyone to have, and it showed he'd spent his life in the air. We can't figure out how something could have happened to him in an airplane that would end his life. Jon was too good of an aviator for anything like this to happen. He was sixty-nine but could pass as a fifty-year-old on most days.

You can see how things go in your seventies, dear Jason and Jodi. I will do my best to keep a positive attitude, and I hope you learn something from all this writing. It seems that an old man would be able to impart some wisdom to his young niece and nephew, but I doubt I can do a whole lot of that. For some reason, for most of my life, I haven't verbalized my thoughts on a whole lot of things. I have preferred to listen to opinions rather than give mine. I liked taking a low-key approach; at least that's how I thought of myself. Some who know me now might disagree with that description.

GUIDANCE FOR MY NIECE AND NEPHEW

I guess I have little guidance for you, and what I have to say is probably very trite, especially with me never having kids. I think having kids probably gets one in shape to *give guidance.* So, with some reluctance, I will say this: love your mates, your kids, and your friends. Try not to be too critical of them; they are human, as you are. Be a model for your children; they will copy many of your methods, whether you want them to or not. Laugh. Embrace humor. Choose to stay positive. Don't take life for granted, for it will go by way too quickly. If you are inclined, be creative. If you are not inclined, try to be creative anyway. I like the notion of striking a balance between the physical, mental, and spiritual aspects of life. Keep smiling. Stay away from drugs. Be careful with alcohol. Try to master one, two, or maybe even three things in this life. Avoid envy. If it is possible, teach your children to avoid envy. At times I think Socialism and Communism are built upon the shoulders of this infection: envy. I worry it can rot our world, our country, or our families from within. Teach your children what you can about economics, capitalism, and even the stock markets. Elementary schools, high schools, and most colleges, as they exist today, likely will not teach these subjects in any meaningful way, and many college professors will show utter disdain for those same subjects.

To All the Mothers, Including My Own

Here, at the conclusion of this memoir, I want to say something else, and I am finding it very difficult to arrive at a reserved, humble, and appropriate message for my thoughts. And this is for you, Jason and Jodi, but it is more for mothers everywhere. It is this: because of all the things my mother instilled in me—chiefly through love, support, and subtle guidance— she provided a road map to help me form goals for myself. I found it amazing that that same love, support, and subtle guidance is what lit a fire within me to strive for those same goals. Mothers, never doubt the influence you have over your children, especially in their early years. Fathers—well, that is another story.

Finally, I love you, Jason and Jodi, probably more than you will ever know.

My last comment about mothers has to be reserved for my own mother, Alice Marie Gilmore. Thanks for your love and your discipline. Rest in peace, my dear mother.

SOME PICTURES

Jason's wedding. From left to right, this image
shows me; Patricia; Jack; Jason and his wife,
Carli; my sister-in-law, Judy; and Jodi.
In the upper right are Jodi's husband,
Paul, and my great-niece Ruby.

**My four great-nieces and great-nephews:
Winston, Ruby, Will, and Ellie**

**My Friday breakfast buddy for the past twenty years, Jerry (*sitting
center*). Next to Jerry is his wife, Vicki. Pat and I are standing.**

This is the godfather, Mr. Rock. He's a glass expert, realtor/broker, entrepreneur extraordinaire, and friend since the Bowling Green days.

Patricia, Gil, and *Songbird*. The Cessna Skylane 182 had a max speed of about 173 mph and 230 horsepower.

CHAPTER 9

What Do I Think about the Vietnam War?

MIKE AND MAX ASK THE QUESTION

JUST WHEN YOU GOT USED to my chapter formatting with the age thing going on, such as *Ages Ten to Twenty*, etc., I switched this last chapter name to one without an age mentioned in the chapter title. Why? It is because while my involvement in Southeast Asia and the Vietnam War is clear in this memoir, *what I felt or thought about the Vietnam War*, thus far in this memoir, is not clear.

Most Vietnam veterans could write an entire book about their thoughts on Vietnam, and so could I. I will write some of those thoughts here. This is difficult and likely will be a catharsis for me, possibly of interest to you, and likely provocative to many others who might read this. Although the subject is probably too large to include at the end of a memoir, I will persist.

What I think about Vietnam and how it changed me are questions I have been asked through the years in various ways, but I never really gave thoughtful answers. Specifically, and more recently, I was asked these questions by two of my friends' kids, Mike and Max. They were both about seventeen or eighteen years old and were doing class projects with Vietnam as a theme. This was in the 2010 to 2014 time frame. I gave them answers, but as usual, I wasn't satisfied with those abbreviated responses.

To say I disagreed with much of the rhetoric regarding Vietnam was an understatement. My nature had always been to get along with people, but the subject of Vietnam has always tested this principle of mine. Generally I stayed quiet and listened, perhaps for forty years or more. And gradually I came to wonder if anybody was aware of what had really gone on in Vietnam. When these two young men asked their questions about Vietnam for their class study, I found, in retrospect, that my answers were not very forthcoming. I found I had been silent for so long that articulation on the subject was probably lacking, as was any real mastery of the topic.

Before and after these discussions with Mike and Max, I tried to review some articles and books about the subject. As I reviewed a few books, I reflected on a couple things. Many, perhaps most, Vietnam veterans have never answered these questions, especially in any kind of public forum. From a veteran's perspective, the public really didn't much care what he or she, the veteran, thought. That aside, I pondered the questions for years after Vietnam was over, but I considered them even more after these two young guys approached me. So I am going to give a more thoughtful answer to these questions now. The answers are likely at an elementary level compared to the writings of literary scholars, but I think my experiences in Asia count for something—my experiences during two years in Asia and 474 combat missions flown in three different aircraft, operating out of three different locations in two different countries.

These 474 combat missions covered geography from a few miles south of China, through North Vietnam, and to the southern tip of South Vietnam. Laos and Cambodia were very familiar geographically to me also. Of the 474 missions I flew in Southeast Asia, 110 were flights into North Vietnam. Most aviator vets will separate their activities distinctively between North or South Vietnam, because for aviators, the threat level was so much higher, generally, in North Vietnam than it was in South Vietnam. (I pause to recognize all the operators in Laos and Cambodia, such as the Raven FACs, who faced huge threats.)

OTHER CATALYSTS FOR MY VIETNAM DISCUSSIONS

As I continued my search for more literary information regarding Vietnam, to my surprise, I found a catalyst in a book by Thomas Sowell called *Intellectuals and Society*.[6] My lifelong affinity for understanding more about human intelligence was the only reason for my interest in this book at the time. Not military intelligence. It was brainpower intelligence that interested me. I was interested in the title alone and expected to learn something more about intelligence quotients and how the mind works. Neither Vietnam nor this memoir was on my mind at the time. To my surprise, this book turned out to be the Vietnam discussion catalyst I had looked for on many occasions.

If you leaf to the back of this memoir, you will see that I have provided five "Vietnam Appendixes." In order to have you understand the effects that Sowell had on me during this journey I have provided an appendix titled *Appendix B:*

Thomas Sowell on Vietnam. It is the second appendix of five that I present. You should know that Sowell's writings most influenced how I presented my own thoughts on the subject of Vietnam here in this chapter. Similarly, I was greatly affected by the other books detailed in the appendixes: *Stolen Valor* and *Thoughts of a Philosophical Fighter Pilot.* These books, my experiences in Southeast Asia, and the environment that I grew up in are the basis upon which I write the following.

The first image that comes to my mind about *how I feel about Vietnam* is, ironically, a picture I have hanging on a wall in my house. The picture depicts an American sailor kissing a woman in Times Square in New York City, purportedly on Victory over Japan Day (V-J Day). The date of this picture was August 14 or 15, 1945. A US Navy photographer is credited with taking the picture, although photojournalist Victor Jorgensen is also frequently credited with taking a very similar picture.

**"Kissing the War Goodbye"(public domain
photo by Victor Jorgensen)**

You probably wonder how this picture relates to Vietnam
for me. It does so in four ways. First, the sailor is in uniform.

Vietnam vets, for the most part, did not wear their uniforms on public streets in America, because of all the protest riots over the war. Second, in the Times Square picture, there seems to be a celebration of the war being over and a celebration of the veterans too. There was no celebration for the war being over in Vietnam, and certainly there was no celebration for the veterans who had participated in it. Third, we all know WWII had been won, and the picture certainly embraces the notion of winning.

But winning in Vietnam? The subject of winning in Vietnam is largely lost on the American public, and they, on average, have no idea about it. Again, I think the average US civilian alive at the time would blanch at any notion of the United States winning anything in Vietnam. All in all, when I look at this sailor's picture, I feel elation for the veterans and for the United States during this time. They were proud Americans, they had worked together, and they had won. But I am reminded of Vietnam also, because the message sent to Vietnam veterans was that we should *not* be proud. Most would agree that the people of the United States did not work together in the Vietnam War effort. Further, there were people in the United States who seemed determined to ensure we did not win in Vietnam. That last statement sounds provocative, but I will expand upon this notion later.

The fourth thing I think of when I look at this picture is that my father had a uniform just like the sailor's. I had inspected every inch of that uniform as it hung in his closet in Hubbard, Ohio, beginning when I was five or six years old. Of course I had several sailor hats that I wore as a kid too. In short, I felt like I knew the sailor in the Jorgensen/Eisenstaedt photos. Looking back on Vietnam, I yearned for the appreciation, the jubilation, or just the thanks to the veterans—not for me, but at least for all the GIs killed or injured during the war. In general, few positives would ever come from the American public regarding Vietnam. I suppose this is one of the reasons most Vietnam veterans appreciate one another so much. From my perspective, 99.9 percent of any positive comments about Vietnam come at the intersection of Vietnam vets conversing with one another, and respect is the primary feeling that permeates most gatherings of Vietnam veterans.

THE HEART OF THE MATTER

Still you ask, What do I think about Vietnam? (Sorry for the bullet format.)

- What do I think about Vietnam?
  - o I think that, at the time, America was very worried Communism would take over a larger part of the world than it already had.
  - o I think the Domino Theory, as it was called, was valid at the time. The thought was that if South Vietnam went Communist, then so would Cambodia, Laos, the rest of Asia, and other parts of the world.
  - o I think the US military fought most of the war with at least one hand tied behind its back, due to the war being run, in many respects, from Washington.
  - o I feel that if the war had been taken directly to the heart of North Vietnam, Hanoi, in a sustained fashion, and early on, it would have ended very quickly.

Instead, Washington placed its targeting efforts in rural or remote areas too much of the time.

o I think we almost never used the full might of the military in Vietnam. And when we did, we were interrupted with bombing pauses, usually instigated by the Communists and agreed to by Washington. I think a US bombing pause should occur only if or when the United States or a US ally initiates one.

o I think that, for the first time in American history, America showed the world a weak side. The weak side came from the Americans at home and our politicians, not the military. I think the weakness shown by the Americans at home regarding Vietnam will continue to influence international policy in the future, unless somehow checked.

o I feel certain that the *intelligentsia* played a large part in the success of the Communists in Vietnam. Most in this group were Americans. My discussions on intelligentsia appear in a number of locations in this memoir, and thanks to Thomas Sowell, I realized the intelligentsia subject was at the center of my thoughts regarding the *media* versus the war in Vietnam—for years. For now let's just think of *intelligentsia* as professions who deal in the marketplace of ideas (not originators of ideas). Among the *intelligentsia* are media types, professors, and social activists and others. (This is elaborated on extensively in appendix B.)

o I feel badly—very badly—for the more than 58,200 American lives lost there.

o I feel terrible about the estimated 200,000 to 250,000 South Vietnamese lives that were lost during the war, the 165,000 South Vietnamese lost while in reeducation camps, and the 200,000 to 400,000 Vietnamese "boat people" who lost their lives after the war. (These figures vary with the source.)

o I feel very badly for the Canadian, South Korean, Thai, Australian, and New Zealand lives that were lost in Vietnam.

o I feel that few US citizens really know what happened in Vietnam.

o I feel that the US civilian population was convinced by the intelligentsia that the war was unwinnable, and once that happened, politics took over and caused the war effort to be shut down.

o I feel that, although the Vietnam War occurred a long time ago, the divide that became evident in the American populace during Vietnam has only widened since.

o I feel that America has never had a government run by the hard left until recently (2008–2016). I think this evolution of American politics was greatly influenced by the left during the Vietnam War years. Many of the protesters of the Vietnam War *or their ilk* are leading the country now.

o I feel that our school systems, colleges, and news outlets are mostly run by the left, and so the US will continue its decline into socialism or socialistic tendencies unless checked through the emergence of an iconic leadership figure to the political scene. (2016)

o I feel that America's future will continue to be negatively affected by the intelligentsia's success in molding minds in America.

o I feel that draft dodgers were never dealt with, especially those who fled to Canada. As a result, I would be amazed if there is ever a draft in America again. We set precedents of national weakness.

o I feel that the political left has always had a say about wars, but in World War I, World War II, and Korea, the left was marginalized long enough for successful outcomes to occur. In Vietnam, I feel that the political left prevailed, and of course, the outcomes were *not* successful.

o I feel a deep kinship to all who gave their lives in Vietnam, especially those I knew personally:
  - Dick Elzinga
  - Billy Joe Williams
  - Fran Townsend
  - Roger Behnfeldt
  - Bob Lodge
  - David Yokum
  - Paul Bast
  - Dana Dilly
  - George Spitz

o I feel very sad about the outcome of Vietnam, but I feel good that I gave my all in an attempt to have a successful outcome.

* Do I think differently about Vietnam now, as compared to my thoughts during the war? I told Max I feel the same now as I did back during the war. For months afterward I thought about that question. Here is my revised answer.
  o For the most part, I feel the same now as I did then.
  o But now, I feel different about government.
  o But now, I am more aware of politics.
  o But now, I am particularly aware of the politics of the left, what they are doing, and what they stand for.
  o But now, I realize the left never seems to be in favor of military involvement in anything.
  o But now, I realize that if the left is talking about a decrease in government spending, it usually means they are going to decrease spending on defense.
  o But now, I realize that in the blink of an old man's eye, the protestors and lefties, which include many members of the intelligentsia, can be installed in the heart of America's political system, and their values and ambitions can prevail for long periods of time. If they keep playing Santa Claus with the money from the public, this will continue.
  o I guess I will not name them, but I am ashamed of the leadership that has prevailed in America over the last number of years.
  o I have lost some friends over politics. For years I listened. I find that if someone responds to the left, they are stunned, and then they begin their usual demonization process. Sometimes I respond now.

o I now realize how naïve I was to believe that, if my country was at war, the war effort would be the country's top priority.

o But now, more than anything, I realize how *conflicted* our political leaders were during the Vietnam years. President Johnson, Secretary of Defense McNamara, and Daniel Ellsberg—who worked directly for McNamara—are at the top of my list of *conflicted* participants in the politics of the Vietnam War. Johnson was conflicted between the war priorities, his efforts regarding the Great Society, and his aspirations for reelection. McNamara was conflicted for many reasons. Living or operating between Presidents Kennedy and Johnson and military commanders for seven years provided the backdrop for his conflictions. Daniel Ellsberg is unique in his conflictions. While working in the highest parts of the US government and supporting McNamara at first, he later became an activist against the Vietnam War. He was responsible for giving a huge amount of classified material (later referred to as the Pentagon Papers) to media outlets. (See the book *Secrets: A Memoir of Vietnam and the Pentagon Papers.*)

o And now I realize the word *conflicted* pertains not only to the war itself and to our leaders at the time. It defined our culture then and perhaps does so even more now. I think the breadth of confliction has continued to grow within our culture. I wonder how much of the conflicts and division evident in our

American society today began during the Vietnam years.

o And now I realize arguments about Vietnam will persist forever. As someone said, the subject of Vietnam has evolved into an industry.

o I saw recently that a Hollywood mogul is thinking about making a movie about the Pentagon Papers.[7] I also heard about another planning to do a TV series on the subject of Vietnam. I assume both of these presentations will be another elaboration of media-intelligentsia philosophy, similar to what I have heard and seen since I came back to the States in 1973.

o Despite everything said so far, I must recognize a truth about the Vietnam War that is difficult for me. This is not new information, but it is often overlooked when people take sides in the arguments about Vietnam, and I think it's disheartening for most Vietnam vets, whether they learned of it early on or twenty to forty years after the war was over. (Certainly it is disheartening for me.) It is this: in 1964, there were allegedly two attacks on a US destroyer, the USS *Maddox*, in the Gulf of Tonkin. The second attack is the one our government used as an official reason to proceed into the war with Vietnam.

Commonly known as the Gulf of Tonkin Resolution, it gave President Johnson congressional authorization for the use of conventional military force in Southeast Asia. The problem with this is that the second attack on the USS *Maddox* probably never happened. Jim Stockdale describes this reality firsthand in appendix C of this memoir.

o And so now I think and wonder a lot about how the Gulf of Tonkin incident compares with other historic events (that is, historic events that existed prior to this). I believe there certainly was a huge history nudging us, one way or another, into this war in Asia prior to Johnson's being president *and prior to the Gulf of Tonkin incident.*

o There is a case to be made that the United States entered the war incrementally between 1950 and 1965.

   ▪ In 1950 President Truman authorized military aid to the French fighting for control in Vietnam, Laos, and Cambodia.

   ▪ Once the French were defeated, the Communists were in charge in North Vietnam, north of the seventeenth parallel. Noncommunist entities continued in South Vietnam. The United States refused to accept the arrangement.

   ▪ Presidents Eisenhower and Kennedy were involved in South Vietnam. Sixteen thousand US advisers were in Vietnam, and more than a hundred Americans had been killed when Kennedy was assassinated in 1963.[8]

o And so now I can more clearly see that there is a lot of history leading up to our war in Vietnam—it was a long time from 1950 to the Gulf of Tonkin incident in 1964.

o I think we had already been in a war of some sort in Asia since about 1950. To tie our entrance into Vietnam to the Gulf of Tonkin incident is to deny the fourteen years of effort already spent in turning the area from Communist control to anything resembling a free country, and this existed regardless of the reality of the second attack on the USS *Maddox*.

o I think we had a chance to help Vietnam to be free, and we blew it.

o I also wonder what would have happened had the Nixon administration not been involved in Watergate. The proximity in time between the Watergate scandal, June 1972; the Nixon resignation, August 1974; and the final collapse of South Vietnam, April 1975, only gives me more to think about. That is, given the myriad of controversies surrounding the Vietnam War, I find it interesting to contemplate what would have happened in Vietnam if Watergate had never happened and if Nixon hadn't resigned. We'll never know.

o I pause here, at the end, to reflect on some folks who have approached me to tell me *how it was in Vietnam*, when in fact they had never been there. This scenario is a problem for most Vietnam veterans and is almost never resolved through discussion. This is the reason most veterans I know reserve their thoughts and opinions until they are in the company of other Vietnam veterans.

o Well, those two young guys who interviewed me about Vietnam a few years ago would be surprised to see my new answers to their questions. Frankly, I am too. And dear Jason and Jodi, I guess you too will be surprised by the amount of time I have spent on the Vietnam subject.

My last thoughts on Vietnam will rely heavily, if not totally, on some statements made by B. C. Burkett near the end of *Stolen Valor*. He writes that he is often asked why he has completed such in-depth research on Vietnam and what he hopes to gain from it. His responses mimic, in a large way, how I feel about these questions. To the first question—"Why are you doing this?" (I extrapolate this out to include "Why have you spent so much time on the subject of Vietnam in this memoir?")— Burkett's answer is, "I have no good 'sound bite' answer. I know only that I am compelled to draw attention to the truth about Vietnam veterans and to do otherwise would be a violation of some personal code of conduct." As the author of this memoir, I feel exactly, word for word, the same way.

To the second question, "What do you want?" Burkett explains that because of the huge effort he put into his book, some say that he must want something. Similarly because of all the time I have spent on Vietnam, I might be asked the same question. First Burkett's answer, then mine.

Burkett's answer (on page 591 of his book) is this:

I have thought long and hard about that one. Do I want something? The question is usually asked in such a tone that I know the inquisitor considers my "irrational" behavior (effort in discussing Vietnam) to be a prelude to a demand—a demand like a kidnapper or a terrorist might make. Why would I have gone to all this trouble if there was no demand? On reflection, I know they are right. I do want something. I want an apology. In the past, America has expressed regret for diplomatic indiscretions and military blunders. It has asked forgiveness of Native Americans and enemy and friendly nations. Three and a half million Americans—our Vietnam veterans—have been unjustly disparaged, ridiculed, and offended: An expression of regret is appropriate. I want an apology from America to every man and woman who served in Vietnam and to every family who lost a son or a daughter, an apology not for their service or their loss, but for the indifference and disrespect heaped on Vietnam veterans, living or dead, after the war. The dictionary defines an apology as a "statement of acknowledgment expressing regret or asking pardon for a fault or offense." Yeah, I want an apology from America. Not for me but for Connie Wright, who lost two sons. And for Allen Clark, who lost both legs at Dak To. And for Tim Honsinger, who kept protecting his friends even after his arm had been blown off. And to the family of Harry Horton, who knew before it happened that he would give his life for America. An apology not for their loss—there is no compensation for that—but for the lack of honor and respect, both of which were owed but withheld.

My answer is that I want an apology to at least all the families of those listed on the Vietnam Veterans Memorial Wall. Those many families would include the following: the Elzingas, the Williamses, the Behnfeldts, the Townsends, the Dilleys, the Lodges, the Yoakums, the Basts, and the Spitzes. I highlight these because I personally knew these pilots (and one reconnaissance system operator) from these families. Dick Elzinga was my classmate in pilot training and died in Southeast Asia (Laos) as a Raven forward air controller. Billie Williams was my operations officer at Udorn and was an RF-4 pilot killed in North Vietnam. Roger Behnfeldt had been in ROTC with me, was in the same RF-4 squadron with me, and was from Ohio. He was shot down in North Vietnam with a SAM. His remains were returned in 1987. Fran Townsend was an Air Force Academy grad, an RF-4C reconnaissance system operator whom I had flown with many times at Udorn. His aircraft was shot down in North Vietnam, and his remains were returned in 1999.

Dana Dilley was another pilot-training classmate, who happened to die on my birthday in a helicopter in South Vietnam in 1970. Dana was also from Ohio. Robert Lodge was an F-4 pilot at Udorn and gave me one of the most professional tactics briefings I have ever heard. He would eventually shoot down a couple MiGs. But in May 1972, he was shot down. Lodge was then listed MIA until his remains were discovered in 1977. David Yoakum, another pilot-training classmate was an O-2 pilot and forward air controller in Vietnam. His airplane was hit by ground fire in South Vietnam, and his injuries were fatal. His date of death is listed as June 25, 1972. Paul Bast, my friend from my Puerto Rico assignment, was earlier an F-100 pilot and a Silver Star recipient for action in Vietnam. On a second Vietnam tour, on February 1, 1972, Paul had some kind of mechanical problem with his F-4 and was killed in Thailand as a result. That was two months before I got there. George Spitz, another pilot-training classmate, was shot down while flying an EC-47Q in Laos on February 5, 1973. Although controversial, it appears that George Spitz perished in the crash, which occurred after his aircraft was hit by AAA. I knew these and many others who gave their lives in Southeast Asia. As far as I know, their families never got an apology.

Maybe President Reagan, at least, gave some respect to all the Vietnam vets, living or dead, with his homage to a Vietnam vet on May 28, 1984. Speaking at a dedication ceremony for the Unknown Soldier of the Vietnam War, Reagan queried whether the man in question ever played on an American city street or worked with his father on a farm in America's heartland. He wondered if the man had married, had children, or expected to return to a bride. "We'll never know," Regan said, "the answers to these questions about his life. We do know, though, why he died. He saw the horrors of war but bravely faced them, certain his own cause and his country's cause was a noble one; that he was fighting for human dignity, for free men everywhere."[9]

Again, as the author of this memoir, I would be remiss not to acknowledge all the efforts of those veterans who have been in combat, before or after Vietnam. My hopes, of course, are that the mistakes made by government, media, and the rest of the intelligentsia of America are not being repeated in all the years after Vietnam. As I look at our country today (2016), generally I see the war activists of the sixties, or their ilk, now running our country. And I see the intelligentsia acting in a

EPILOGUE

Writing this memoir was a challenge for this old man. Never a student of writing or the arts, I proceeded with experiences, memories, feelings, and a few books as my guides. Like many who attempt a memoir, I found more than one internal struggle going on during this writing. Among those struggles was this:

When I was about fifty years old, I realized arrogance and narcissism were the human traits I loathed most. In my seventies and in the middle of this writing, I eventually realized that writing about one's self seemed a task impossible to accomplish without eventually being judged and deemed either arrogant or narcissistic. Given the dilemma, I finally gave up and stopped worrying about it. I have lived a life, and I decided to tell my story to my niece and nephew as best I could. But to be honest, I still found the process to be too self-involved. I'm envious of you mystery writers, or novel writers, or any other writers except autobiography or memoir writers.

With that said, I'll proceed with a few more reflections. People use the word *arc* now as a metaphor for things occurring over a period of time, either in the past or projected to occur in the future. The arc of history I became acutely aware of, for most of my life, is one that began with the end of World

War II when I was a child. This arc proceeded through the Korean and the Vietnam War eras and times when US bomber-tanker aircrews were on alert 24-7 to forestall the threats of Socialism and Communism. That arc proceeds from there, of course, until today. Many thought that while Socialism and Communism were not thwarted in the Vietnam years, at least they were not dominant forces in America.

Eventually the arc took us to the times when people like Bill Ayers and Bernardine Dohrn, associated with the bombing of the US Capitol, the Pentagon, and several police stations in New York, were later employed as professors or associate professors within universities in America. They both were listed on the FBI's most-wanted list…and yet each became a professor within the American education system. Let me repeat that: they went from being wanted by the FBI to being professors within our education system. A cursory review of legal action against the two of them seems to indicate that Bill Ayers never spent any significant time in jail for his actions, and Bernardine Dohrn was incarcerated for less than a year. I know this Ayers/Dohrn thing is not big news now, but these two individuals are superb examples of members of the intelligentsia elaborated upon earlier in this memoir. Both also spent a lot of time protesting the Vietnam War. Doesn't the Ayers/Dohrn story serve as a metaphor for possible things to come or things that have already happened in the 2009–2015 time frame? Or after the 2015–2017 time frame?

The same historical arc then runs through an era in which we are now being attacked on our own soil by radical Islamic terrorists. Aside from 9/11, this would include attacks in Little Rock, Arkansas; Fort Hood, Texas; Boston, Massachusetts;

Moore, Oklahoma; Queens, New York; Brooklyn, New York; Garland, Texas; Chattanooga, Tennessee; San Bernardino, California; Orlando, Florida; Saint Cloud, Minnesota; and Columbus, Ohio.[10] And aside from 9/11, all the attacks just mentioned occurred between 2009 and 2015. This seems an appallingly long list of places where terrorist attacks have taken place in the United States. The historical arc I am talking about concludes with an avowed Socialist running for president of the United States of America in 2016. The Socialists and Communists continue to chip away at America from the inside. Many inhabit our universities and our media, seemingly in growing numbers, influencing the youth of our country. And now we also have radical Islamic terrorists undermining America from within. Where does the arc go from here?

Of the many things worthy of mention that have happened since I wrote this memoir, three immediately stand out. The first is the presidential election of 2016. The second is the publication of J. Harvie Wilkinson III's book *All Falling Faiths: Reflections on the Promise and Failure of the 1960s*.[11] The third is the 2017 publication of the book *The Smear* by Sharyl Attkisson.[12] All three events are of significance and relate in a large way to things I have commented on in this memoir.

The election results directly challenge the socialistic, militant, and anarchist tendencies of our culture; media included. The aspirations of future terrorists are going to be challenged as well. Many would say this has been a long time coming.

I find it very interesting that many of Wilkinson's personal feelings about the 1960s seem to converge with mine. I don't agree with him on many of the Vietnam aspects, but I do agree with his take on many of the negative cultural aspects that

The Smear by Sharyl Attkisson, reflects, to me, a more up-to-date version of many of the things that Thomas Sowell wrote about regarding the intelligentsia, primarily the media. And if you didn't realize it, her focus on the media is also the primary issue that I wrote about in my last chapter of this memoir.

Honestly, by the end of 2016, my life in America felt much like the Vietnam years did—but with Islamic terrorism added to the mix. It feels to me that the intelligentsia—mostly media, many college professors, and some judges—are adding fuel to that lethal mix. I especially wonder if those same institutions will have a continued negative impact on our society regarding Socialism, Communism, and radical Islamic terror as time moves forward. And I am worried about it.

As regards philosophy, at least I outlived Socrates! He only got to seventy, though I wonder how long he would have lived had he not taken the hemlock.

As regards the financial markets, I'll stop giving numbers for the Dow Jones Industrials as of May 19, 2017. On this date, it was at 20,804.84. (Yes, I know the pros like to use the S&P 500 or other indexes of choice.) If you had invested in the Dow Jones Industrials in 1942 and reinvested the dividends until now, your inflation-adjusted return would have been roughly 7.6 percent. I did this rough calculation and had it verified by a professional friend in the finance business.

In the end, as in the beginning, I have written this for my niece and nephew. I want them to know what I did with my life and how I thought about a few things. If other readers came along, great!

VIETNAM APPENDIXES

Photo licensed via Getty Images.
April 29, 1975, at 22 Gia Long Street in Saigon, South Vietnam

Many photos epitomize the last days of a noncommunist
South Vietnam, but this is one of the most popular.
Still unbeknown to many, the people getting on the CIA
helicopter are South Vietnamese fleeing the coming
onslaught by the Communists. The city of Saigon, of
course, has been renamed Ho Chi Minh City.

INTRODUCTION TO THE
VIETNAM APPENDIXES

THE VIETNAM APPENDIXES ARE MEANT to be supporting material or historical reference material for what I have written throughout this memoir but mostly for what I wrote in chapter 9.

A. The Six-Minute Vietnam Explanation. This is the shortest synopsis of the Vietnam War I have seen, and I am sure intellectuals will have a field day debunking it; however, I enjoyed its obvious simplicity. See what you think. You will have to load an Internet address into your computer, tablet, or cell phone in order to watch the video. Alternatively, I have provided a transcript of the video.

B. Thomas Sowell on Vietnam. I relied heavily on the writings of Thomas Sowell, an American economist, social theorist, political philosopher, and author to frame and present my thoughts on Vietnam. His book *Intellectuals and Society* served as background material for much of what I have written on the subject of Vietnam.

C. **Vice Admiral Stockdale and B. G. Burkett (and Glenna Whitley) on Vietnam.** This is an elaboration on thoughts and studies on Vietnam by these authors. Stockdale was a naval officer, fighter pilot, seven-year prisoner of war, philosopher, vice-presidential aspirant, and Medal of Honor recipient. His thoughts and writings are given in the book *Thoughts of a Philosophical Fighter Pilot.* B. G. Burkett is a retired army officer, Vietnam veteran, and author of the book *Stolen Valor.* Glenna Whitley, Burkett's coauthor, used to be an investigative reporter and was a senior editor at *D Magazine* in Dallas, Texas, when she and Burkett wrote *Stolen Valor.* As she said to me on the phone one day, "The story [in *Stolen Valor*] is [Burkett's]."

D. **Aftermath of Paris Peace Accords.** This appendix provides a very short discussion of what happened after North Vietnam was driven to sign the Paris Peace Accords. It concludes that, two years after signing the Paris Peace Accords, the North Vietnamese proceeded to take over South Vietnam. And this appendix should lead you to understand that the aftermath of Vietnam lead to a whole new set of crises, a whole new death toll, and a whole new elaboration on the meaning of the fall of South Vietnam.

E. **The 432nd Tactical Reconnaissance Wing** offers a summary of the unit to which I was attached from April 1972 to April 1973. The 432nd was the parent organization of the Fourteenth Tactical Reconnaissance Squadron

(RF-4s), other F-4 fighter squadrons, and other entities. I have presented this only to add some context
and meaning to the 432nd Tactical Reconnaissance
Wing, which I have mentioned several times within this
memoir.

APPENDIX A: THE SIX-MINUTE
VIETNAM EXPLANATION

WHAT FOLLOWS IS A TRANSCRIPT of Bruce Herschensohn's presentation, which is available on a Prager University website. (See my references for additional information about accessing this video.) Mr. Herschensohn was an adviser to President Nixon. The information in this transcript previously was available online in a video titled "The Six-Minute Explanation of the Vietnam War," but in its more recent iterations, I have seen it titled "The Truth about the Vietnam War."

"The Truth about the Vietnam War" by Bruce Herschensohn[14]

Decades back, in late 1972, South Vietnam and the United States were winning the Vietnam War decisively by every conceivable measure. That's not just my view. That was the view of our enemy, the North Vietnamese government officials. Victory was apparent when President Nixon ordered the US Air Force to bomb industrial and military targets in Hanoi, North Vietnam's capital city, and in Haiphong, its major port city, and we would stop the bombing if the North Vietnamese would attend the Paris Peace Talks that they had left earlier.

The North Vietnamese did go back to the Paris Peace talks, and we did stop the bombing as promised. On January 23, 1973, President Nixon gave a speech to the nation on prime-time television announcing that the Paris Peace Accords had been initialed by the United States, South Vietnam, North Vietnam, the Viet Cong, and the Accords would be signed on the twenty-seventh. What the United States and South Vietnam received in those accords was victory. At the White House, it was called VV Day, or Victory in Vietnam Day. The US backed up that victory with a simple pledge within the Paris Peace Accords saying: should the South require any military hardware to defend itself against any North Vietnam aggression we would provide replacement aid to the South on a piece-by-piece, one-to-one replacement, meaning a bullet for a bullet; a helicopter for a helicopter, for all things lost—replacement. The advance of Communist tyranny had been halted by those accords. Then it all came apart.

And it happened this way: In August of the following year, 1974, President Nixon resigned his office as a result of what became known as Watergate. Three months after his resignation came the November congressional elections and within them the Democrats won a landslide victory for the new Congress, and many of the members used their new majority to defund the military aid the US had promised, piece for piece, breaking the commitment that we made to the South Vietnamese in Paris to provide whatever military hardware the South Vietnamese needed in case of aggression from the North. Put simply and accurately, a majority of Democrats of the Ninety-Fourth congress did not keep the word of the United States. On April 10, 1975, President Gerald Ford appealed directly to those members of the congress in an evening joint session televised to the nation. In that speech he literally begged the Congress to keep the word of the United States. But as President Ford delivered his speech, many of the members of the Congress walked out of the chamber. Many of them had an investment in America's failure in Vietnam. They had participated in demonstrations against the war for many years. They wouldn't give the aid.

On April 30, South Vietnam surrendered and reeducation camps were constructed. If the South Vietnamese had received the arms that the United States promised them, would the result have been different? It already had been different. The North Vietnamese leaders admitted that they were testing the new president, Gerald Ford, and they took one village after another, then cities, then provinces, and our only response was to go back on our word. The US did not resupply the South Vietnamese as we had promised. It was then that the North Vietnamese knew they were on the road to South Vietnam's capital city, Saigon, that would soon be renamed Ho Chi Minh City.

Former Arkansas Senator William Fulbright, who had been the chairman of the Senate Foreign Relations Committee made a public statement about the surrender of South Vietnam. He said this, "I am no more distressed than I would be about Arkansas losing a football game to Texas." The US knew that North Vietnam would violate the accords, and so we planned for it. What we did not know was that our own Congress would violate the accords. And violate them, of all things, on behalf of the North Vietnamese. That's what happened. I'm Bruce Herschensohn.

APPENDIX B: THOMAS
SOWELL ON VIETNAM

MOST OF THE MATERIAL IN this appendix comes from the writings of Thomas Sowell in *Intellectuals and Society*. Those interested should read Sowell's chapter 8, "Intellectuals and War: Repeating History."[‡] I rely heavily on the section about the Vietnam War for my effort here.

Let me first give you some of Sowell's words on intellect in a brief summary of just who represents the intellectuals and then a discussion about the intelligentsia—the users and disseminators of what the intellectuals produce. Then I'll go on to the Vietnam discussion by Sowell. Taken in total, his presentations helped me frame and present my thoughts on what I think about the Vietnam War. What follows is lengthy, but I want you to understand how those described as the *intelligentsia* and I stand on opposite sides of the Vietnam argument. The easiest way for me to do that is through examining Sowell's book, highlighting and defining who the intelligentsia are,

---

[‡] From *Intellectuals and Society* by Thomas Sowell, copyright 2010. Reprinted by permission of Basic Books, an imprint of Perseus Books, LLC, a subsidiary of Hachette Book Group, Inc.

and then following up with the effects they have had on culture, society, and the Vietnam War. Again, I revert eventually to a bullet format.

Sowell says we must be clear about what we mean by *intellectuals*. Here, *intellectuals* refers to an occupational category, people whose occupations deal primarily with ideas—writers, academics, and the like. Most of us do not think of brain surgeons or engineers as intellectuals, despite the demanding mental training each goes through, and virtually no one regards even the most brilliant and successful financial wizard as an intellectual.

Sowell goes on: "At the core of the notion of an intellectual is the *dealer* in ideas, as such—not the personal application of ideas, as engineers apply complex scientific principles to create physical structures or mechanisms."

Other points that Sowell makes to define intellect include the following:

* The output—the end product—of an intellectual consists of ideas.
* An intellectual's work begins and ends with ideas.
* Adam Smith never ran a business, and Karl Marx never administered a gulag. They were intellectuals.
* Ideas as such are not only the key to the intellectual's function but are also the criteria of intellectual achievements and the source of the often-dangerous seductions of the occupation.

  Sowell goes to great length to dispel the notion that the term *intellectual* relates necessarily to the production of *wise* ideas. That is, like cops, there are good ones and bad ones. Just because someone is identified as an intellectual doesn't mean he or she is a *wise* intellectual.

* Intellect is *not* wisdom.[15]
* There can be *unwise* intellect.[16]
* Sheer brainpower—intellect, the capacity to grasp and manipulate complex concepts and ideas—can be put at the service of concepts and ideas that lead to *mistaken* conclusions and *unwise* actions.
* Karl Marx's *Capital* was a classic example of an intellectually masterful elaboration of a fundamental misconception.
* Intelligence minus judgment equals intellect.
* Wisdom is the rarest quality of all—the ability to combine intellect, knowledge, experience, and judgment in a way that produces a coherent understanding. Wisdom is the fulfillment of the ancient admonition "With all your getting, get understanding."
* Wisdom requires self-discipline and an understanding of the realities of the world, including the limitations of one's own experience and of reason itself.
* The opposite of intellect is dullness or slowness, but the opposite of wisdom is foolishness, which is far more dangerous.
* George Orwell said that some ideas are so foolish only an intellectual could believe them, for no ordinary man could be such a fool.
* Lenin, Stalin, Mao, and Hitler all had their admirers, defenders, and apologists among the intelligentsia in western democratic nations, despite the fact that these dictators each ended up killing people of their own

countries on a scale unprecedented even by despotic regimes that preceded them.

Sowell says, in essence, not to misunderstand the title of intellectual. It's an occupational description, not a qualitative label or honorific title.

Intelligentsia are the *users* and *disseminators* of ideas that come from intellectuals. Sowell lists these users and disseminators of ideas. Among them are

- teachers,
- journalists,
- political aides,
- social activists,
- judges' clerks,
- others who base their beliefs or actions on the ideas of intellectuals,[17] and
- journalists in roles as editorial writers or columnists. Here Sowell says, "Originality is not essential to the definition of an intellectual, so long as the end product is ideas."[18]

As the author of this memoir, participant in the Vietnam War, and citizen of America, I've found through the years that I very often disagreed with the mainstream journalists, social activists, and professor elements of the intelligentsia Thomas Sowell has outlined, though not all of them. That disagreement began for me in the '60s and has only grown since. It is interesting to note the similarities in the tone of the discourse now versus the tone of the discourse going on years ago.

The 1960s and the Vietnam War brought a more general return to the intellectual and ideological climate that had reigned during the 1920s and 1930s. Indeed, many of the very words and phrases of that earlier time reappeared in the 1960s, often put forth as if they were fresh new insights, instead of old notions already discredited by the course of history. Disarmament advocates once again called themselves "the peace movement" and called military deterrence an "arms race." They argued again that "war solves nothing." Manufacturers of military equipment were called the military-industrial complex. Again, they were regarded as a threat to peace, rather than suppliers of the means of deterring aggressor nations. The Oxford Pledge by young Englishmen of the 1930s to refuse to fight for their country in war was echoed during the '60s by young Americans of draft age who said, "Hell no, I won't go."

Few who espoused these and other ideas from the 1930s recognized their antecedents, much less the disasters to which those antecedents had led. Most of the notions among the pacifist intelligentsia of the 1960s and later had appeared in British prime minister Neville Chamberlain's speeches back in the 1930s, which were published as a collection in his book *In Search of Peace*, which appeared just months before the outbreak of the Second World War.

More importantly, as too often happens, words became preemptive—disarmament being axiomatically equated with peace, for example. To disarmament advocates of his day, Churchill had said, "When you have peace, you will have disarmament"—not the other way around—but there was seldom even an attempt to test this hypothesis against that of those who automatically transformed disarmament advocates into "the peace movement."[19]

Sowell writes, "The role of the intelligentsia is illuminated during Vietnam as they ended up playing a role in influencing the policies of a society and the course of history." He illuminates another truth I felt constantly during the Vietnam years, saying, "In modern democratic nations, the intelligentsia can have influence—sometimes decisive influence—by creating a general climate of opinion in which it becomes politically impossible for the wielders of power to do what they believe needs to be done."

Sowell spends a few pages showing in detail how ideas from intellectuals are often unverifiable and unaccountable. *Academic tenure, academic freedom,* and *academic self-governance* are a few terms that describe how an intellectual can often live in a bubble that is very limited when it comes to anything verifiable or accountable. Sowell summarizes, saying, "In short, constraints which apply to people in most other fields do not apply even approximately equally to intellectuals."

Sowell spells out how some in Europe around 1933 dared not talk about how Germany was rearming, because for some, this would be bad politically and would require a rearming of Britain.

To sound the alarm about impending dangers from Germany could bring to power the oppositional Labor Party, which was totally opposed to military preparedness and would make the nation even more vulnerable than it was.

In short, Sowell continues, the climate of opinion of the times made it politically difficult for Britain to rearm adequately, as either a deterrent to war or as a means of defending itself in the event of war, even though its highest officials were fully aware of the dangers of what was, at the time, clandestine

German rearmament, at least in the sense that the general public was not aware of it. Thus the influence of the intelligentsia was decisive.[20]

Although the Vietnam War involved very different issues and different facts, its outcome reflected the influence of the intelligentsia on public opinion. More than fifty thousand Americans died *winning* military victories in Vietnam that ended in political defeat because the climate of opinion created by the intelligentsia in the United States made it politically impossible to continue the involvement of American troops in the fighting there or even to continue to supply the resources needed by the South Vietnamese government to defend itself after American troops were withdrawn. With one side (North Vietnam) receiving aid from outside and the other side (South Vietnam) not, the outcome was inevitable—the conquest of South Vietnam by North Vietnam.[21]

The decisive turning point in the Vietnam War, says Sowell, came with a massive 1968 uprising of Communist guerrillas in South Vietnam during a Vietnamese holiday called Tet. This uprising, which became known as the Tet Offensive, was launched during what was supposed to be a holiday truce. After many optimistic statements by American political and military leaders about how well the war was going, it came as a shock to the American public that the Communists were able to launch such a massive effort in the heart of South Vietnam. Moreover, and I will add emphasis to this Sowell comment, many in the media depicted what happened as a defeat for the United States, when in fact the Communist guerilla movement was decimated in the fighting and was never the same again. [22] Communist leaders openly admitted in later years that they had lost militarily in their war with American troops in Vietnam, including during Tet.[23]

Some key takeaways:

* These Communist leaders pointed out that they had won politically in America.
* James Stockdale, an American POW, was told the following by his North Vietnamese captor:
  o "Our country has no capability to defeat you on the battlefield."
  o They expected to "win this war on the streets of New York."[24]
* General Vo Nguyen Giap, who had defeated the French in the battle of Dien Bien Phu in 1954 and later commanded North Vietnamese forces against the Americans, said a few things:
  o "We are not strong enough to drive out a half-million American troops, but that wasn't our aim. Our intention was to *break the will of the American government* to continue the war."
  o "Westmoreland was wrong to expect that his superior firepower would grind us down. If we had focused on the balance of forces, we would have been defeated in two hours."[25]
* One of Giap's aides said this:
  o The North Vietnamese lost at least a million troops, killed mostly by American troops. This was a death toll almost twenty times that of the Americans'.
  o "Communist losses during the Tet offensive (were) devastating."[26]

- A North Vietnamese staff officer, Colonel Bui Tin, makes some of the following points:
  o The American antiwar movement was essential to our (North Vietnamese) strategy.
  o He says they listened to world news every day to follow the growth of the American antiwar movement.
  o "Visits to Hanoi by people like Jane Fonda and former attorney general Ramsey Clark and ministers gave us confidence that we should hold on in the face of battlefield reverses. We (North Vietnamese) were elated when Jane Fonda, wearing a red Vietnamese dress, said at a press conference that she was ashamed of American actions in the war and that she would struggle along with us."
  o The Politburo paid keen attention to these visits, because those people represented the conscience of America.
  o America lost because of its democracy; *through dissent and protest, it lost the ability to mobilize a will to win.*[27]
  o "Tet was designed to influence American public opinion," an interviewee remarked.
  o Another Communist commented, "Our losses were staggering and a complete surprise." Giap later said Tet had been a military defeat (for North Vietnam), though North Vietnam had gained the planned political advantages when Johnson agreed to negotiate and did not run for reelection.
  o Giap again said, "Our forces in the South were nearly wiped out by all the fighting in 1968," in an interview of Bui Tin.[28]

My point of all the discussion about the intelligentsia is backed up by this Sowell comment: "This paradoxical combination of overwhelming American military victories in Vietnam and devastating political defeat in Washington was crucially dependent on the climate of opinion in the US, a climate to which the intelligentsia made a major contribution."[29]

Sowell says, "The Communists' political success consisted precisely in the fact that media outlets like the *New York Times* declared their (North Vietnam's) military offensive successful. The inaccurate military assessment *by the media* carried more weight in shaping public opinion than the accurate assessments made by national leaders in both Hanoi and Washington."[30]

I guess I must stop quoting Sowell and move on, but this glimpse into *Intellectuals and Society* goes to the heart of the questions Max and Mike asked me regarding how I felt about Vietnam. How many journalists ever served in the military? How many college professors? How many activists? How many of the intelligentsia? Yet the members of the intelligentsia were a major cause for the final outcome of Vietnam. I find it interesting that many do not realize that very soon after the US bombing in North Vietnam, the Communists signed the Paris Peace Accords. But after this, the United States withdrew, and soon thereafter, the Communists began another offensive that eventually took them all the way to the capturing of the capital of South Vietnam, Saigon. The United States was supposed to intervene, but the Democrat-controlled Congress had taken away the money to continue fighting or even supporting South Vietnam, and the United States had lost its will to fight. The intelligentsia had won the war in Vietnam for the Communists. And so it was that, despite winning all major battles in Vietnam, we now say we lost the war. What a tragedy.

During the Clinton presidency, I had a T-shirt that illustrated, literally, some of the angst I felt about Vietnam. It said, in large letters, "Only in America can you have veterans sleeping in a cardboard box and a draft dodger in the White House." Not the real protester, I wore the shirt only once. Ironically, a member of the intelligentsia remarked to me that day, "You've got balls, wearing that."

The next appendix is a bit more of the same, but with information coming from three other authors. That is, I am going to present the writings with the same type of bullet formatting, and once again I consider the material presented as some backup material for my chapter 9.

APPENDIX C: VICE ADMIRAL STOCKDALE, B. G. BURKETT AND GLENNA WHITLEY ON VIETNAM

MATERIAL FOR THIS APPENDIX COMES primarily from two different books: *Thoughts of a Philosophical Fighter Pilot* by Jim Stockdale and *Stolen Valor* by B. G. Burkett and Glenna Whitley.

Thoughts of a Philosophical Fighter Pilot by Jim Stockdale[31]

Source: http://www.usna.edu/Ethics/bios/stockdale.php

Who was Jim Stockdale?

* He was a naval officer, test pilot, instructor, and fighter pilot.
* He attended graduate school at Stanford University for two years.
* He was shot down over North Vietnam on his second tour in Vietnam. He
  o became a prisoner of war (POW) for eight years,
  o was put in leg irons for two years,
  o was put in solitary confinement for four years,
  o was the highest-ranking naval officer held during the Vietnam War, and
  o retired as a vice admiral in the US Navy.
* He was a recipient of the Medal of Honor.
* As a civilian, he was a college professor and president and a senior research fellow at the Hoover Institute. He held eleven honorary doctoral degrees.
* His writings all converge on the theme of how man can rise with dignity to prevail in the face of adversity.
* He ran as a vice-presidential candidate with Ross Perot in 1992.
* He died in 2005. His wife died at age 90 in 2015, and she was a force in her own right.

Here are some of the important points Stockdale makes in *Thoughts of a Philosophical Fighter Pilot*:

* Americans don't seem able to grasp the politics and psychology of terrorism and hostage taking.[32]

* As regards the worldview of the Stoics, Professor Rhinelander, Stockdale's teacher and friend from Stanford, once joked that their environment was a buzz saw in which human will was the only salvation.[33]

* To me the greatest educational fallacy is that you can get it without stress.[34]

* "Honor," writes Stockdale, "is often what remains after faith, love, and hope are lost."[35]

* Three months after Stockdale was shot down, he had a conversation with an officer in charge of the prison camp. Here Stockdale quotes the officer: "Through propaganda, we will win the war on the streets of New York."[36]

* In the early 1960s, a fourth leadership style emerged. John F. Kennedy and his whiz kids took center stage, explaining that we had made this whole business of running a country too hard. Maccoby, a Harvard psychoanalyst, identifies practitioners of this style as "the gamesmen." The gamesmen, impatient under the yoke of their paternalistic and authoritarian fathers and educated more often than not in the game-theory-oriented elite business schools in the country, turned over a new page in leadership practices. These gamesmen were relaxed, objective, open-minded, detached, and cerebral. The gamesmen, concluded Maccoby, were basically "men of the head": cool, intellectual types—walking calculating machines. Men of the head do many things well, but they usually have trouble coping with unpleasantness. The typical gamesman craves to be admired

and can't stand not to be loved, and that is a great leadership weakness.[37]

* The cheapest escape route of modern times: jump on the bandwagon of a social determinism that holds that all men are victims of their environment.[38]

* The notion that human beings are always victims of their circumstances is an affront to those bold spirits who, throughout history, have spent their lives prevailing over adversity.[39]

* When it comes to resolve, staying power is the name of the game.[40]

* The only time I ever saw real anger at news in the prison was when we were told on the loudspeaker, convincingly, that "McNamara and Johnson had quit and that the bombing would stop. That was personal. That was betrayal."[41]

* So what about national resolve? It's too valuable, it's too hard to come by, it takes too much out of us, to commit it to any cause that is not worthy of our nation... what goes for a man going into torture (i.e., his need for resolve) should apply to a leader sending his troops off to shed their blood. Intellectualism won't cut it, bureaucratic maneuvering won't cut it, and arguments from reason are insufficient. To profess resolve means you are willing to make the cause part of you, part of the nation. It must come from the heart of the nation. Who was tracking the heart of the nation as we dabbled in Vietnam as war clouds gathered over Southeast Asia?[42]

* Here are some Stockdale comments on the Gulf of Tonkin:

o No longer a place, it was a buzzword—a symbol.
o Different groups had different ideas about it.
  ▪ Why the term "the Gulf of Tonkin" elicited so much reaction will be explained below in further Stockdale writings. He says that the term became a buzzword for Johnson's duplicity and betrayal to some, and alludes to people using "the Gulf of Tonkin" as a catalyst for untruthful antiwar discussions.
o Here is a summary of Stockdale's account of the Gulf of Tonkin incident:
  ▪ August 2, 1964, he took off from the *Ticonderoga* with four F-8 Crusaders.
  ▪ Stockdale shot up three North Vietnamese PT boats that had fired a couple of torpedoes at the *Maddox* and missed.
  ▪ Forty-eight hours later, Stockdale was the first plane up there and watched it all. This time there were two destroyers, *Maddox* and *Joy*.
    • The North Vietnamese never showed up. No boats. No attack. False alarm.
  ▪ "I am the only person in the world who was an eyewitness to both the actions of the real PT boats on Sunday (August 2) and the phantom battle on Tuesday night (August 4)," says Stockdale.[43]

Much is made of the Gulf of Tonkin and the Gulf of Tonkin Resolution, which the US Congress passed on August 7 (some say August 9), 1967, in response to the incident. The resolution gave President Johnson authorization, without a declaration of war by Congress, for use of conventional military force in Southeast Asia. Only one or two members of the Senate did not vote for the resolution. Some say that since attacks on August 4 had not actually occurred, the resolution should not have been passed, and by inference, the troop buildup in Asia should never have occurred.

Stockdale's comments, continued:

* "Those whiz kids and their mentors played games with the great goodwill of middle America, squandered it, got religion, bugged out, left a generation of their sons face down in the mud and got away with it."[44]
* "[T]he history of the war as seen from Hanoi (North Vietnam) consisted of two separate wars."
  o "When Lyndon Johnson threw in the towel and stopped all bombing, 1968."
  o "Then began a three-year and two-month hiatus—there were no bombs (in North Vietnam)."
  o "Then came the short one-year-plus second war, culminating in that beautiful December 1972 plastering of Hanoi with B-52s, something that could have been safely done and produced the same result—*North Vietnam's virtual surrender*—seven years earlier, in 1965."[45]

I could go on and on with the Stockdale book. I will just say that you should read the book if you want a glimpse into an aviator, leader, and Vietnam vet who was very aware of the

Stolen Valor by B. G. Burkett and Glenna Whitley

For the years after Vietnam, most publications and media comments on the subjects of Vietnam or Vietnam vets made little sense to me, the author of this memoir, as compared to my experiences during the years from 1968 to 1973. What the media was saying simply didn't jive with what I had seen and felt while flying combat missions in three different aircraft out of three different locations in Southeast Asia. I viewed the war and its veterans differently from how the media did. Most of my Vietnam veteran friends went on to continue very successful lives after the war was over. They were not dropouts, druggies, or ne'er-do-wells. On the contrary, most were very successful and productive in their post-Vietnam years.

In 2015 retired colonel Karl Polifka, a friend, recommended I read a book called *Stolen Valor*. Karl had been a Raven forward air controller, flying mostly the O-1 Bird Dog, and later authored the book *Meeting Steve Canyon...and Flying with the CIA in Laos*.[46] After his Raven days, he had been a squadron mate of mine as an RF-4C pilot operating out of Thailand. After the Vietnam years, he flew the B-52 and spent considerable time in the Pentagon. *Stolen Valor* was another revelation to me, despite the fact that I read it some seventeen years after its copyright date.

Stolen Valor explains why and how things were distorted by the myriad of publications, media, and political comments on the Vietnam War and the Vietnam veteran. Again, as I did with the books by Sowell and Stockdale, I will highlight some comments by Burkett. If I were to try to summarize what I gleaned from this book it would be this: The media and many others—including the intelligentsia described so well by Thomas Sowell—seemed to have a vested interest in diminishing the Vietnam veteran's experience in Southeast Asia, as well as our country's war effort there. Because of the negative drumbeat of the media and others regarding veterans and the war, many vets retreated totally from the Vietnam dialogue and went about their lives. Many vets, including me, seldom read anything that had to do with Vietnam, for thirty years or more. When I did read anything on Vietnam, especially soon after I got back from Asia, the message within never coincided with my experience.

The irony brought out to me by *Stolen Valor* is that many civilians have pretended to be Vietnam veterans so they could feed at the government trough—the one set up and intended to help those veterans who did have difficulty adjusting to life upon return. For whatever reason, there were also many veterans who never served in Vietnam but pretended to have done so. They also fed on the government trough. And our government grew. I think, in the beginning, there was proper US government intent to help our Vietnam vets. But in the end, the government was growing to support not only Vietnam vets but also civilians and veterans that pretended to have served in Vietnam. My opinion is that this cost was huge, and the overall process had the effect of showing the Vietnam veteran as a victim. The last thing I want—or any vet I know wants—is to be shown as a victim.

At first I thought some of the accusations in *Stolen Valor* were a bit overboard, but as I read, I was astounded at the quantity of fraud going on in this area, as well as the huge amount of documentation that filled *Stolen Valor* to demonstrate and substantiate these points. The book is almost seven hundred pages long and contains nearly a thousand footnotes to substantiate findings. Here are just a few excerpts from hundreds within *Stolen Valor* (mostly quotes from the authors):

* "Americans think they know the truth about Vietnam veterans because they constantly see the traumatized men who fought the war portrayed in all their pathetic anguish in the nation's most prestigious media—the *New York Times*, the *Washington Post*, and the nightly network news. It never occurs to most of us to ask: Were these men really there?"[47]

* On Jane Fonda: "She epitomized everything we (veterans) hated about the antiwar movement: She had wealthy parents and knew nothing of the reality of the war. To me, protesting government policy was legitimate; but traveling to North Vietnam and making broadcasts saying you supported the people trying to kill American troops and destroy a democratic nation was nothing short of collaborating with the enemy."[48]

* On the truth about eighteen-year-olds and Vietnam: "When people are asked how many eighteen-year-old draftees died in Vietnam, they invariably answer with a number such as 'seven thousand' or 'ten thousand.' The correct answer is 101."[49]

* On comparing support for World War I, World War II, and the Vietnam War:
  o A 1937 poll showed 64 percent of Americans regarded our entry into World War I as a blunder.

o Even World War II, "the good war," was *not* universally popular. Two years after the fighting ended, an October 1947 poll indicated that 25 percent of Americans regarded US participation in World War II as a mistake.

o "The Gulf of Tonkin Resolution—the quasi-official start of the Vietnam War...was opposed by only two US senators."[50]

* On drug use: A study, the Vietnam-Era Research Project, concluded that drug use was more common among nonveterans than Vietnam-era veterans.[51]

* On desertion: In World War II, the army's overall desertion rate was 55 percent higher than during Vietnam.

* On thoughts about serving in Vietnam—from a *Washington Post* survey: 91 percent of those who served in Vietnam were "glad they served their country."[52]

* On Dan Rather, a reporter during and after the Vietnam War:

o Although the press often refers to Rather as an "ex-Marine," he did not finish marine-recruit training. He joined the marines on January 22, 1954, but was discharged less than four months later, on May 11 for being medically unfit. (As a boy, Rather had suffered from rheumatic fever.)[53]

* On John Kerry, 1971: Kerry flung a handful of medals over the fence (in front of the US Capitol) and spoke later that week before the Senate Foreign Relations Committee.

o Years later, after his election to the Senate, Kerry's medals turned up on the wall of his Capitol Hill office. When a reporter noticed them, Kerry admitted the medals he had thrown that day were not his.[54]

- On Senator Tom Harkin of Iowa[55]:
  - o "During a 1992 bid for the presidency [he] claimed that he had served as a pilot in Vietnam. His claim had surfaced eight years before, during a 1984 bid for reelection to the Senate, when Harkin boasted that he had served one year in Vietnam flying F-4s and F-8s on combat air patrols and photo-reconnaissance support missions."
  - o Challenged by Senator Barry Goldwater, Harkin did a quick shuffle, claiming he had actually flown combat sorties over Cuba during the sixties.
  - o Harkin finally admitted he had not seen combat but had served as a ferry pilot in Atsugi, Japan, flying aircraft to be repaired from Atsugi to the Philippines. When pressed by reporters to explain how much time he'd really spent in Vietnam, Harkin estimated that, over a year, he flew in and out of Vietnam a dozen or so times.
  - o Harkin's military record showed no Vietnam service decorations.
  - o He finally conceded he had not flown combat air patrols in Vietnam and began describing himself as a Vietnam-*era* vet.
- On "pretenders," people who pretended to be Vietnam veterans or who made up stories about their service:
  - o "Patterns emerge when comparing pretenders and why they lie about Vietnam service. While some use

it to excuse their failures, others use it to polish their professional image, to hide criminal behavior, to get attention, to extort money from sympathetic people even to get elected."[56]

* More on pretenders, referring to a proposed study (eventually shelved) to compare actual military records with interviews between the veteran and doctors:
  o "I suspect the real reason (for the shelving of the study) is because the VA does not want to acknowledge that as many as three-fourths of those receiving PTSD compensation are pretenders."[57]
* On suicide: 2.7 million served in-country, and 384 men killed themselves in Vietnam.
  o That is lower than their stateside peer group.[58]
  o That is far lower than the number of army personnel in the European theater during World War II who committed suicide.[59]

The following items are discussed in *Stolen Valor* and emphasized on a website: http://www.miafacts.org/stolenvalor.htm. Reader, please note: this site is a summarized version of much of the material in *Stolen Valor*. It contains information, perhaps marketing information, that might entice the reader to buy the book.

* The rate of Vietnam veterans suffering psychological and emotional trauma from combat is lower than that for veterans of World War II.

* African Americans did *not* die in Vietnam in far greater proportions to their percentage in the American population.
* Vietnam veterans do *not* make up a greater proportion of the homeless than do non-Vietnam veterans.

APPENDIX D: AFTERMATH OF
THE PARIS PEACE ACCORDS

THE PARIS PEACE ACCORDS EFFECTIVELY removed the United States from the conflict in Vietnam; however, the agreement's provisions were routinely flouted by both the North Vietnamese and the Saigon government, eliciting no response from the United States and ultimately resulting in the Communists enlarging the area under their control by the end of 1973. North Vietnamese military forces gradually built up their military infrastructure in the areas they controlled and two years later were in position to launch the successful offensive that ended South Vietnam's status as an independent country.

Nixon had secretly promised Thieu he would use airpower to support the Saigon government should it be necessary. (Thieu was the elected president of South Vietnam in 1967and was eventually forced to flee when North Vietnam took over the country in 1975) During his [Nixon's] confirmation hearings in June 1973, Secretary of Defense James Schlesinger was sharply criticized by some senators after he stated that he would recommend resumption of US bombing in North Vietnam if North Vietnam launched a major offensive against South Vietnam, but by August 15, 1973, 95 percent of American troops and their allies had left Vietnam (both North and

South), as well as Cambodia and Laos, under the Case-Church Amendment. The amendment, which was approved by the US Congress in June 1973, prohibited further US military activity in Vietnam, Laos, and Cambodia unless the president secured congressional approval in advance. However, during this time, Nixon was being driven from office due to the Watergate scandal, which led to his resignation in 1974.

When the North Vietnamese began their final offensive early in 1975, the US Congress refused to appropriate additional military assistance for South Vietnam, citing strong American opposition to the war and the loss of American equipment to the North Vietnamese by retreating South Vietnamese forces. Thiệu subsequently resigned, accusing the United States of betrayal in a TV and radio address: "At the time of the peace agreement the United States agreed to replace equipment on a one-by-one basis. But the United States did not keep its word. Is an American's word reliable these days? The United States did not keep its promise to help us fight for freedom and it was in the same fight that the United States lost 50,000 of its young men."[60]

Saigon fell to the North Vietnamese army supported by Viet Cong units on April 30, 1975. Schlesinger had announced early in the morning of April 29 the beginning of Operation Frequent Wind. This entailed the evacuation of the last US diplomatic, military, and civilian personnel from Saigon via helicopter and was completed in the early morning hours of April 30. Not only did North Vietnam conquer South Vietnam, but the Communists were also victorious in Cambodia when the Khmer Rouge captured Phnom Penh on April 17. Likewise, the Pathet Lao were successful in capturing Vientiane on December 2. As in Saigon, US civilian and military personnel were evacuated from Phnom Penh, US diplomatic presence in Vientiane was significantly downgraded, and the number of remaining US personnel was severely reduced.[61]

Let's take a closer look at what happened after the Communists took over South Vietnam. Below is a very small sampling of the history after 1975.

Between two hundred thousand and three hundred thousand Vietnamese were sent to reeducation camps. Many endured torture, starvation, and disease while being forced to perform hard labor.[62]

In 1977, *National Review* alleged that some thirty thousand South Vietnamese had been systematically killed using a list of CIA informants left behind by the US embassy.[63]

The "Indochina Refugee Crisis" was the large outflow of people from the former French colonies of Indochina, comprising the countries of Vietnam, Cambodia, and Laos, after Communist governments were established in 1975. Over the next twenty-five years and out of a total Indochinese population in 1975 of 56 million, more than 3 million people would undertake the dangerous journey to become refugees in other countries of Southeast Asia or China. Hundreds of thousands may have died in their attempt to flee. More than 2.5 million Indochinese were resettled, mostly in North America and Europe. Five hundred thousand were repatriated, either voluntarily or involuntarily.[64]

Thousands of Hmong, US allies in the Vietnam War, and other highland people from Laos died on a journey trying to flee to Thailand after the war.[65]

Starting in about September 1978, many escaped Vietnam via makeshift boats with the intention of going to Malaysia, Thailand, Indonesia, Hong Kong, and other countries.[66] The United Nations High Commission for Refugees estimated that between two hundred thousand and four hundred thousand boat people died at sea.[67] Other estimates compiled are that 10 to 70 percent of the 1 to 2 million Vietnamese boat people died in transit.[68] The boat people comprised only part of the Vietnamese resettled abroad from 1975 until the end of the twentieth century.

A total of more than 1.6 million Vietnamese were resettled between 1975 and 1997. Of that number, more than 700,000 were boat people; the remaining 900,000 were resettled under the Orderly Departure Program, in China or in Malaysia.[69] The three countries resettling most Vietnamese boat people and land arrivals were the United States with 402,382, Australia with 108,808, and Canada with 100,012.[70]

You get the picture. I have not presented a full disclosure of what happened to others: the people fleeing Cambodia after April 1975; the Montagnards, originally of the Central Highlands of Vietnam, who did a lot of work with our US Special Forces; or the Hmong, who assisted our CIA in Laos for many years. I know my old RF-4 squadron mate Colonel Karl Polifka made a dedication to the Hmong in his book *Meeting Steve Canyon…and Flying with the CIA in Laos.* He wrote, "To the Hmong, whose population fought a brutal war for fourteen years with resolute courage and dedication but at a terrible cost."

The stories of the Cambodians, the Laotians, the Montagnards, and the Hmong are all stories unto themselves and are still being told. That these people were dependent in many ways on a positive US outcome in SEA is still very bothersome to me. We let a lot of people down.

APPENDIX E: THE 432ND TACTICAL RECONNAISSANCE WING

I WAS ASSIGNED TO THE Fourteenth Tactical Reconnaissance Squadron, a unit of the 432nd Tactical Reconnaissance Wing, while flying the RF-4 out of Udorn, Thailand, in 1972 and 1973. I include this description of the 432nd only to give you some historical perspective and understanding of this wing, which I have mentioned a few times in this memoir. The following fact sheet from the Creech Air Force Base website describes the 432nd Wing:

> The illustrious history of the 432nd "Hunters" began with the activation of the 432nd Observation Group on Feb. 22, 1943, at Alachua Army Air Field, Fla., to train cadres for new groups and squadrons as the nation continued to prepare forces for war. After redesignation as the 432nd Reconnaissance Group, and a transfer to Keystone Army Air Field, Fla., a revamped training program offered basic and flying training, and instruction on subjects that included chemical warfare, aircraft recognition, security and censorship. The Army Air Force inactivated the group on Nov. 1, 1943, shortly after its redesignation as the 432nd Tactical Reconnaissance

Group. Just over a decade later, on March 18, 1954, the group returned to active status at Shaw Air Force Base, SC, to provide tactical reconnaissance capabilities. In early 1959, after consolidating its lineage with the 432nd Tactical Reconnaissance Wing's, the unit ran the US Air Force Advanced Flying School, Tactical Reconnaissance, briefly before inactivating on May 17, 1959.

Activated once again on Aug. 19, 1966, the 432nd TRW formed up a month later on Sep. 18, 1966, at Udorn Royal Thai Air Force Base, Thailand. Thus began the most defining era of the unit's history, one that forged a legacy of valor, courage and steadfastness that buttresses the warfighting traditions carried on by today's "Hunters." As before, the role that initially personified the "hunt" in Vietnam for the 432nd was tactical aerial reconnaissance in support of other combat operations. This changed one year later, with the arrival and assignment of seven tactical fighter squadrons to the wing, as its mission expanded to include combat air patrols against MiGs and ground strike operations. To be sure, the Hunters embraced the intensification of their combat role. Between Dec. 17, 1967, and Jan. 8, 1973, the wing's squadrons received credit for 36 confirmed MiG kills. Sixteen of those came from the air force's only Vietnam era "Aces," each one a Hunter. Three in all, they included Capt. Charles B. DeBellevue, of the 555th Tactical Fighter Squadron, credited with downing two MiG-19s and four MiG-21s; Capt. Jeffrey S. Feinstein, of the 13th TFS, credited with downing five MiG-21s; and

lastly Capt. Richard S. Ritchie, of the 555th TFS, credited with five MiG-21s.

Not all landmark events in that war occurred in the
air, as with the case of Capt. Roger C. Locher of the
555th TFS. Shot down on May 10, 1972, Locher evaded
captivity for 23 days before being rescued. The rescue
itself, the deepest such mission into North Vietnam territory by American forces, is still deemed one of the most
successful combat evasion chapters of the war. After participating in 14 of the 17 air campaigns of the Vietnam
War, in Jan. 1973, the 432nd officially ended operations
in that country. Still, combat air operations continued
that year in Laos until February and in Cambodia until
August. After implementation of the cease-fire accords,
the 432nd remained in Thailand to conduct routine
reconnaissance and training missions. In belated recognition of its new mission, it became the 432nd Tactical
Fighter Wing on Nov. 15, 1974. In April 1975, the wing
supported the evacuation of American and Allied personnel from Cambodia and South Vietnam. That same
year, the 432nd played a key role in finding and recovering the American freighter, SS *Mayaguez*. Relieved of all
operational duties on Nov. 30, 1975, the 432nd inactivated on Dec. 23 of the same year.

This time the highly decorated flag of the 432nd
did not remain furled for long. After redesignation
as the 432nd Tactical Drone Group, the unit activated May 24, 1976, at Davis-Monthan Air Force Base,
Ariz., to conduct follow-on and evaluation testing of
the AQM-34V unmanned drone. The 432nd carried

out parallel initial operational testing of the drone's DC-130H "mothership" as well. This brief venture into yet another mission area ended, for a time at least, with the group's inactivation in 1979. On July 1, 1984, the unit activated at Misawa Air Base, Japan, as the 432nd Tactical Fighter Wing. Serving as the host base unit, the 432nd TFW flew F-16 Viper aircraft in support of a tactical employment mission. Using Misawa as a test base for a new wing organizational structure, popularly referred to as the "one wing, one base, one boss" concept, the air force redesignated the unit as the 432nd Fighter Wing on May 31, 1991. This concept led to the assignment of a third flying squadron to the 432nd FW, with operational control of the 39th Rescue Squadron's four HH-60G Black Hawk helicopters ceded to the wing by the Air Rescue Service on Feb. 1, 1993. On Oct. 1, 1994, the 432nd FW inactivated at Misawa as the 35th FW stood up there.

The veteran combat unit returned to active service on May 1, 2007, at Creech AFB, Nev., as the 432nd Wing, and formed the US Air Force's first unmanned (later, remotely piloted) aircraft systems wing. In doing so, the 432nd took charge of existing and rapidly expanding unmanned precision attack and intelligence, surveillance, and reconnaissance combat missions there in support of overseas contingency operations. On May 15, 2008, the provisional 432nd Air Expeditionary Wing activated at Creech to offer the fullest possible spectrum of leadership to these fights, while complementing the operate, train, and equip efforts of the 432nd Wing.[71]

Just a side note here: I repeatedly sat in the same briefing room and flew in the same airspace with those listed in this fact sheet: Capt. Charles B. DeBellevue, Capt. Jeffrey S. Feinstein, Capt. Richard S. Ritchie, and Capt. Roger C. Locher. (And so did most of my Fourteenth TRS buddies.) This was in the 1972–1973 time frames. Can't say I got to know them personally, but it is all interesting to me and perhaps to you, Jason and Jodi, from a historical perspective. I also remember the names and some of the faces of MiG killers Olmstead, Cherry, Lodge, Baily, and Madden.

GLOSSARY

AAA   Antiaircraft artillery.

Afterburner   A component present on some jet engines
                      with the purpose of increasing thrust,
                      usually for takeoff, supersonic flight, and
                      combat situations. The advantage of using
                      afterburners is significantly increased
                      thrust; the disadvantage is its very high fuel
                      consumption. Jargon often used in place
                      of the term among aviators is *ABs*, *burners*,
                      heaters, or *reheat*. (With current technol-
                      ogy, some aircraft are capable of super-
                      sonic flight without using afterburners.)

AGL   Altitude above ground level.

Air to Air   A mission where fighter pilots are pri-
                      marily dedicated to destroying airborne
                      enemy aircraft.

ACM   Air combat maneuvering. The tactical
                      art of moving, turning, and/or situating
                      one's fighter aircraft in order to attain
                      a position from which an attack can be
                      made on another aircraft.

Airman   Within the US Air Force, it describes an
                      enlisted person below the rank of sergeant.

Often used to describe most anyone who flies.

Air to Ground
A mission where pilots are employing or dropping ordinance on a ground-based target.

ANS
Astro-inertial navigation system. A navigation system installed on the SR-71 that basically looked at stars to figure out where it was.

AR-15
A lightweight, magazine-fed semi-automatic rifle.

Bogey
Unidentified and potentially hostile aircraft.

Call Sign
Identifying words assigned to an individual, aircraft, ship, unit, or facility for the purpose of radio communications.

CAS
Close air support. Air action against hostile targets that are in close proximity to friendly forces.

DMZ
Demilitarized zone.

F-4
A twin-engine all-weather tactical fighter aircraft.

RF-4	The reconnaissance version of the F-4. (The RF-4 had a longer, more pointed nose. The fire-control radar of the F-4 was replaced by cameras, mapping radar, and infrared-imaging equipment for the reconnaissance role.)
FAC	An individual who, from a forward ground or airborne position, controls aircraft engaged in close air support of ground troops.
FCF	Functional check flight. As the name implies, an FCF is a flight conducted for the primary purpose of checking the functionality of an aircraft after an engine change, a major control surface change or other system change, or a single significant maintenance action.
GCI	Ground control intercept. A method of vectoring or giving direction to one aircraft for the purpose of intercepting another aircraft via a radar interpretation.
G-Force	Force of gravity. Sitting or standing on the ground, you are experiencing one G. Fighter-type aircrews regularly experience four Gs and higher during air operations.

Gib	Guy in back. Usually a term associated with navigators that occupied the back seat in fighter type aircraft. Most were trained as navigators but also had a lot of training in other technical specialties such as in reconnaissance system operations, weapon system operations, radar operations or electronic warfare operations. Despite the term "guy in back", the pilots relied very heavily upon them for the survival of the mission, the aircraft they were flying, and for the survival of the crew itself.
GPS	Global Positioning System. This is a global navigation satellite system that provides geolocation and time information to a GPS receiver anywhere on or near the earth where there is an unobstructed line of sight to four or more GPS satellites. GPS is available to most aircraft, assuming they have a GPS receiver, and is accurate and reliable from this author's perspective.
Habu	A deadly venomous snake native to the island of Okinawa, Japan. Over time the term came to be associated with SR-71crews that had completed an operational assignment to Okinawa.
Helo Driver	Slang for helicopter pilot.

INS   Inertial navigation system. A navigation
                       aid that uses a computer, accelerometers,
                       and gyroscopes to continuously calculate
                       position, orientation, and velocity without
                       the need for external references. This sys-
                       tem was on the RF-4.

KIAS   Knots indicated airspeed.

Knot   One knot is a nautical mile per hour.
                       One nautical mile equals 1.1508 statute
                       miles.

LORAN   A "long-range navigation" system that was
                       employed on the RF-4. This system was
                       more accurate than the INS on the RF-4
                       but, due to a limited supply, was available
                       on only a few aircraft (1972–73). This sys-
                       tem measured the time-of-arrival differ-
                       ence between two signals transmitted from
                       two geographically separated ground
                       stations.

Mach   The ratio of the speed of a body to the speed
                       of sound in the surrounding medium.
                       (Mach 1 equals 1x the speed of sound,
                       Mach 2 equals 2x the speed of sound,
                       and so on.)

MIA   Missing in action.

O-1 Bird Dog

For our purposes here, a single-engine reciprocating-engine aircraft used by the air force and others during the Vietnam War, mostly as a FAC aircraft, but also for reconnaissance, artillery adjustment, radio relay. It was a stalwart aircraft for use by the Raven FACs operating in Laos.

O-2

A twin-engine, reciprocating-engine aircraft used primarily by the Air Force for FAC operations in Vietnam, including reconnaissance, artillery adjustment, and radio relay. One engine in the front, one engine in the back, commonly referred to as a *push/pull* configuration. This airplane is the military version of a Cessna 337 Super Skymaster.

Officer

When used without further detail, the term almost always refers to commissioned officers, the more senior portion of a force that derive their authority from a commission from the head of state of a sovereign nation-state.

Within the US Air Force, the officer ranks consist of the following:

Second Lieutenant (2nd Lt.)
First Lieutenant (1st Lt.)
Captain (Capt.)

Major (Maj.)
Lieutenant Colonel (Lt. Col.)
Colonel (Col.)
Brigadier General (Brig. Gen.) (One Star)
Major General (Maj. Gen.) (Two Stars)
Lieutenant General (Lt. Gen.) (Three Stars)
General (Gen.) (Four Stars)

Ops   Operations. Here this mostly refers to an operations officer, an officer generally in charge of the operations of a flying squadron.

Phantom   Another name for the F-4 or as used in the more encompassing moniker...*the F-4 Phantom.*

POW   Prisoner of war.

Raven   The call sign associated with FACs operating out of Laos during the Vietnam War, usually flying the O-1 Bird Dog.

ROMAD   Radio operator, maintainer, and driver. The term has often referred to an enlisted airman who moves, at times, with army units to assist in providing close air support (CAS) for associated units.

RPG | Rocket-propelled grenade. Intended as an antitank weapon, it could penetrate ten inches of armor with its shaped-charge warhead and then incinerate anything in an enclosed interior. It had a minimal shrapnel effect when it burst in the air.

SAC | Strategic Air Command, an air force major command organization dedicated to strategic concerns of the United States, responsible for land-based strategic bombers and intercontinental ballistic missiles, strategic reconnaissance aircraft, and most USAF refueling aircraft, with a few exceptions. By 1992 this organization underwent major reorganization including associated name changes to identify various missions. For the most part Air Combat Command and Air Mobility Command became the new creations. All mentions of SAC in this memoir refer to its original structure, prior to the Air Combat Command and Air Mobility Command.

SAM | Surface-to-air missile.

SA-2 | The primary SAM used by the North Vietnamese to attack US aircraft during the Vietnam years.

SAR	Search and rescue. For our purposes here, this usually pertains to the search and rescue of downed airmen in Vietnam.
SEA	Southeast Asia.
Sergeant	Generally, a noncommissioned officer in the armed forces.
Sgt	Sergeant.
SSgt	Staff sergeant.
TSgt	Technical sergeant.
MSgt	Master sergeant.
SMSgt	Senior master sergeant.
CMSgt	Chief master sergeant.
Sled	A nickname for the SR-71.
Speed of Sound	For our purposes, we are talking about the speed of sound as it travels through air. Keep in mind that this depends on factors such as temperature, humidity, and air pressure. A National Weather Service website computes the speed of sound at 767.74 mph with a temperature of 60 degrees

Fahrenheit. At eighty thousand feet above sea level, the standard temperature is about - 62 degrees Fahrenheit, which the National Weather Service says converts to 666.35 miles per hour. Another way of thinking about it is that at sea level and 70 degrees Fahrenheit, under normal atmospheric conditions, the speed of sound is 770 miles per hour.

TAC   Tactical Air Command. A major command of the US Air Force. Dedicated to tactical concerns of the United States. Historically, it was responsible for large contingents of fighter aircraft and some tactical reconnaissance aircraft, but its missions included a number of different types of aircraft and missions. In about 1992 most TAC and SAC resources were merged. This merger resulted generally in the creation of two new major commands: Air Combat Command and Air Mobility Command. All mentions of TAC in this memoir generally pertain to the original TAC, prior to the Air Combat Command and Air Mobility Command.

TASS   Tactical air-support squadron. This unit has administrative control over those assigned to FAC operations. During Vietnam, we had five in Southeast Asia.

Vector

For our purposes, this is getting a heading or a direction to proceed for various purposes, such as to intercept another aircraft, to join up with a refueling aircraft, and so on.

VOR

VHF omnidirectional radio range. This was an older type of short-range radio navigation system for aircraft, enabling aircraft with a receiving unit to determine their positions and stay on course by receiving radio signals transmitted by a network of fixed-ground radio beacons.

Willy Pete

Willy Pete, or Willy Peter, is slang for the white-phosphorus rockets FACs carried on their aircraft to mark targets for their fighters during close air-support missions. Fighter pilots could visually acquire a target marked with Willy Pete very easily because of the white smoke emanating from the ground.

NOTES

1. Joe Yoon, "Convert Thrust to Horsepower," Aerospaceweb. org, http://www.aerospaceweb.org/question/propulsion/q0195.shtml, September 26, 2004.

2. Richard H. Graham, *SR-71 Blackbird Stories, Tales, and Legends.* (St. Paul, MN: MBI Publishing Co., 2002), 25.

3. *Wikipedia,* s.v. "Pratt & Whitney J58," last modified March 2, 2017, https://en.wikipedia.org/w/index.php?title=Pratt_%26_Whitney_J58&oldid=768275905.

4. *Wikipedia,* s.v. "McDonnell Douglas MD-80," last modified March 13, 2017, https://en.wikipedia.org/w/index.php?title=McDonnell_Douglas_MD-80&oldid=770067339.

5. "The History of Ferocious Frankie," North American P-51D Mustang: Ferocious Frankie, accessed April 13, 2017, http://www.ferociousfrankie.com/the-history-of-ferocious-frankie/.

6. From *Intellectuals and Society* by Thomas Sowell, copyright 2010. Reprinted by permission of Basic Books, an imprint of Perseus Books, LLC, a subsidiary of Hachette Book Group, Inc.

7. Paul Szoldra, "Spielberg Is Making a Film on the 'Pentagon Papers' That Exposed Lies about the Vietnam

War," *Business Insider,* March 6, 2017, http://www.businessinsider.com/steven-spielberg-pentagon-papers-2017-3.

8. Andrew J. Rotter, "The Causes of the Vietnam War," in *The Oxford Companion to American Military History,* ed. John Whiteclay Chambers II (New York: Oxford UP, 1999).

9. President Ronald Reagan, Speech Honoring the Vietnam War's Unknown Soldier, May 28, 1984, in Sandra Scanlon, *The Pro-War Movement* (Amherst, MA: University of Massachusetts Press, 2013), 341.

10. James Barrett, "A Complete List of Radical Islamic Terror Attacks on US Soil under Obama," *The Daily Wire,* Dec. 7, 2016. http://www.dailywire.com/news/11410/completelist-radical-islamic-terror-attacks-us-james-barrett.

11. J. Harvie Wilkinson III, *All Falling Faiths: Reflections on the Promise and Failure of the 1960s (*New York: Encounter Books, 2017).

12. Sharyl Attkisson, *The Smear* (New York: HarperCollins, 2017).

13. J. Harvie Wilkinson III, *All Falling Faiths,* Loc 2608.

14. Bruce Herschensohn, "The Truth about the Vietnam War," PragerU, June 23, 2014, https://www.prageru.com/courses/history/truth-about-vietnam-war.

15. Thomas Sowell, "Intellect and Intellectuals," in *Intellectuals and Society* (New York: Basic Books, 2009), 1–9.

16. Ibid.

17. Ibid.

18. Ibid.

19. Thomas Sowell, "Intellectuals and War: Repeating History" in *Intellectuals and Society* (New York: Basic Books, 2009), 241–80.

20. Ibid.

21. Ibid.

22. Ibid.

23. Peter Braestrup, "Big Story: How the American Press and Television Reported and Interpreted the Crisis of Tet 1968 in Vietnam and Washington (Garden City, NY: Anchor Books, 1978), 49–54.

24. Jim and Sybil Stockdale, *In Love and War: The Story of a Family's Ordeal and Sacrifice during the Vietnam Years* (New York: Harper and Row, 1984), 181.

25. Thomas Sowell, "Intellectuals and War: Repeating History" in *Intellectuals and Society* (New York: Basic Books, 2009), 248.

26. Ibid.

27. Ibid.

28. "How North Vietnam Won the War," *Wall Street Journal*, August 3, 1995, 62.

29. Thomas Sowell, "Intellectuals and War: Repeating History" in *Intellectuals and Society* (New York: Basic Books, 2009), 249–50.

30. Ibid.

31. Jim Stockdale, *Thoughts of a Philosophical Fighter Pilot* (Hoover Institution Press Publication No: 431, Stanford University, Stanford, CA, 1995).

32. Jim Stockdale, *Thoughts of a Philosophical Fighter Pilot* (Hoover Institution Press Publication No: 431, Stanford University, Stanford, CA, 1995), 9.

33. Stockdale, *Thoughts of a Philosophical Fighter Pilot*, 22.

34. Stockdale, *Thoughts of a Philosophical Fighter Pilot*, 26.

35. Stockdale, *Thoughts of a Philosophical Fighter Pilot*, 27, quoting from *The Civilization of the Renaissance in Italy, London, 1929*, 428.

36. Stockdale, *Thoughts of a Philosophical Fighter Pilot*, 28.

37. Stockdale, *Thoughts of a Philosophical Fighter Pilot*, 34.

38. Stockdale, *Thoughts of a Philosophical Fighter Pilot*, 41.

39. Ibid.

40. Stockdale, *Thoughts of a Philosophical Fighter Pilot*, 48.

41. Stockdale, *Thoughts of a Philosophical Fighter Pilot*, 49.

42. Stockdale, *Thoughts of a Philosophical Fighter Pilot*, 52.

43. Stockdale, *Thoughts of a Philosophical Fighter Pilot*, 54.

44. Stockdale, *Thoughts of a Philosophical Fighter Pilot*, 55.

45. Stockdale, *Thoughts of a Philosophical Fighter Pilot*, 72.

46. Karl L. Polifka, *Meeting Steve Canyon...and Flying with the CIA in Laos* (North Charleston, SC: self-published thru CreateSpace, 2013).

47. B. G. Burkett and Glenna Whitley, *Stolen Valor* (Dallas, TX, Verity Press, 1998).

48. Burkett and Whitley, 23.

49. Burkett and Whitley, 48.

50. Burkett and Whitley, 48–49.

51. Burkett and Whitley, 62.

52. Burkett and Whitley quoting from "Poll Finds Veterans Are at Home Again," *Washington Post*, April 11, 1985, A-11.

53. Burkett and Whitley quoting from military record of Dan Irvin Rather, National Personnel Records Center, FOIA request by B. G. Burkett, August 23, 1990.

54. Burkett and Whitley quoting from Phil Duncan, ed., "Congressional Quarterly's Politics in America," 102nd Congress, 1992, 678.

55. Burkett and Whitley, 182.

56. Burkett and Whitley, 176.

57. Burkett and Whitley, 279.

58. Burkett and Whitley, 303, quoting from Department of Defense Casualty Records.

59. Burkett and Whitley, 303, quoting from *Listing of Army Personnel Who Died by Suicide or Execution, 7 December 1941 through 30 June 1946*, National Archives.

60. "1975: Vietnam's President Thieu Resigns," *On This Day*, BBC News, April 21, 1975.

61. *Wikipedia*, s.v. "Paris Peace Accords," last modified March 12, 2017, https://en.wikipedia.org/w/index.php?title=Paris_Peace_Accords&oldid=769930066.

62. Gareth Porter and James Roberts, "Creating a Bloodbath by Statistical Manipulation," review of *A Methodology for Estimating Political Executions in Vietnam* by Jacqueline Desbarats and Karl D. Jackson, eds., *Pacific Affairs* 61, no. 2 (1988): 303–10; Edward P. Metzner, *Reeducation in Postwar Vietnam: Personal Postscripts to Peace* (College Station, TX: Texas A&M University Press), xiii; Ginetta Sagan and Stephen Denney, "Re-education in Unliberated Vietnam: Loneliness, Suffering and Death," *The Indochina Newsletter*, October–November 1982.

63. Le Thi Anh, "The New Vietnam," *National Review*, April 29, 1977. "According to Frank Snepp, a CIA analyst who served in Saigon, the American Embassy wasn't able to destroy its top-secret files during the frantic evacuation, and among the information that fell into Communist hands was a list of 30,000 Vietnamese who had worked in the Phoenix

Program, a U.S.-sponsored operation responsible for the elimination of thousands of Communist agents. A full report on the massacre of those 30,000 Phoenix cadres is said to have reached the desk of the French ambassador to Saigon by late 1975; he communicated it to Washington, where nothing was done with it."

64. *Wikipedia*, s.v. "Indochina Refugee Crisis," last modified May 27, 2017, https://en.wikipedia.org/wiki/Indochina_refugee_crisis; United Nations High Commissioner for Refugees, "The State of the World's Refugees, 2000," UNHCR, 81, 102.

65. Grit Grigoleit, "Coming Home: The Integration of Hmong Refugees from Wat Tham Krabok, Thailand," *Hmong Studies Journal* 7 (2006), http://hmongstudies.org/Grigoleit.pdf; W. Courtland Robinson, *Terms of Refuge: United Nations High Commissioner for Refugees* (London: Zed Books, 1998), Appendix 2.

66. *Wikipedia*, s.v. "Indochina Refugee Crisis: Boat People."

67. Associated Press, June 23, 1979, *San Diego Union*, July 20, 1986. See generally Nghia M. Vo, *The Vietnamese Boat People* (2006), 1954 and 1975–1992, McFarland.

68. Rudolph Rummel, "Statistics of Vietnamese Democide," in his *Statistics of Democide* (Wissenschaftliche Paperbacks, 1997), Table 6.1B, lines 730, 749–51.

69. Robinson, *Terms of Refuge*, Appendix 1 and 2; *Far Eastern Economic Review* (June 23, 1978): 20.

70. Robinson, *Terms of Refuge*, Appendix 1 and 2.

71. Creech Air Force Base, "432nd Wing, 432nd Air Expeditionary Wing," May 16, 2013, http://www.creech.af.mil/About-Us/Fact-Sheets/Display/Article/449126/432nd-wing-432nd-air-expeditionary-wing/.

Made in the USA
San Bernardino, CA
15 November 2017